# FILM
# PRODUCTION
# THEORY

THE **SUNY** SERIES

**CULTURAL STUDIES IN CINEMA/VIDEO**

**WHEELER WINSTON DIXON** | EDITOR

# FILM
# PRODUCTION
# THEORY

JEAN-PIERRE
GEUENS

STATE UNIVERSITY OF NEW YORK PRESS

Published by
State University of New York Press, Albany

© 2000  State University of New York

For information, address State University of New York Press,
State University Plaza, Albany, N.Y., 12246

Production by Marilyn P. Semerad
Marketing by Dana E. Yanulavich

**Library of Congress Cataloging-in-Publication Data**

Geuens, Jean Pierre.
    Film production theory / Jean-Pierre Geuens.
        p.  cm. — (The SUNY series, cultural studies in cinema/video)
    Includes bibliographical references and index.
    ISBN 0-7914-4525-9 (HC : alk. paper) — ISBN 0-7914-4526-7 (PB : alk. paper)
        1. Motion pictures—Production and direction. 2. Motion pictures—Philosophy. I. Title.
    II. Series.

PN1995.9.P7 G437 2000
791.43′0232—dc21
                                                                99-057804

10 9 8 7 6 5 4 3 2 1

*This book,*
*in André Bazin's spirit,*
*is for cinema.*

# CONTENTS

# ACKNOWLEDGMENTS

At IDHEC, Gaston Mundwiller trusted me with a camera.

At USC, Marsha Kinder guided me through the riddles of critical studies. She gave me room to explore, struggle, and rebel. Without her continuous encouragement, this book would never have been written.

Throughout the two years of research and writing, Michaela Tork offered me invaluable insights and incredible support.

All have my profound and lasting gratitude.

To the aspiring filmmaker:

My goal in this book has been to fire up your imagination, to kindle in you a desire for new and powerful combinations of images and sounds beyond the Hollywood formula.

Rather than go through the text systematically, I invite you to leaf through the pages and find the topics that immediately speak to you.

Then, go for broke!

# CHAPTER ONE

—————————— ◉ ——————————

## *Cinema:*
## *The State of the Art*

I

To all appearances, the business of cinema goes on as usual. Yes, movies are being made. The production lines in the studios keep churning out their images. The digital effects specialists stay up late at night to meet endless deadlines. Films open in Berlin or Cannes. Critics write their reviews. People talk about the latest releases at work or during dinner with friends. More than ever the filmmaking industry is part of our everyday cultural landscape. *Premiere* tells us what is going on. Critics on TV give thumbs up or down. *Hard Copy* and *Entertainment Tonight* keep us abreast of the successes and distresses of the stars and would-be stars. Even the historians of the medium regularly bring out fresh editions covering recent developments in the field. Once a year, the Academy Awards are seen the world over. Week after week, *Variety* tabulates the receipts. The money keeps pouring in. Another blockbuster year for the motion picture industry is in the works!

On the surface indeed, nothing has changed and it is business as usual in Hollywood. If we dig a little deeper, though, it is not difficult to see that this background of continuing normality, glamour, and professionalism in the industry in fact hides radical transformations that have influenced the conception, production, distribution, and reception of films in the last thirty some years. Anyone who has lived this period of history knows what I am talking about. On the one hand, blockbusters now totally dominate the scene, technology is big business, budgets go through the roof, and celebrities are all over the place. On the other, foreign films are rare and tame, the art cinema has disappeared, and real independents are out of luck. But it is not just the movies that have changed, audiences have changed as well. Once upon a time, difficult films by Jean-Luc Godard could attract a sizable crowd in a first-run theater, whereas today, apart from mediocre productions made to order for the American market, foreign films have a hard time playing one week in a small run-down theater. Some say it is the subtitles, others blame difficult narratives. More generally, there seems to be a lack of interest in the U.S. today for serious filmmaking. Whatever the reason, this restructuring of both the business and the market presents aspiring filmmakers with poor alternatives. Let me offer a quick example from the class room. To illustrate time condensation in the cinema, an instructor shows the last scene of *2001* (Stanley Kubrick, 1968). The classical beauty of the shots mesmerizes everyone even though, for most, this is not their first viewing of the piece. But then someone breaks the mood by questioning the slow pace and the ambiguity of the scene, saying that today not even Kubrick would be allowed to shoot it this way. And even if he did, there is no doubt that it would be struck from the final cut of the picture. And if it were still in the release prints despite the odds, audiences would not stand for it, leaving the theater in droves, impatient, unwilling to confront the challenges of a more demanding kind of cinema.

What this example attempts to make clear is that, today, the choices for a young filmmaker are rather limited. The themes must be explicit, the action relentless. The language of cinema has shrunken. The possibilities of using the medium fully have been considerably narrowed. Sure, the entertainment industry requires yearly infusion of creative talent, fresh blood necessary to keep itself at the cutting edge of style and technology. But that is as far as it goes, for each talent will be harnessed so as to produce only what is needed to turn the project into an exciting package. At this point the classroom becomes silent, each student reflecting about his or her future: stereotyped characters, car chases, people shooting at each other, endless explosions, stunt people flying through the air, an orgy of fast cuts, and loud, loud music throughout. Options are not attractive either: truly independent films (not low-budget Hollywood movies) have a hard time raising capital. And, when released, they can manage only token advertising so that, even with good reviews, these films come and go in a week, without a fighting chance of reaching their potential audience. For the filmmaker then, it is back to square one, once again raising money for the next project that will barely get any release, etc.

I believe it is important to face this impasse. I also think that to learn from what is presently going on in the industry, one needs to understand how and why these changes came about. Rather than moaning about the lack of taste of audiences or complaining about the greed prevalent in the business, one needs to go back and analyze what brought us here in the first place. But even this is difficult for there is no single nefarious decision that can be pointed to, no malevolent conspiracy between the big players in the field as would be the case in a Hollywood script. Rather, we are dealing with isolated events, each one giving rise to consequences whose exact breadth and particulars could be noted only after the fact. All together, using Wayne C. Booth's words, the circumstances we find ourselves in make up "an *un*controlled experiment of vast proportions, the results of which we will never fully know."[1]

My view is that three factors contributed the most to the present situation. First, there was the rapid evolution of Hollywood into a winner-take-all economic model which made it very difficult for independents and foreigners to compete. Second, the thrust of the counterculture movement in the sixties pushed Hollywood into embracing a cinema of experience rather than one of reflection. Third, in the arts themselves, the debasement of aesthetic values made possible by postmodernism undermined both the artist's self-confidence and the value of material created outside the culture industry's immediate concerns.

It may be true, as Perry Anderson suggests, that "no class in history immediately comprehends the logic of its own historical situation."[2] Disoriented and confused we surely are. In cinema, the forces of entertainment appear indeed to have won the day. Yet, the medium is too important to be abandoned without a fight to the barons of the culture industry who see no distinction between it and Coca-Cola, popcorn, or any other product of mass consumption. My story is a rather circuitous one. Please, bear with me.

## II

Although Hollywood earned its global ascendancy mostly by chance— World War I devastated the European cinemas and ended their dominance in world markets—there was also, no doubt, a better business acumen here than elsewhere. Most formidably, the system was rationalized early on so as to be able to deliver time and time again products that would be of interest to a large audience for a reasonable cost. The industry's success, Janet Staiger convincingly writes, was due to two major factors. On the one hand, those in charge were able to "simplify, standardize and consolidate" the entire production process so as to make it as efficient as possible. On the other hand, each project could lay claim to some textual differences, some unique production values.[3] Indeed, if Hollywood never looked back after World War I, it is because it was able most of the time to avoid getting stuck in norms so rigid they bored spectators. The system thus remained eclectic throughout its history, welcoming foreign personalities and experimenting with ideas and styles that had proved themselves elsewhere.

Internally Hollywood evolved from a system of filmmaking controlled by cameramen working on their own to a unit of specialists operating under the leadership of a director. Quickly though, to combat inefficiency and reduce production costs, the core operation shifted to someone who could coordinate these matters from the outside—a central producer for each studio. By the thirties, following a sharp drop at the box office, decentralization became popular, each studio now employing a number of producers, each in charge of eight to ten films per year. By the fifties, the forced breakdown of the studio system saw the beginning of a series of structural changes whose consequences are still with us today.[4]

For the first time, the studios lost their corporate independence. Paramount became a part of Gulf and Western, United Artists was absorbed by Transamerica, Warner Brothers was taken over by Kinney National Service, etc. That these particular marriages did not last long is inconsequential. Each studio became merely the leisure time division of a conglomerate made up of radically different industrial concerns (an oil company, an insurance business, etc.). Although the change was seen at first as having little impact beyond bookkeeping, it turned out to have a profound influence on the entire studio culture. Think about it: the old rivalry between studios had now been complicated by the fact that each studio had to compete—in attention, financing, and revenues—with the other money-making ventures within each industrial group. Much more scrutiny than before was thus brought to the entire process of manufacturing and marketing the products of the film division. In other words, the new owners were not going to repeat the mistake of the studios which, early on, failed to acknowledge television as a potential source of income for their products.[5] Rational business practices were therefore forced upon an industry that had grown in relative protection from outsiders. "Hotshot" CEOs were suddenly surveying their new domains with calculative eyes: was it possible to extract new profits from movies, conquer new markets, and generally increase filmmaking revenues?

III

The answer remained in doubt until an entirely new breed of players replaced the ill-fitted combines. You are familiar with today's names: Disney, Sony, Seagram's, Time-Warner, etc. The new owners differentiated themselves from their predecessors because their joint interests stood in related areas: television networks, cable companies, printing presses, publishing houses, bookstore chains, radio stations, record companies, newspapers and magazines, advertising and billboard companies, etc. Instead of remaining autonomous, each company could now be used to help the others reach maximum audience exposure. Indeed it is the effective "synergy" between them that made possible a vast increase in receipts and profits, and helped redefine a movie as a lead item for a variety of ancillary goods.

Typically a big picture's opening is now accompanied by the simultaneous release of a book based on the film's story and a CD of its music. At the same time, all sorts of merchandise—clothing, toys, lunch boxes, etc.—become suddenly available in stores everywhere. The film's animated characters inevitably pop up on McDonald's packaging. And eventually, the picture's "concept" or characters are exported to theme parks, television shows, video games, CD-ROM's, etc.[6] With a campaign in full swing, the "product" can now be encountered not only on theater screens but also in all areas of daily life: in advertisements on TV, billboards, magazines and newspapers, in book and record stores, in restaurants and department stores, in supermarkets, even on people themselves as they advertise the film on their T-shirts and baseball caps. Or vice versa, the picture itself can function as a billboard for other products, for instance when a protagonist "happens" to smoke a Marlboro cigarette, shop at Macy's, or eat some Häagen Dazs ice cream. All these gimmicks and alliances have clearly expanded the reach and visibility of a film, turning it into an event that one needs to see in order to participate in the cultural exchange of daily life. To orchestrate the multitudinous possibilities of each product, each media company affiliate employs synergy managers "whose job it is to work out how their division can add value to others, and others to theirs." Through this kind of saturation then, the big movie did not just increase its share of the market, it aimed at monopolizing it. As noted by Theodor Adorno, greedy expansion fits the logic of the capitalist enterprise, for its ultimate objective is "to handle, to manipulate, to absorb everything," leaving "[no]thing beyond itself untouched."[8]

The new communication companies were certainly helped in their marketing expansion by the technological changes of the last twenty years. The introduction of the VCR and pay cable technologies, for instance, fattened the gross revenues of films to the point that, today, more money is made from these distribution circuits than from the theatrical box office alone. In economic terms, all of this meant that the old law of diminishing returns for a product, once postulated by Alfred Marshall and others, had finally been overruled.[9] Although depending upon the success of a film in its initial theatrical release, the new markets could in fact generate exponential returns for its producers. Clearly, the economic tables have been dramatically turned around with only big movies and global marketing now capable of consistently delivering rich monetary rewards, a situation described by W. Brian Arthur as the law of *increasing* returns, "the tendency for that which is ahead to get further ahead, for that which loses advantage to lose further advantage."[10]


## IV


The amount of attention and money involved in all these synergies required a radically new kind of product: the blockbuster. As Robert H. Frank and Philip J. Cook point out in their analysis of the new economic trend, there are only a few books on the *New York Times* best-sellers list.[11] These are the books which will be reviewed in the press, these are the books which will be advertised and financially supported by the publishers, these are the books which people will hear and read about, see displayed in bookstores, and buy. Only so many books make it, the others don't. Each time a book manages its way into the charts, another is removed. To turn a profit at all, a book must make the list and stay there for a while. That is where the rewards are. The more copies that are sold, the more a publisher can lower the cost per volume. Twenty books that sell five thousand copies each lose money for the publishing house, one that sells one hundred thousand copies guarantees that the company will be in the black at the end of the fiscal year. The same situation applies to films. Only so many films become hits at the box office. For the lucky ones, each print, each video, each release venue effectively lowers its overall distribution cost per viewer.

Whereas studio movies were put together from the inside out (the script largely determining the choice of the director, the actors, etc.), blockbusters are assembled from the outside in. They may originate, for instance, in a company's need for a big movie for Christmas or the Fourth of July.[12] That is followed by lumping together actors, writers, directors, musicians, etc., big names, recognizable names, names that can be counted on in a global marketing campaign. No one seems to care "whether or not [these people are] right for the material."[13] Worse, "the script is the last thing that people focus on."[14] Everything is based on which personality, what genre, what theme, what kind of action, cutting style, or special effect is popular with the audience right now. Not surprisingly, this approach has often resulted in "high concept" scripts, super heroes, cardboard characters, nonstop action, an ultrafast pace, and a brassy score. The purpose, remember, is no longer to make a film but to generate a short-lived but omnipresent brand name whose contents can be exploited in as many venues as possible. The difference between the studios of yore and today's corporate structures is not unlike that between an old county hospital and a modern HMO. Sure, doctors, nurses, and staff people made a living out of caring for people, but turning a profit was not the organization's primary reason for being.

According to Lawrence Kasdan, director-producers George Lucas and Steven Spielberg must bear responsibility for the industry's evolution. They "changed every studio's idea of what a movie should do in terms of investment versus return. It ruined the modest expectations of the movie business. Now every studio film is designed to be a blockbuster."[15] Practically speaking, the need for blockbusters has pushed the industry to go with known quantities only, regardless of cost. Harold Vogel puts it this way:

It may be less risky to pay a star $1.5 million than to pay an unknown $100,000; the presence of the star may easily increase the value of the property by several times that $1.5 million salary through increased sales in theatrical and other markets, whereas the unknown may contribute nothing from the standpoint of returns on investment.[16]

Absolute performance (how good someone actually is) has become less important than relative performance (how much additional money can this person generate as opposed to someone else), with the winner grabbing most of the rewards. This way of doing things has been characterized by Frank and Cook as "the winner-take-all society."[17] While Bruce Willis, Arnold Schwarzenegger, Michael Douglas, Sylvester Stallone, Eddie Murphy, and others are paid millions for their participation in a film, only twelve percent of the actors registered in Hollywood find work in any given year and barely ten percent of the lucky ones earn more than $5,000 a year for their efforts.[18] For the three large agencies which dominate Hollywood life—Creative Artists Agency, William Morris Agency, and International Creative Management—the lesson does not go unnoticed: the value of a film is no longer located in the worth of its drama or the talent of those working in it. What matters most of all is the participants' fame, their celebrity status, their ability to support a package with global economic potential. Selling stars, writers, and directors as private labels, these agencies assemble and reassemble their pawns in ever more exciting combinations. "The goal," Arthur suggests, "becomes the search for the Next Big Thing."[19] The agents may speak warmly of creative personnel and talented individuals, but that carries as much resonance as Jack Valenti talking about art during the Academy Awards. Who you are as a human being, how much talent you have means little to the agents. What they need is brand appeal, someone they can sell.

For Hollywood then, the huge stars, the big script, the state-of-the-art technology, the one hundred million dollar budget, and the ubiquitous advertising campaign make plenty of economic sense. To be sure, this gambling is not for the faint of heart. As the stakes keep increasing, the producers end up putting all their chips on one big bet without knowing really what the odds are.[20] But that is Hollywood's problem. For its competitors at home and abroad though, the increase in production and distribution costs has been devastating. Working with small budgets, unable to match the scale of Hollywood's products on any level, these producers can no longer meet the demands of spectators jaded by extravaganzas. For the customer, because a theater ticket, video rental, and cable subscription cost the same regardless of the kind of film being watched, a blockbuster movie appears to give more entertainment value for the money. Put differently, one could say that the big Hollywood movies have redefined the audience's expectations of what a film is. "Market norms" in effect, Robert Kuttner writes, "drive out non-market norms."[21] Small projects with an unknown cast, a more adventurous narrative, maybe even an idiosyncratic style, will find it increasingly difficult to reach the finish line. So while it is possible for a filmmaker to produce a film on a mini-budget with the help of actors and crew (and the continuous support of farsighted equipment companies like Clairmont Camera), the release of a film involves an entirely different group of players. Newspapers, magazines, and billboard companies are not likely to give you a rebate on your ads because you're a nice guy and your film got good reviews. The same with networks, local TV stations, and cable companies. As for Jay Leno, David Letterman, and the gossip press, your unknown actors have nothing to offer that could possibly interest them. All in all, if it costs the same to release a genuinely independent film as it costs to release a run-of-the-mill Hollywood movie, and the latter will far outperform the former in the marketplace, why go through the effort? For independent producers then, the temptation is to play the only cards that will guarantee them at least some distribution time: the sleaze, the freaky, the outlandish, sex and violence beyond the norms Hollywood is comfortable with. In the end, the winner-take-all environment has polluted the air, infecting most with jackpot fever, leaving independents with few options but to look for shock value.


V


My second point has to do with the changes in filmmaking brought about as a result of the counterculture movement in the sixties. As far back as 1962, Tom Hayden of the Students for a Democratic Society was claiming that the national power structure excluded ordinary people from the "basic decisions affecting the nature and organization of work, rewards, and opportunities."[22] Before long, the sixties saw the radical rejection by the younger generation of all the values held by their elders. Every entrenched segment of society came under attack: the political power, the world of business, the conventional social virtues, traditional morality, consumerism, the whole "Eisenhower-Disney-Doris Day façade" as a *Rolling Stones* editor was eventually to put it.[23]

But we need to slow down here. Why this sudden rebellion by the young? First there was the excitement provided by a young president in the

White House, following eight years that had been dominated by older men who stuck to views shaped by their experience in the forties: Dwight Eisenhower as President, Foster Dulles as Secretary of State, and Charles Wilson from General Motors in charge of the economy. Not only was Kennedy young—and his wife beautiful—but his vitality, liberal social ideas, and an economic policy resolutely directed toward growth, resonated well with a generation disenchanted by the ever-present social conformity propounded by families, churches, businesses, and the media. For a while, the Peace Corps and other New Frontier programs were able to quench the idealistic thirst of the young. The failed invasion of Cuba and the shock of multiple political assassinations, however, quickly reawakened doubt about who was really in charge of the country. Were there conspiracies after all? LBJ replaced Kennedy. The Great Society got moving. The war on poverty blitzed through Congress: school lunches, Head Start, etc. With the Civil Rights Act, the Administration assuaged some of the shame of segregation that had been exposed to the world by Martin Luther King Jr. and his marchers in Birmingham and elsewhere. Yet explosion after explosion continued to rock the land. Racial unrest destroyed parts of many cities. An unpopular war was raging in Asia. Draft cards were burned on campuses. ROTC recruiters were expelled from colleges and universities. Dow Chemical came under attack for manufacturing napalm. Other businesses were indicted for being socially or ecologically irresponsible. There were sit-ins everywhere. Large demonstrations in Chicago, Washington, and elsewhere united all those who demanded not only an end to the war but also radical changes in the way this country was run.

On the cultural front, hair grew longer, clothing loosened up, jeans were everywhere, the pill pushed sex out of the closet, film and book censorship disappeared, and rock music exploded on the scene, at Woodstock and in the record stores' cash registers. More ominously, drugs became prevalent. Ken Kesey perfectly summarized the mood of the times when, in *One Flew Over the Cuckoo's Nest*, he portrayed the United States as an asylum-society with nefarious leaders bullying and domineering the rest of the population.

## VI

Through it all, Hollywood remained aloof, incapable of addressing the issues that were tearing the country apart. Although in the past, the studios had learned to use the screen quite effectively to mobilize not only GIs but also the population at large against foreign villains, they now faced their worst nightmare: an impossible topic and a divided audience at home. There was simply no way to entertain people on these issues. And to talk about them concretely was risking alienating those in the audience who saw things differently. Let us remember: from the beginning, the entire system had been built around a mass audience whereas it was now facing ideologically fragmented groups. Caught by surprise by the rapid shift in mores and the dissension in the land, the studios' more conventional products felt flat, banal, out of touch with what was happening. Rock Hudson romancing Doris Day simply would not do when Kent State students were being shot by the National Guard on campus lawns and the mayhem in Vietnam was brought fresh every night into people's living rooms.

But what else was there? Well, there was the foreign cinema. The numbers speak by themselves: during the fifties when the major studios released an average of 250 films per year, there were about 170 imports available yearly. By the sixties, in a moment of crisis for the American film industry, these figures were turned around—Hollywood now producing only about 150 movies on a year-to-year basis while there were about 250 imports available for distribution.[24] The herald year for foreign films was 1964 when 303 features were offered to the market place! These numbers, however, should be taken with a grain of salt. Not every foreign film was actually released during that time and not every film was memorable.[25] In fact many were no better than Hollywood's run-of-the-mill products.

Nevertheless, there is no doubt that a segment at least of the general public (the younger audience mostly) was now interested in exploring a different kind of cinema, subtitled though it may have been. In retrospect, it is clear that this tentative move toward more mature themes and styles was a marriage of convenience rather than anything else. The appeal of these films at the time may have been based primarily on their sexual frankness. Furthermore, following the New Wave in France and elsewhere, many characters were decidedly younger and their faces, refreshingly, were allowed to remain ordinary, a far cry from the glamorous treatment usually given stars in Hollywood. Finally, it is also possible that the stylistic immediacy of these films (e.g., hand-held camera work and jump-cutting) appealed to the young because it felt anarchistic and was perceived as a joyful violation of the aesthetic norms of the past.

Even though the films created by François Truffaut, Federico Fellini, Vera Chytilovà, and many others slipped into the mainstream, gaining market share against their Hollywood opponent, it took some time for American independents to take advantage of the situation. Dennis Hopper's *Easy Rider* eventually pulled it off in 1969, aligning the film thematically and stylistically with the rest of the revolutionary culture enjoyed by the younger audience. Faced with this visual upheaval, it was easy at the time to believe that the modernist revolution that had seized music, painting, and literature at the turn of the century had finally reached film as well. In film in particular, for the very first time, what was perceived as the avant-garde dominated the cultural scene.[26] Surely no turning back was thinkable at this junction. Filmmakers here and in the rest of the world were going to keep probing the limits of the medium. A film Renaissance was finally at hand.

## VII

This view of things turned out to be dead wrong after all. The support of high culture by what was after all mostly middle-class youth proved as lasting as its endorsement of the new left and black radicals. Most observers at the time got it wrong because they interpreted mere experimentation for lasting conviction. More specifically, once American films were able to provide novelty without subtitles, outrageous homegrown characters rather than aloof foreign ones, boisterous sex encounters in lieu of refined erotics, and quick cutting as a substitute for genuine aesthetic experimentation, spicing it all with a newly charged but uniquely American violence, the passing endorsement of the foreign cinema came to an end. It had been but a misalliance from the beginning.

In the other arts too, the current was flowing from stateliness toward confrontation, energy, and immediacy. Happenings were in vogue. The Living Theater in New York fostered performance art, breaking down the traditional boundaries between actors and spectators. "Action painting" and the quick, bright, colorful, iconoclastic pop art of Andy Warhol became the rage in many galleries. And, of course, the rock music of the Rolling Stones, Jim Morrison, Jimi Hendrix, Janet Joplin, and so many others attracted all those rebelling against the stifling rigidity and conformism of the previous generation's mores. Certainly, in the long run, rock had a lot more to offer to the kids than the rest of culture put together. You didn't have to bring anything to it for it spoke to the body rather than the intellect. As a music manager put it then, "rock and roll music is one of the most vital revolutionary forces in the West—it blows people all the way back to their senses and makes them feel good, like they are *alive* again in the middle of the monstrous funeral parlor of Western civilization."[27] Not only were you able to experience the sound's vibrations running through your entire body, a huge crowd could respond identically to a given beat, generating a Dionysiac sensation in everyone. Sharing marijuana surely helped. As Todd Gitlin remembered it, "the point was to open up a new space, an *inner* space, so that we could *space out*, live for the sheer exultant point of living."[28] More so than the other arts then, rock epitomized what was going on. Yet, if we look at its undercurrents, we cannot fail to notice how in tune it was with a consistent characteristic of the American psyche: although the celebration may have been pagan in its effusive bodily displays, it nevertheless remained thoroughly evangelical in spirit. It was, in other words, a populist reaffirmation of natural instinct, of vital impulse over the need for ratiocination. In the end, the culture industry had no trouble hijacking this audience, taking it for a ride, giving the kids an illusion of antiestablishment rhetoric while simultaneously reaffirming traditional distrust toward rationality and artistry.[29] This point, however, requires some elaboration.

## VIII

In a remarkable essay now largely forgotten, Richard Hofstadter once emphasized the continuing importance of anti-intellectualism in American life.[30] Working from the point of view of the fifties (they feel just like the nineties), Hofstadter focused his attention on the continuing values in the history of this country that militate against those who elevate the life of the mind. Foremost in his judgment was the influence of the Protestant evangelical movement which, early on, rebelled against the mediation of the learned clergy, insisting that the common man was naturally capable of understanding right from wrong without the help of any special learning. Uniting these believers, Hofstadter wrote, was "the feeling that ideas should above all be made to work, the disdain for doctrine and for refinements in ideas, the subordination of men of ideas to men of emotional power or manipulative skill."[31] The sense of independence, of having but oneself to count on was nurtured as well by the Westward movement which, as Alexis de Tocqueville noted, not only rewarded fast-thinking individuals but also insulated them from the reach of the New England elite.[32] These two forces eventually combined to produce a popular ethos that stood in deeply felt opposition to the acquired learning of the educated classes. By the end of the nineteenth century, the mentality was solidly anchored throughout much of American society. According to this view, Hofstadter summarized, "the plain sense of the common man, especially if tested by success in some demanding line of practical work, is an altogether substitute for, if not actually much superior to, formal knowledge and expertise acquired in the schools. . . ."[33] Integral then to the American spirit is the notion that the common man can do no wrong. Anyone can judge a situation and take action. Just show me how to use a gun, I'll know when and whom to shoot. Those who flaunt their intellect on the other hand are seen as a dangerous aristocracy most ready to discriminate against, take advantage of, and oppress common folks. Hence they are to be distrusted, rejected, and opposed.

Not surprisingly, antiestablishment feelings present in the counterculture turned against intellectualism in the arts. Theodore Roszak made this particularly clear when he wrote that the thrust of the movement was aimed at the previous generation's "egocentric and cerebral mode of consciousness." He continued, "In its place, there must be a new culture in which the non-intellective capacities of the personality—those capacities that take fire from visionary splendor and the experience of human communion—become the arbiters of the good, the true, and the beautiful."[34] In practice, this meant that high art, especially in music, painting, and literature, but also, eventually, in the art cinema of Europe and elsewhere, was not in sync with the mood of the times. It was perceived as theoretically grounded, abstruse, and unnecessarily demanding. Difficulty and obscurity had been elevated at the expense of all other artistic values. And that was the case only because artists had to please the mannered taste of pretentious older critics, totally cutoff from the joy and dynamism of life. In *Against Interpretation*, Susan Sontag certainly reflected the mood of the times when she took a shot at the then dominant New Criticism school in literary studies. Typically, what these critics enjoyed most was to argue endlessly about the meanings articulated through the organic unity of a text, turning the work into an exegesis that sucked all life out of the material. Not addressed by that process was "the pure, untranslatable, sensuous immediacy of some of [the] images."[35] In film, *Last Year in Marienbad* (Alain Resnais, 1961) would offer a good example of pure visual pleasure. Sontag also mentions the sudden intrusion of a tank rumbling through a city street at night in Ingmar Bergman's *Silence* (1963). These images in her view should not be explained symbolically; they had to be experienced on a pure phenomenological level. The critical practice of the times simply did not do justice to such immediacy of the art. In fact, Sontag went on, "to interpret is to impoverish, to deplete the world."[36] Such cerebral disposition merely flaunted "the hypertrophy of the intellect at the expense of energy and sensual capability. . . ."[37] In other words, critics had seriously narrowed the possible play made available by the work of art. Not only that, David Steigerwald makes clear, "by turning art into an intellectual activity, interpretation denied the artist access to everything that could not be rationally understood, which is to say, nearly everything that comprised life itself: nature, impulse, desire, madness, passion."[38] For Sontag, moreover, it was important "to recover ours senses. We must learn to *see* more, to *hear* more, to *feel* more," for a work of art, after all, was an experience first, it was "a programming of sensations" before anything else.[39] The direct physical or emotional effect on the spectator was the important factor. It did not matter therefore whether an effect originated from a Rauschenberg painting or a record by the Supremes, the impact was equally valuable.[40] But we must be fair to Sontag: her views were inclusive rather than prescriptive in spirit. She had recognized that the old standards for the arts were fully out of tune with contemporary cultural demands and she was making a bid to keep them afloat within the new paradigm. "From the vantage point of this new sensibility," she wrote, "the beauty of the machine or of the solution to a mathematical problem, of a painting by Jasper Johns, of a film by Jean-Luc Godard, and of the personalities and music of the Beatles is equally accessible."[41] Only today do we know that these different aspects or luminaries of modern culture were incompatible after all, that, for instance, the success of the Beatles sent Godard packing. Likewise her celebration of the "luminousness" of images in the films of Alain Resnais, Ingmar Bergman, or Yoshiro Ozu failed to carry the day after all. Far from it, the general agreement that images could be immediately felt, directly experienced, undermined artistic complexity in texts. As Steigerwald points out, Sontag's push against interpretation "left herself no way to fend off the corrupting force of the market place."[42] Art in the long run got ransacked while business profited mightily from all the protest songs.[43]

## IX

All in all then, the counterculture radical demand that art could be directly apprehended by the senses, without any training, any research, or any effort by the mind, fell in step with the anti-intellectualism in American life that Hofstadter had so convincingly described. Yet the counterculture's attack against what it saw as impersonal, abstract, stuffy, intellectual art seriously misfired insofar as this was not bourgeois art at all. In fact, as Daniel Bell argued in his book on the cultural contradictions of capitalism, the original bourgeois social values, those that stemmed from the Protestant ethic and Puritan beliefs, were no longer even operating in society at the time, having been progressively engulfed, since the beginning of the century, within other ideas intimately linked to business.[44] Whereas

> the basic American value pattern emphasized the virtue of achievement, defined as doing and making, and a man displayed his character in the quality of his work . . . by the 1950's, the pattern of achievement remained, but it had been redefined to emphasize status and taste. The culture was no longer concerned with how to work and achieve, but with how to spend and enjoy.[45]

Instead of attacking the encroachments of business values into the realm of culture, the radical movement hit the wrong target, assaulting modernism, an artistic style born out of distaste for the bourgeoisie and rejection of capitalism. Tragically, the counterculture's profound dislike of aesthetic distance made it an ally, on this point at least, of the culture industry. Certainly, the easy consumption and immediate pleasure already programmed in the products of the latter were not out of line with the demand for immediacy sought by the former. Although stuck creatively at the time, the entertainment industry eventually found a way to provide participatory thrill without the foreign cultural baggage of the sixties. To keep the new audience turned on, it was discovered, all you needed was a great display of energy speaking directly to the senses. And that is what we got.

## X

At first, Hollywood was quite incapable of matching the kind of immediacy and involvement that could be generated in happenings, rock concerts, etc. Typically, since Griffith, viewers had learned to identify with a film's principal characters. The classical cinema manipulated this involvement through techniques (preferential staging and lighting, more close-ups, etc.) integrated into a plot that progressively restricted the world to a series of action sequences that put the protagonist at risk. Through it all though, the point of view remained respectfully spectatorial in tone: one essentially *looked* at an action unfolding out there, in the diegetic world.[46] Much more than this therefore was needed for the movies to release the kind of punch, the physical absorption, the immediate rush, that other types of contemporary entertainment were now able to deliver. For the jaded younger audience certainly, partial identification with a character in an otherwise placid, detached spectacle, was no longer enough. They groped for total involvement, absolute participation in the show. How could this be achieved? More so than any other techniques, motion within the frame and camera movement were found to provide just the kind of visual stir needed to grab the spectators' attention.

## XI

But let me go back for a moment. Action scenes had always been Hollywood's forte. Faster cutting, violent motion on the screen typically took over when characters stopped talking. All at once the visual activity on the screen swelled. The pace sharpened as a result of someone's chasing someone else. Or there could be an outburst of frenzied action with one character hitting another, the crashing of a body against a piece of furniture, with general mayhem ensuing, etc. When analyzed, an action scene can be said to work on two levels. First there is the interest in the diegetic action: what is happening to the protagonist, how much danger is involved, how will everything turn out. But second, there is also, for the eye, a series of quick responses to multiple stimuli. The eye indeed is programmed to react at once to any change in the peripheral vision area. The flurry of activity therefore punches the optic nerves all the way to the visual cortex. Although essentially a disturbance, the sensory staccato raises the stakes, sending a thrill to otherwise inactive little conduits. As a result of this twin maneuvering, the psychological identification with the character in danger is intensified by a visceral reaction based on the quickening of the stimuli. But whereas the first response benefits from careful character conditioning and narrative buildup, and is thus dependent on the craft of the filmmakers, the payoff of the second is fully automatic in nature: one has no choice but to react.

Let us focus on this reflex action for a moment. What does it mean? How does it work? More than a hundred years ago, much research focused on what happened to a body in the grip of strong experiences like grief or fear. Darwin, among other scientists, carefully noted the physical results of fear: there was the widening of the mouth, the stretching of the eyes, and the raising of the eyebrows. The heartbeat would quicken and the skin could get pale. In addition, the individual would often perspire, muscles might shiver, etc.[47] The prevalent idea at the time was that the sight of something fearful was communicated to the mind, which responded accordingly by activating all kinds of responses in the body. William James, however, reordered the terms of this scenario. In his essay on psychology, he contended that "the bodily changes follow directly the perception of the exciting fact," that "our feeling of [these] . . . changes as they occur *is* the emotion."[48] His conclusion was truly radical:

> We feel sorry because we cry, angry because we strike, afraid because we tremble. . . . Without the bodily states following on the perceptions, the latter would be purely cognitive in form, colorless, destitute of emotional warmth. We might then see the bear and judge it best to run, receive the insult and deem it right to strike, but we should not actually *feel* afraid or angry.[49]

To go back to Darwin's example, one's experience of fear was now construed as a direct bodily reaction to specific stimuli, a sensation that does not immediately involve the mind. Insofar as film is concerned, this would mean that the spectator can in fact be agitated through bodily stimulation rather than mental apprehension.

## XII

Years later, James's ideas would find their application in the cinema thanks to Slavko Vorkapich. In a remarkable article published in 1972 in *American Cinematographer*, the famous montage specialist isolates "kinesthetic or implicit motor impulses" which are passed through joints, muscles, and tendons so that at the end we duplicate internally whatever it is we are watching. "To kinesthetically feel," he explains, is to somehow reproduce these movements [a door opening, a billowing curtain, a wave breaking, etc.] within our body."[50] Motion, construed as the key to the visceral response of spectators, could now be generated in all kinds of ways. The point can be made clear using the last scene in *Thelma and Louise* (Ridley Scott, 1991), when the two women have been cornered by the police on a canyon plateau. There are a few camera movements in the scene but they are not particularly spectacular, and neither is the editing. The excitement rather originates from within the shots themselves: in each of them something is astir that grabs the eyes' attention. Let us take a look. An extremely long lens first dramatizes the sudden rise of the helicopter from within the canyon walls, emphasizing its size, making us feel that it is literally on top of the women. The turbulence of the blades immediately raises a storm of dust all around and throws the women's hats out of the car. Their hair now waves freely in the wind. Tight close-ups of the actresses make us share their confusion. Long shots frame tens of police cars rushing to the scene, with all their lights flashing. The women panic: there is an extreme close-up of Susan Sarandon's foot pushing on the accelerator followed by a tight shot of a tire screeching forward with dust being kicked up. As they realize they are trapped, the film cuts to a series of extreme close-ups showing bullets being loaded in the barrel of a shotgun, a magazine being shoved into a chamber, fingers tightening on a trigger. The lead cops argue in front of the rotating blades of the helicopter. A cross-bar targets the back of the women through a long lens. More bullets are loaded. As the women decide their fate in tight close-ups, the sun which backlights Geena Davis's head is reflected off the face of Susan Sarandon. Their hair continue to flutter in the wind, etc., etc. In all these shots, the emphasis is no longer on storytelling (conveyed through conventional staging and editing) but on creating an internal tension within the images through a visual displacement of some sort.

This kind of filmmaking is as different from Eisenstein's notion of shocks as it is from standard action scenes in the classical cinema. Eisenstein indeed also looked at ways to infuse his images with kinetic stimulations of all kinds, but his goal was to help the audience expand beyond the present action to the larger meaning of the scene. A shock, he wrote, is anything "that is known and proven to exercise a definite effect on the attention and emotions of the audience and that, combined with others, possesses the characteristic of concentrating the audience's emotions in any direction dictated by the production's purpose."[51] In *Strike* (1924), the Russian director crosscuts the Cossacks shooting the demonstrators with cattle being butchered in a slaughterhouse. Our visceral reaction to the real blood gushing from the bodies of the animals thus provides a powerful simile for the workers' "massacre." In Scott's film to the contrary, the kinetic flux leads nowhere, its only function being to intensify the viewers' attention on the moment itself, shot after shot. The hair fluttering in the wind mesmerize our eyes. The blades of the helicopter rotating behind the police energize what would otherwise remain but a dull confrontation with undeveloped characters. Daniel Bell, I believe, has sharply pointed out the difference between the two types of shocks. "The effect of immediacy, impact, simultaneity, and sensation as the mode of aesthetic—and psychological—experience is to *dramatize* each moment, to increase our tensions to a fever pitch, and yet to leave us without a resolution, reconciliation, or transforming moment, which is the catharsis of a ritual."[52] So whereas Eisenstein's shocks lead us toward revolutionary solidarity, Scott's keep us hyperventilating during the scene but deflated a moment later when the credits roll and we leave the theater without instructions as to what to do with our excess emotions.

When compared to the classical cinema, today's movies can be seen as belonging to another breed altogether.[53] Then, spectators remained essentially aloof witnesses watching the action from afar. Now, the scene is organized for the sake of effects. By focusing on the physical action of a scene, the buildup of character is eliminated. In other words, one goes immediately for the jugular and stays there. Additionally, still in *Thelma and Louise*, what is seen of the action is shown impressionistically, as if the entire events were now perceived from the women's own point of view. The viewers thus experience the helicopter's surge as the women do, immediately, viscerally. The faces of the protagonists appear very close as they would be were we standing just next to them. The police action becomes nothing but moving vehicles, dust, lights flashing, bullhorns, guns, and cross-bars. Every shot is articulated to emphasize some motion or the dance of light. Identification with characters out there has given way to an incestuous relationship with them. Viewers react to the action at the same time and with the same subjectivity as the characters do. Put another way, spectators can be said to access the scene on a first-person basis. They are excited by the images first, they process the information second. Immersed in the scene, our eyes vibrate in response to the pulsating stimuli. The diegetic world has become our world as well.

# XIII

A second attack on the senses was made possible by Garrett Brown's invention of the Steadicam in 1976. At first the new stabilizing device was used to supplement regular filmmaking rather than as an alternative to it. More specifically, it integrated both the convenience of handheld shooting (a practice somewhat inimical to the Hollywood spirit) and the steadiness of the dolly.[54] One could now follow a protagonist past sharp turns and up a flight of stairs without any shakiness marring the image. Beyond this, the Steadicam focused the attention of filmmakers on camera motion as a device capable of engaging audiences' participation. But, unlike the views which emanate from the camera when it is handheld (when one feels the pressure of the air as it surges ahead) or from a dolly which is weighed down by gravity, there is a definite insubstantiality to Steadicam shots. In fact, the Steadicam look can be described as pure penetration of space, a zero degree of kinetics. Its effect, speed, Jean Baudrillard wrote, "is itself a pure object, since it cancels out the ground and territorial reference-points, since it runs ahead of time to annul time itself, since it moves more quickly than its own cause and obliterates that cause by outstripping it."[55] In other words, camera motion could now separate itself from the world of the characters and address the senses on their own. Suspended in midair, whirling around, the camera could make itself known and provoke reactions unconnected to the limited, diegetic space occupied by the protagonists. Rock videos showed the way by using the new possibilities to the hilt, capturing the attention of the younger audience and redefining visual style for the rest of the industry in the process.

To strengthen its hold over its young customers, Hollywood had no choice but to follow suit, adapting its filmmaking to the virtual world made possible by the Steadicam and all the other devices that similarly helped disembody the camera style. Whereas, in the classical cinema, camera movement and action scenes were used as visual punctuation mostly, with the regular, more sedate narrative resuming just afterward, in contemporary filmmaking, motion of one type or another could be added at any time to spice up a shot. In *Bound* (The Wachowski Brothers, 1996), for instance, as a protagonist is making a phone call, the camera abruptly takes off and rushes along the long telephone cord, all the way to the plug on the wall, and through the plug, to the other side, onto the cord again, the telephone, and the character who answers the ring in the apartment next door. Viewers are thus taken on a totally arbitrary but irresistible ride through space. The faster the motion, the quicker the reaction by the eyes. The eyes have no choice but to respond to the visual changes. They are thus engaged—James-like—independently from the mind which reacts by storing momentarily story and characters on the back burner. And the more often this kind of motion is used, the less time the mind has for ordinary mental activity

It is this hijacking of the eyes by the camera style that has defined the American cinema since the eighties and made it so successful here and abroad. There is no way indeed for anyone to reject the powerful immersion in pure space. The engagement is reflexive before all else. We are made to experience abrupt and novel sensations. Whereas in the classical cinema, one would look at the screen from a seat in the theater, partly identifying with the world of a character, the new camera style forces viewers within that world. William James described a similar phenomenon when he recalled that "if our friend goes near the edge of a precipice, we get the well-known feeling of 'all-overishness', and we shrink back. . . ."[56] Today the film technique keeps us on the edge as well, even when we do not care much about the well-being of the character involved. Witness for instance, the last sequence preceding the arrest of the main protagonist in *Goodfellas* (1990). Martin Scorsese keeps the juices flowing by forcing the camera to fly through space, surging toward a pot of pasta or rushing to the protagonist's car without conventional cue or motivation. Whether we want to or not, he makes us experience the world through the coked head of the character. What matters is the flux of it all.

These are the kind of shots that have transformed our cinema. The key factor here is that spectators are made to participate and become accomplices of the action rather than its witnesses. Aesthetic distance has been eliminated. For directors, this means being in charge of a roller coaster, and their talent is now gauged in terms of their ability to produce as many thrills as possible. For audiences bred on such effects, different kinds of filmmaking, say *Secrets and Lies* (Mike Leigh, 1996), will feel terribly slow, dull, uneventful, unbearable even. Abroad too, this boisterous cinema is altering local taste, destroying independent film cultures. All in all, the deintellectualization of art and the primacy given to sensual responses by the body—the guiding principles of the counterculture movement in the sixties—have led to a filmmaking style today that is entirely driven by stimuli which mesmerize and keep audiences coming back for more.

## XIV

Whereas counterculture assaulted the leading principles of art from the outside, postmodernism has undermined them from the inside. I do not intend here to provide a full-fledged account of the postmodern movement, for this has been done very successfully elsewhere.[57] Rather, I will focus on those ideas that have most impacted the welfare of artists and filmmakers. But before we proceed with the current trend, we need to reacquaint ourselves with the foundation and ethos of modernism, the art movement that came under attack.

At the beginning of the century, the situation for artists was without historical precedent. Believing they could escape neither the ravages of the industrial revolution nor the dominance of art by the market place, artists carved up special places where serious and controversial art could still be exhibited: galleries, museums, concert halls, art cinemas, etc. These modern sanctuaries were established to protect art from the general commodification of life. Emerging from the creative will of dissident artists, beautiful and unique works could be appreciated there by the public, without the coarse pressure of buying and selling found everywhere else in society. Modern art was thus strongly romantic and affirmative in its nature: individual creators standing against the low standards pushed by the flourishing mass culture.

In achieving these goals, however, modern art alienated itself from popular support. Its texts became highly formal, theoretical in nature, often abstract or dissonant, and a great deal of time, education, and effort were required before their complex formal structures could generate a gratification of some sort for those willing to engage them. Artists came to be resented by many as pretentious parasites who had little to offer to common folk. As Adorno put it: "While people resign themselves to the unintelligibility of theorems of modern physics, trusting that they are rational just the same, they tend to brand the unintelligibility of modern art as some schizoid whim."[58] Why can't I just look at this painting and understand what it shows, just like I see and recognize the things around me? Why all these sounds in this music? Why this complexity, this difficulty in this book? Why be so hermetic? What's wrong with plain speaking?

Modern art's liberation then, as Horkheimer and Adorno were quick to point out, turned out to be a costly one. "The purity of [this] art," they wrote, "which hypostasized itself as a world of freedom in contrast to what was happening in the material world, was from the beginning bought with the exclusion of the lower classes. . . ."[59] By escaping to a new world of forms, artists abandoned their ability to speak directly about issues that were the concern of the masses. They now exclusively addressed specialized audiences, a situation which pushed them further and further afield. Eventually this led to the adoption of an "international" style that retained few connections with the different national cultures within which artists in fact worked. For all of that, it remained that modern art, by its very nature, posited a field of activity, a world whose values were very much at odds with those pushed by the mass media. The mere presence of that art offered a possible refuge from the crass commodities of the consumer industry everywhere on display. This is why Adorno, in his *Aesthetic Theory*, insisted that modern art, for all its shortcomings, nevertheless produced the only works which countered the presence of commercial interests. "Works of art," he wrote, "are plenipotentiaries of things beyond the mutilating sway of exchange, profit and false human needs."[60] High art, by its very presence, implied that not everything in life was for sale. It even had the potential to reveal their alienated existence to those caught up in the ideological spin of the times. Modernism, at least in Adorno's eyes, had thus an utopian social effect: "Art respects the masses by presenting itself to them as that which they might become, instead of adapting itself to them in their degraded state." "Culture," he concluded, momentarily "keeps barbarism in check."[61]

## XV

What was possibly an admirable solution at the beginning of the century was less clearly so at its close. Artists became disillusioned with museum culture as well as with self-imposed exile from daily life. Beyond that, some unexpected applications of semiotics, psychoanalysis, Marxism, etc., in the sixties and after, suddenly exploded the conventional ways through which art and artists were viewed. Semiotics, to take a single example, was revisited long after Charles Sanders Peirce and Ferdinand de Saussure proposed their seminal insights about the working of language. First, Peirce made us realize the distance between a referent (what is out there) and a sign (a word, for instance). For Peirce, although we have direct contact with the world, our signs are merely the *interpretants* of that world. They cannot by definition bring across the fullness of material objects. Because of this, our knowledge about the world cannot ever quite encompass our experience of it. As for Saussure, he demonstrated the absence of link between a word (a signifier) and what is meant by it (its signified). Take any word and you will find no connection between it and the concept it denotes: what is the rapport between the four letters t-r-e-e and the mental association we get from that word? Or between t-r-e-e, a-r-b-r-e, and b-o-o-m, the same idea in different languages? The language system which is our link to the real world out there is thus arbitrary from the start.

In practice though, Saussure reassured us, the fact that signifiers and signifieds were not securely linked did not keep us from communicating effectively. Those who followed him disputed this assertion. For the post-structuralists indeed (Roland Barthes, Jacques Derrida, and Michel Foucault among others), the fact that "in language there are only differences,"[62] that there is no such thing as an unimpeachable connection between a signifier and its signified, puts great stress on the entire system. At least "tree" could refer to something solid. But what about a "lie"? Where is it? And what happens when a word has meanings beyond the one chosen by a speaker? A bias, for instance, refers not only to prejudice but also to an oblique cut in clothes making, a special twist given to a bowling ball causing it to change direction, and the voltage inherent in a microphone design. Which is the correct meaning? Context most often is counted on to save the day. Additionally, we find our sentences infiltrated by slips of the tongue, puns, allusions, eponyms, synecdoches, symbols, metaphors, words hiding within other words, slang which playfully deforms and reforms meanings at will, all extras that function within language like banana peels in a Laurel and Hardy movie. Barthes had no trouble seeing the consequences of such a polyphonic thrust: "Everything signifies ceaselessly and several times," he wrote, "but without being delegated to a great final ensemble, to an ultimate structure."[63] Each word then resonates with idiosyncratic inconsistency and the longer the sentence the more difficult it becomes to keep the meaning in check. Sometimes not even the immediate context surrounding a word is capable of determining what is being said in the first place. We have to grasp the whole before being able to go back and specify the meaning of each part—a bewildering proposition to be sure. If language is thus shown to be so radically imprecise in its functioning, maybe our assumptions about how we construct meaning needed to be thoroughly reassessed as well.

The cultural revisionism was thorough. To start with, without strong links between referents and what we use to represent them, how could we be sure of a smooth transition from one realm to the other? Could we really be confident that even images were truthful to the event one wished to evoke? The old notions of historical truth and documentary objectivity were logically among the first to come under attack.[64] With language such a questionable ally, how could we ever get to the truth of any event indeed? Isn't the writing of history only a genre that owes more to internal narrative demands than to the brute facts they claim to relate? And what are the consequences of this for documentary filmmaking? Doesn't any recording automatically alter an event's authenticity? Shouldn't we rather acknowledge the subjectivity of the process and limit ourselves to first-person inquiries? Or perhaps, sensing that documentary fact is a fiction anyway, present reconstructions of the way things might have been (as in *The Thin Blue Line*, [Errol Morris, 1988])?

Second, if language is a figurative operation, it is foolish to expect ideas to navigate within a discourse without being deformed by it. This is made clear on an everyday basis when we attempt to correct an obvious misunderstanding by telling our listener: "What I meant to say is. . . ." What happens in such cases is that the other party placed our words within another context, a set of references different from our own, a situation which altered the intended communication. In the plane of art, therefore, texts were now said to be coproduced by readers and viewers who inevitably experience new texts within their own specific frame of reference, modulating them accordingly in the process. The integrity of any text is thus only wishful thinking. Stable meanings cannot in fact be controlled by the writer or the artist, for no meaning can ever be said to be actually present, right there, at that moment, in this word, this sentence, or this image. Meaning emerges rather as a consequence of a certain construction within the text and a specific context outside of it. Hence, as soon as a text enters the public domain, it becomes the object of universal play, something Derrida called *différance,* a combination that continually delays and defers meaning as the original signifiers of a text encounter other signifiers in other texts and realms elsewhere, those brought in fortuitously by historical circumstances, by listeners, readers, and viewers everywhere. Reading and viewing texts thus become creative activities that contribute to their actual meaning.

All in all, postmodernism activated a shift of interest from the question of meaning in a text to the operations of language itself. How we construct this meaning out of this text became more important than understanding the intentions of an author or the limited interpretation mandated by a carefully structured work. Not surprisingly, the hierarchical ranking between complex meaningful works and more accessible ones, that is to say between high art and low art, also flattened under the weight of all these connotative influences. High art in particular became to be seen as a power play by the elite to endow their personal values and tastes with universal significance. No works could any longer be said to possess some transcendental creative *Geist* in their core. How good or valuable anything is essentially became a matter of local culture and personal taste. All texts, good and bad, were basically equal and could be appreciated as mere cultural documents, crisscrossing scores of other texts, famous or mediocre, past and present. Casting and recasting different webs between a myriad of texts became far more exciting than analyzing the limited viewpoint of a single author or the attempt by one work to control meaning through its structural unity. In the long run then, semiotics (as used by the post-structuralists) thoroughly subverted our access to a stable referential world, the certainty of meaning, the intrinsic value of high art, and the importance of an artist working in isolation from the utilitarian interests of most people.

## XVI

Post-modernism was just plain fun, at least at the beginning. Its spirit made it possible to dismantle the boundaries that carefully contained and defined fields of investigation in theory as well as in practice. Barthes could talk about wrestling, Foucault about insane asylums. The field of critical studies exploded, opening the way to fresh writing about film. And in the cinema itself, Dusan Makavejev (to take a single example) was able to crosscut through disparate film sources to come up with his tour de force, *Innocence Unprotected* (1968). With time though, some other aspects of the cultural revolution came more sharply into view. Most importantly, it became clear that modern art was not the only victim of the revisionist attack, art *tout court* was. For, beyond the ideas that art could be created and displayed in the most unusual places, postmodernism also embraced the notion of the artist as some kind of public entertainer.

Although artists had worked under conditions that alienated them from the rest of society, this exclusion had for the most part benefited them. Their very opposition to the social system had in fact infused them with enough confidence to create vital works. To find one's voice, one simply had to go inside and dig deep. Eventually, the quintessential self would be discovered amidst the debris that had accumulated over the years. This long-lasting, romantic fantasy finally came crashing down under the assault of postmodernist thinking. For Jacques Lacan indeed, our very idea of ourselves—who we think we are—is in every respect organized, conditioned, and modulated by language. As developing infants, we become aware of ourselves and make sense of our beingness in the world through the sieve of language. Language thus infiltrates our innermost being, the core we identify with. It becomes the exclusive channel between the inside and the outside. Only that which can be processed as a word or a thought can actually reach consciousness. Heidegger expressed these ideas most succinctly when he suggested that human beings did not possess language, but were spoken by it.[65] To illustrate this point in the cinema, one could say that any actual practice of the medium is filled with billions of images already in place in the visual discourse. Filmmakers thus become mere channels for the endless reorganization of texts.

Similarly, because we have no direct access to the magma that lies inside of us, only reactions to external stimuli are in fact recoverable to our consciousness. The person we think we are ends up therefore to be no more than a regurgitation of foreign input: its orchestration to some extent, maybe a tone of voice, at best a special feel, but always a recombination of imported material. On the social front too, an individual could be said to function in society very much like a word in a dictionary, his or her identity defined through a range of similarities and differences with other human beings. Since every qualifier points to a different facet, what is there changes color with the speed of a chameleon. Nothing can ever be named once and for all. This person is a son, a brother, a parent, a relative, a friend, a lover, a neighbor, a man, an African-American, a New Yorker, a Catholic. That person likes jazz, fast cars, computers, Italian food, etc. Rather than pointing to an internal, unchanging, united (and largely imaginary) self, these characterizations (a selection in a menu) cannot but bring out incidental qualities. As a result of all this, artists were now asked to think of themselves no longer as free agents but as crossing points, accidental intersections between thousands of cultural threads.

Needless to say, all of this severely undermined the artists' traditional approach to the creative process. Without a stable identity to support them, unable to originate fresh material, it is not surprising that they started quoting each other. Playful manipulation of known forms and styles became the most important stuff of their discourses. In time, independence, strength, and artistic integrity gave way to detachment, irony, and quick eloquence. Personality took precedence over soul. Today these affectations are so prevalent, so taken for granted, that few artists realize they actually still have a choice. In fact the very breadth of the new paradigm guarantees a wide variety of artistic determinants. We do not therefore have to accept discourses as the only influences that make their mark on one's creative output. From the moment of birth onward, live encounters affect us as well. Even though their vital impact cannot be accessed without the symbolic ordering of language, it remains that the resulting formation (our continuing transformation as human beings) is metamorphic in nature and thus largely unpredictable, personal if you will. Hence there is no reason why one's creative reach should not concentrate, as before, on the more intimate strata that also bespeak one's direct experience in the world. In other words, one should not despair because one's cultural makeup is not unique and the chosen artistic treatment only one set among a variety of available arrangements. Think of it: Ingmar Bergman was certainly not the only little boy in his days to build a puppet playhouse. The difference between him and the rest of his generation is that he was able to turn that experience into memorable material while others were not. And today we respond emotionally to these scenes in his films not because he does them better than anyone else but because they feel genuine. Yes, his take is but one possible illustration of a child's lively imagination, but the reason it plays so well is that Bergman managed to remain faithful to the special set of emotions and circumstances connected with that moment of his life. Although one cannot deny the pull of intertextuality, it does not have exclusivity in the fount of art.

## XVII

Too often unfortunately, artists have evolved into agile players who seize, manipulate, and reframe ideas, texts, and images already in circulation. Style ceases to be the outgrowth of a sensibility honed in a specific human context and sharpened by time. It becomes a choice within a gallery of many. A software program can give your image the Van Gogh look (minus the misery of course) or the Seurat touch. Tarkovsky's personal and religious imagery can be appropriated and made to serve a rich man with a guitar in a music video. This is exactly the problem Karl Mannheim warned us about fifty years ago. He argued that style needed time to mature, away from the public light, in order to reach its potential, that is to say, its ability to display meaningfully a deeply felt situation. "The new impulses, intuitions and fresh approaches to the world," he wrote, "if they have no time to mature in small groups, will be apprehended by the masses as mere stimuli. . . ."[66] Isn't this where we are today? A breathtaking figure in a film is imitated even before the release of the original text, and the whole undertaking is quickly discarded by audiences as a mere gimmick. The motif's latent power to break through the barriers which suffocate our apprehension of life through cinema is cut short. Through it all, a posture of disengagement is a must for the postmodern artist. To be cool is the thing. Best of all is to wink at a hip audience which appreciates the wit of the package and recognizes the quotes in the text. No one, it is argued, should take too seriously these surface reflections, these artificial refractions, these mirror games. Seen in this light, to create (or embrace as a viewer) passionate, meaningful, or engaging material becomes the equivalent of an artistic faux pas.

The snag in postmodernism is that it has relocated art within the market place. Cut from its traditional amphitheater where it could more or less control the rules of the game, art is now forced to fight it out at street level against two powerful gangs: Madison Avenue and Hollywood. As a result, in Gerald Graff 's words, "the values, ideas, artworks, and other products of the spirit are assimilated into the logic of the fashion industries."[67] Certainly the barons of the culture industry must be amused by it all. Where previously their control of the streets was tempered by the knowledge that there existed somewhere a place where works were created to reflect a higher standard, now for the first time all the players share the same field. Did the naïve uptown people really believe that their poorly advertised, severe-looking booths would have a chance of attracting passers-by when experienced barkers have made a career of pushing street traffic toward the glittery productions controlled by the mob? The end result was all too predictable: the industrialists took advantage of the situation to expand their market share at the expense of the newcomers.

The free, nonhierarchical circulation of images elevated the products of the culture industry at the same time as it cheapened art. Adorno, as usual, was the first to point out the consequences of this superficial democratization when he wrote that "the commercial character of culture causes the difference between culture and practical life to disappear. . . ."[68] At the very least, this meant that the representation of daily life could be homogenized. Everything could now be the same everywhere. Fredric Jameson describes the resulting culture as "the surrounding environment of philistinism, of schlock and kitsch, of TV series and Reader's Digest culture . . . that whole landscape of advertising and motels, of the Las Vegas strip, of the late show and Grade-B Hollywood film, of so-called paraliterature with its airport paperback categories. . . ."[69] The "democratization" thus confirmed the view that there is only one "real" world and that all texts, regardless of their source, share the same views about it. What previously would have been recognized as art now vanishes into the thin air of the consumer culture. Even on a purely technical level, commercial art had no problem appropriating the most formidable redoubt of art: its formal avant-garde.[70] That the superb imagery of rock videos fails to question reality in the way its prime movers, say, surrealism or expressionism, did, remains unimportant for an audience which has no memory or knowledge of these original movements. What matters here is that rock videos have preempted the need for a real avant-garde. A dose of MTV indeed fills up whatever urge one may have for a different sort of visual exploration.

## XVIII

The nonstop babble of the advertising industry, what Jean Renoir so judiciously called the "cancer" at the core of our society, our culture, our life, now fills the air free of interference.[71] From park benches and city buses to magazine pages and television commercials, the culture industry surrounds its potential consumers with thousands of messages each day. It does not matter that such interpellations are nonthreatening or that people see through the ads. Ubiquity is the thing. Everywhere we turn, images confront us. Print and electronic pictures satiate our gaze, making it more difficult to create or even want to experience other images, images that could actually benefit our lives. The point of advertising indeed is less to sell this, now, to this person, than to occupy the subject's entire life. At no time should one be able to reflect on what the discourse of capitalism in fact excludes. For Madison Avenue, a fastidious nanny towering over us day and night, insists that she knows what is good for us, that all our aspirations and yearnings can be effectively represented in its permanent theater-in-the-round, and that the solution inevitably involves the buying of yet another consumer product. Gallo captures in less than a minute all the warmth of a large and loving family. Charlie helps young women come into their own. AT&T knows the power of reaching out and touching someone. Gentle admonitions from the U.S. Army and American Express keep us on track: we should be all we can be and never travel without it. And, although we are normally in good hands with you know whom, conflict, when it occurs, can be limited to a festive joust between brand names: Coke or Pepsi, Mac or IBM. Which side are you really on? The group which cheers for "good taste" or those who look for the "less filling" quality of Miller Light? Real-life conflicts fade in comparison for they lack the wit and the visual puns to make them entertaining. As for the social struggle, it is nowhere in sight. At the end of the day, exhausted, we are only too happy to retire to Marlboro Country.

Lost in the shuffle of a winner-take-all economy, banged up by a competition that aims at the senses rather than the intellect, abandoned by the culture of the mass media, young artists today have few places to go. It is difficult indeed to imagine points of entry where filmmakers would be able to nurture their art away from immediate commercial concerns. Indeed, the global homogenized culture pushed by Hollywood, Madan Sarup tells us, "robs individuals of 'languages' for interpreting self and world by denying them the media for organizing their own experiences."[72] Let us remember: it took Balzac twenty mediocre novels before he was able to master his material. And, in film, who remembers the many movies John Ford directed before *Stagecoach* (1939)? Shamefully, film schools, whose mission should be to provide such sanctuary for budding filmmakers, have become mini-studios. Almost immediately, the emphasis is on devising a portfolio piece that industry people will be able to relate to. Agents must see something they can sell to clients. Otherwise, forget it. You won't get a job. You'll have spent all that money for nothing.

But what if these independent films are not made anymore, what if they stop coming down the pipeline? After all, why go through all the pain associated with creative integrity if nobody gives a damn at the other end? Why do so if a titillating show on television gets more play in the press and academe than a demanding film that tried its best? Commenting on the fragility of art and the artist, Wayne C. Booth once noted that "the [television] tube will not die: the company I keep as I watch it will go on eternally. Reading any beloved author, in contrast, I know that I dwell with someone whose powers are finite."[73] Artists are taken for granted as if the rest of us were permanently entitled to their work. In fact they no longer enjoy the support of any group in society. In the feast of plenty provided by a spectacular industry, it is easy to forget Adorno's warning, that "art will live on only as long as it has the power to resist society."[74] That power has by now been dangerously eroded. Sure, good films are still being made, but for how long? Some independents still try, shooting in 16mm, on video, without permits, with friends, with the help of a community. You have to admire these filmmakers. They go to Sundance. They travel with their films. They rent a theater and do a modicum of advertising. They struggle to get a favorable review. . . . Bigger independent productions that do not fit the mold also have the same kinds of problems. Take Maggie Greenwald's *The Ballad of Little Jo* (1993) as an example: the film was poorly released and died after a couple of weeks. Yet you can feel throughout the director's labor of love: her care for the story, her respect for the era, her love of the medium. Somewhat shockingly, the film makes you realize how little one knows about the West after watching ninety some years of Westerns made by male directors. Because of its quick demise though, the film did not help Greenwald's budding career. For her, unfortunately, it was back to square one.

The new environment I have described pushes earnest filmmakers aside. Little by little, they are being replaced by another brand of director, people with a different mentality altogether. Robert Heilbroner once described our American business civilization in these terms: "The end is profit, income, consumption, economic growth, or whatever . . . the act of labor itself is regarded as nothing more than an unfortunate necessity to which we must submit to obtain this end."[75] Nowadays, more and more young filmmakers make films in order to promote themselves, their careers, get recognition, live in Malibu, and drive a Porsche. Their ultimate goal is to join the "in" crowd, attend Hollywood parties, and be seen at the Academy Awards with an attractive date—anything at all but contribute to cinema. These filmmakers of course have it all wrong: when you make a film you celebrate the miracle of cinema. You partake in something that is much larger than yourself. You join a community of artists who labored at filmmaking before you. And, however small, your contribution is welcome there. The joy of thinking, creating, and assembling images and sounds that mean something is your entire reward. For when it is all over, you can look back at the project in amazement: "God! I made a film! I did it! My film!" You can be proud. The rest is humbug.

# CHAPTER TWO

## *Art/Entertainment*

### I

Today, apart from a few enclaves in New York and San Francisco, the forces of entertainment clearly have the field to themselves. "And what's wrong with that?," many defenders of the system would aggressively counter. "What is wrong with entertainment?" I have heard that question asked many times by students and it deserves an answer. To help understand the ideological role played by entertainment, it may be worthwhile to take a step back for a moment and analyze the function of entertainment in another nation at another time in history. By doing so, it may become easier to recognize the part Hollywood plays in the management of social life. The locale I have chosen is Spain, the time the baroque era.

### II

Imagine a great and powerful country in the thrust of severe internal changes. A strong upsurge in the population has forced masses of people to move from the countryside, where the local economy could no longer absorb them, to the larger towns and cities where work was still available. In moving away from their ancestral abode, the laborers shed their traditional subservience to the local gentry, selling only their manpower to their new urban employers. Indeed, as they established themselves in the cities, the immigrants no longer demonstrated in their behavior the kind of respect the noble and leisured class expected from such a group. Worse, the pressure of the new arrivals also caused the old communal ties that had previously united the different classes in the cities to unravel. Finally, because too many had left at the same time, not all those searching for work were able to find jobs. Some joined the military, most simply remained in the cities, forming a permanent group of vagabonds, beggars, or even bandits. "A day does not dawn," a chronicler writes, "without someone being wounded or murdered, by thieves or soldiers; houses are broken into and young women and widows cry about assaults and robberies."[1] "Things are such," adds another, "that one can't even go out at night without being heavily armed or with a lot of company."[2] Eventually, even the large city jails could not contain the ever-increasing number of inmates. Elsewhere, on the economic front, inflation played havoc with people's savings, and foreign monetary speculation (Dutch tulips) became the only way to stay ahead of the game. At the same time, a plague raged through the land taking the lives of many. All together, the country was experiencing much restlessness and the future looked dark indeed. There was the fear that the established values were out-of-date, incapable of containing the civic changes, and that the entire social structure was doomed to crumble.[3]

Realizing that its policing powers alone would not be able to curb these sweeping social disruptions, the ruling order focused its efforts on an ideological campaign to enlist the minds of the recent immigrants, so as to tame their energy and domesticate their demands. The overall goal, José Antonio Maravall tells us, was "to penetrate into the innermost interiority of the [people's] consciousness."[4] An entire cultural program was thus set up to integrate the newcomers, to "shape types, form mentalities, and group masses ideologically."[5] The idea therefore was to provide the recently arrived with a new cultural identity, to incorporate their way of thinking within the existing culture, and to direct their aspirations toward areas not threatening to society as a whole. By "interpellating" them as subjects, by giving them a place where they could gather and have fun, by providing cultural productions they could enjoy, the existing order hoped to limit the danger to society brought about by the immigrants.[6]

In addition to building large public fountains and plazas and offering fiestas and fireworks (places to go to and things to do when not at work), theater was invested with the principal task of organizing the new mentalities. The stage plays that resulted from this, in marked change from the more established art favored by the elite, thrived on action beyond anything else. Often violent, even cruel, it was populated by easily recognizable types moving through what would quickly become a familiar series of events. This reiteration combined with "sentimentalism, easy passions that valorize the self, subordination to a recipe book of human solutions, and literary poverty . . ." eventually prevailed over Calderón, the versed opponent.[7] To make things even more attractive to the populace, much effort was exerted to highlight the technical stagecraft of the shows. Indeed, the ultimate goal of the spectacles, carefully monitored through previews and audience responses, was to awe the spectators so that, in the thrill of the moment, they would "forget to doubt and question" their actual conditions of existence.[8] One last point: to appreciate fully the ideological impact of such material, we must go beyond single texts to a body of works, we must look beyond individual artistry to what is shared by all. In a word, we must assess their combined effect to capture its significance.

III

If the scenario sounds familiar, it is because Spain in the seventeenth century stands as a good precursor for the United States in the twentieth. In both times, waves of social and economic disruptions, and the baffling problem of what to do with the lower classes, proved themselves a threat to the existing order. And likewise for the solution: the popular fiestas giving way to professional sports and the commercially successful theater of Lope de Vega predating Hollywood moviemaking.[9] Even the theatrical recipe did not change much through the centuries: the characters still being easily recognizable, the situations well-known, the tone emotional, the technique self-flaunting, and the style not straying far from a set of familiar norms—a formula guaranteed to keep the spectacle accessible to all.

Still, "What's wrong with that?" It may be useful at this point to clarify the concept of entertainment. Etymologically, the word originates from the French *entretenir*. And *entretenir* means to keep in good shape, to provide what is necessary to maintain a certain readiness of being, to make sure that nothing inimical happens during some intervening time. The concept thus talks of preserving a situation, of keeping it from deteriorating. But, in our case, what situation are we talking about? That most people have a job they find thoroughly alienating will not come as a great surprise to anyone. Regardless of the economic organization of a society and the political beliefs at its core, most jobs being performed are simply very dull in nature, repetitive, burdensome.[10] Others, less today because of the automation of the production line, still require undue physical force. Early on, well-meaning social scientists like Hugo Munsterberg (also one of the first cinema theorists) attempted to counter the tough regimen recommended by Frederick Taylor and his disciples by attempting to find the right person for each job. "Only when the mental mechanism, the individual dispositions, associations, and reactions are made clear," he suggested, "can it be possible to overcome inner resistances and to avoid frictions, which are in most cases equally to the disadvantages of the employer and the employee."[11] In his research, Munsterberg attempted to match specific work characteristics with agreeable individuals, those for instance for whom monotonous work could provide "overflowing joy and inner harmony."[12] At one point, he interviewed a woman who had wrapped lightbulbs in tissue paper for twelve years in a row. At the rate of twenty-five bulbs every forty-two seconds, she regularly managed to wrap thirteen thousand bulbs a day. As this woman found her job "really interesting," Munsterberg stated that this was probably the case because of her particular ability to observe minute changes in her daily routine. Employers only had to test for similar psychological patterns to determine the right individuals for equally numbing jobs. Quite rightly, Matthew Hale Jr. takes exception to this:

> It never occurred to Munsterberg whether there were enough men and women with a sense of 'inner manifoldness' to fill all the boring jobs. Nor did he ask whether the mental state that allowed the woman to find her job interesting was inherent or whether it developed as a result of twelve years of wrapping. And it never occurred to [him] . . . that she might be lying. Instead he elevated to the level of a science a self-serving and unexamined myth—that menial laborers, because of their special traits of mind, were at least as happy at their worldly duties as the highly pressured professionals were at theirs.[13]

Such well-intentioned efforts eventually went for naught. And today as yesterday, week after week, in factories and offices, people's bodies are continuously disciplined, made to provide just the attention needed to perform the precise gestures demanded by the work at hand. In *Chronicle of a Summer* (Jean Rouch and Edgar Morin, 1961), for example, an interviewed Renault worker complains that his life is being swallowed up by the daily grind of work. How does one deal with such a situation? For Oskar Negt and Alexander Kluge, a countermeasure is needed to withstand the loss, to survive the day: "the unbearable real situation experienced by the worker leads to the creation of a defense mechanism that shields the ego from the shock effects of an alienated reality."[14] In other words, because their labor negates their full personality, workers defensively shut off all psychological functions not essential to the immediate experience in front of them. Only after work or during the weekend, is the individual able to shake off that conditioning and feel whole again. Only then do workers finally have some time to be themselves, to take stock of their personal world: What is going on here? What is happening to my life? What about the dreams I once had? Should I abandon them? Can I still do something about my situation?

This is where the culture industry comes in, providing nonstop diversion to fill in the dangerous time. First off, for Hanns Eisler, its role is "to mask the heartlessness of late industrial society by late-industrial techniques. . . . It attempts to interpose a human coating between the reeled-off pictures and the spectators."[15] In other words, entertainment is counted on to provide the "human" environment that is missing eight hours a day, five days a week. For all that, such content, far from reenergizing the spirit, detracts attention from immediate real-life issues. In *Dialectic of Enlightenment*, Max Horkheimer and Theodor W. Adorno convincingly argue that entertainment in fact "cheats its consumers of what it perpetually promises. . . . [Although] it is sought after as an escape from the mechanized work process, and to recruit strength in order to be able to cope with it again, [it ends up as] prolongation of work."[16] Likewise, Herbert Marcuse describes entertainment products as "modes of relaxation which soothe and prolong [the] stupefaction" created by work, a sort of modern day *Assommoir*.[17] Seen this way, Hollywood movies end up dispensing a time-out when much stronger medicine is needed: a genuine, positive, and permanent escape from conditions of work that generate alienation. This much we have known for quite some time. What sharpens the issue today is that the culture industry aims at occupying the entire field, leaving no ground whatever to alternatives offering more demanding but also more rewarding material. In that sense, even when a commercial product fails at its primary task, it is still successful in that it has kept other works from being created, disseminated, and enjoyed by audiences.

Workers (today, white-collar as well as blue-collar, everyone really because we all drink from the same well) are thus kept from using their re-creation/recreation time to reflect upon their life situation. Insofar as culture "is the very material of our daily lives, the bricks and mortar of our most commonplace understandings," not to find characters, situations, conflicts that could be helpful in defining one's life deprives viewers of a truly valuable support at a time when assistance from the immediate community (family, friends, church, etc.) is on the wane.[18] The distraction offered by the culture industry can therefore be said to be a flight not just "from a wretched reality," still quoting Horkheimer and Adorno, "but from the last remaining thought of resistance. The liberation which amusement promises is [actually] freedom from thought and from negation. . . . [Moviegoers] are assured that they are all right as they are."[19] Insofar as such works take for granted the existing social and political state of affairs rather than question or oppose it, viewers are comforted into accepting their lot.[20] Understood this way, movies and the rest of the mass media—television and pop music mostly—shortchange their consumers, keeping workers on a short leash, delivering them back on the job Monday morning without a harmful idea in their heads. In Paul Tillich's view, the system aims at nothing less than to "standardize" human beings, to keep them consistent seven days a week, to make them, in the long run, as reliable as machines.[21]

## IV

For the system to work, entertainment must be brilliant. There is no doubt that a lot of talent, effort, and work go into the making of many commercial ventures. Typically though, in each case, the film itself monopolizes the attention. And that is true even in the work of a great director like Alfred Hitchcock. The suspense and the mise en scène of *North by Northwest* (1959), for instance, can surely thrill us. One can appreciate the visual wit that permeates the project and comparisons can be made between this film and others like it. What such a film does not do, however, is open possibilities outside itself. That is to say, it does precious little for the viewer's own life apart from keeping reality at bay for two hours. By its very presence, this film may even render inoperative the viewer's own ability to fantasize. We have all read how children have substituted television programming and video games for make-believe situations of their own invention. With adults too, Negt and Kluge insist, fantasy creation is necessary for mental well-being. Playacting operates as "the organizer of mediation. It is the specific work process whereby libidinal structure, consciousness, and the outside world are connected with one another."[22] Seen in this light, personal daydreaming or fantasizing during or after a film is one means through which we help ourselves survive the daily grind and play out various scenarios for the future. Just as with children then, the products of the culture industry fill up the space that could be used for personal rejuvenation. Indeed, Negt and Kluge conclude, "the libidinal fantasies of human beings, their hopes, wishes, needs, are no longer set free, are no longer capable of developing themselves in accordance with random interests. . . ."[23] The "better" the film, the less chance there is that the viewer will daydream (hence the highly controlled, dynamically sustained, closed-end narratives which leave little room for personal intervention). From all of this, it can be inferred that entertainment is not a neutral arrangement. Like magnets, the commodified spectacles capture the gaze of spectators. For Hollywood certainly, a good film is one where all eyes are riveted on the screen at all times. And a good show is one which leaves the real world behind and makes reverie difficult for the audience. Like vacuums, the packages of the culture industry suck up leftover aspirations and desires. Like roller coasters, they exhaust the riders, dissipating their surplus energy. Through the years, generation after generation of filmmakers have made the trip to Hollywood with the idea of changing all of that. The system has defeated them all.[24] Each time, the ideological premise at the core of entertainment prevented them from implementing story elements or techniques that could possibly awake defiant personal fantasies in viewers, possibly even usher in notions of social resistance.

## V

In opposition to entertainment stands the work of art. It is not my intention here to recall the many interpretations that art has evoked through history. Let us just say that, regardless of whether the connection involves God, a Platonic world, nature, beauty, truth, a fierce geniality, or sublime emotions, art opens a space away from the ordinariness of daily life. The shock of something truly genuine provokes a *Rausch,* a rupture, a transcendent state in those lucky enough to encounter it. In Nietzsche's terms, it is the artist alone who benefits from such activation. [25] For others, the work of art can also shock spectators into a rethinking of themselves. Hans-Georg Gadamer expressed the latter view very well, I think, when he wrote that "the power of the work of art suddenly tears the person experiencing it out of the context of life, and yet relates him back to the whole of his existence. In the experience of art is present a fullness of meaning that belongs not only to this particular content or object but rather stands for the meaningful whole of life."[26]

Today, even to raise the issue of the work of art seems pompous if not downright elitist. In fact, Alain Finkielkraut complains, our society has gone to such an extreme that "there is no longer any place to receive these pieces of art and give them meaning. Thus they float absurdly in space without coordinates or points of reference."[27] True enough, yet it is good to remember that a work of art can be modest, quite accessible, and does not have to hang in a museum or be applauded by a crowd of well-wishers. Let me address Nietzsche's point first. Putting it simply, to be involved in making a work of art sparks the artist into a tumultuous process of self-discovery. Whether at once or gradually, *Rausch* takes hold, grabs, seizes the body of the creator. It is "an explosive state" that propels the being out of itself, making it reach for what is not yet there, forcing it to bring back unfamiliar concepts or forms. Because the itinerary is uncharted, the digging hard, and the outgrowth sovereign, the artist shapes him/herself anew through the creative process. This entire operation, however, is paradoxical for, as Martin Heidegger reminds us, "it is the work that first lets the artist emerge as a master of his art. The artist is the origin of the work, [yet] the work is [also] the origin of the artist."[28]

A will to create can originate in a variety of circumstances. Again, no one would deny that a Hollywood spectacle requires a great deal of labor from those who make it come alive, thus providing a well-deserved release when it is complete. The illusion of a spaceship taking off may require endless hours of meticulously shooting models and making a myriad of digital adjustments. You may be exhausted at the end of the day but, when all is said and done, your life does not change as a result of what you just did. You used your creativity, you worked with your peers, you got paid, and now it is time to go to the Bermudas while waiting for the next assignment. On the contrary, the impact of the work of art realigns the artist profoundly and lastingly, along lines not previously foreseen. Once the work of art you have created challenges you, you no longer know yourself. Something inside you has changed forever. In that way, "artists are also always the victims of the talent they possess."[29]

What appears is also very different. When the work of art is complete something that was not there before has emerged. What is it? It is a construct made up of forms. But these forms are unlike those we take for granted all around us. They absorb the attention because, as Nietzsche insists, "to be an artist forces one to experience what non-artists call 'form' as content, as 'the matter itself.'"[30] Because of this, the strange structure or *Gestalt* stands out in the midst of daily life, unfastened from the artist, defiantly itself, thoroughly on its own. One cannot pretend that it is useful. It serves no obvious purpose like the rest of the objects, furnishings, or appliances that accompany us throughout our life. And yet, as Heidegger puts it in his illuminating essay on "The Origin of the Work of Art," its very presence "breaks open an open place, in whose openness everything is other than usual."[31] And this is so because, within the work of art, beings are brought forth out of concealment, "as they never were before and never will be again."[32] In other words, you recognize a work of art through its ability to disclose a world that is like and yet unlike the one you are familiar with. Most works merely reify daily experience. There, people do the things they are supposed to do. Boy meets girl. The city is busy. Night succeeds day. Everything makes sense. Yet this common everyday landscape is also a delusion. Think of the beginning of *Blue Velvet* (David Lynch, 1986), where it is possible to discover dark, frightening, unsuspected layers of life lurking under pictures of normality. In short, works of art present the world anew. They bring into presence aspects of reality we were not cognizant of. Unlike mainstream productions that aim at replicating what is known only too well (even in science fiction), works of art bring forth some other realm of existence—their utopian provision if you wish. By breaking open the reified continuity of one's experience, works of art can also shake those who experience them out of their typical quiescence, Gadamer's point. Because "the existing society is reproduced not only in the mind, the consciousness of men, but also in their senses . . . ," Marcuse reminds us, "no persuasion, no theory, no reasoning can break this prison, unless the fixed, petrified sensibility of the individuals is 'dissolved,' opened to a new dimension of history. . . ."[33] And this is precisely what happens when a viewer sensually witnesses in a work of art a world that radically refashions the belief system held by that individual.

## VI

Let us now look at the entire process in action. Imagine Paul Cézanne in the field with his easel, painting again and again the elusive shapes of Mont Sainte Victoire. Nature remained impregnable though and, for the longest time, the face-to-face encounter continued. But eventually Cézanne managed to understand something of it and curious forms began to appear on his canvas. What emerged in the end was not a mimetic reproduction of the rugged landscape but a questioning of the thing itself. What is that mountain after all? What attracts me to it? Why am I unable to paint it? Why is it that it continually escapes every one of my efforts? Cézanne's paintings then function as reminders that the thing in itself cannot ever really be captured, that there always remains something in reserve despite one's best efforts. One measure of this artist's worth in fact can be located in his acknowledgment that the world, after all, is not for us to seize. But that alone would not bring us very far. So we must go back to the idea that Henri Bergson's words convey so well: "the art of the painter gets modified under the very influence of the works he produces."[34] "Work" here also connotes the labor of creation, not just the finished painting. In other words, the greater the resistance of the world, the more extensive the artist's mutation. Indeed if Werner Heisenberg is correct when saying that a physicist always alters the object of his/her experimentation, the reverse argument must be true as well: the person doing the experimenting cannot escape being affected by it. To come to terms with the world then is a strenuous operation and the artist is reshaped as a result. He/she ends up a different person.

Once the work is complete though, the art separates itself from the environment and the period of time that gave it birth. Indeed when we look at a Cézanne exhibit today, neither Mont Sainte Victoire nor the painter stands beside it. Yet, as long as the meaning of the great changes in painting at the end of the last century still resonates within us, the work itself will somehow manage to recall something of the artist's original struggle.[35] It is as if the painting itself—the new forms on the canvas—is able to make manifest something of that tension. These forms (poetry/language) call up a world that is not unlike other sights familiar to us, yet the picture itself remains disturbing, for what we see eventually trips us up: it makes us realize our tenuous hold on things.

To draw out this aspect of the work of art (its other "work") and its impact on those who witness it, it may be best to shift to Heidegger's own example: the painting of a pair of shoes by Van Gogh. In the painting, the old, decrepit shoes, the laces dangling pathetically on the floor, are depicted closeby, by themselves. The surrounding brushstrokes do not make anything else discernible in the painting: the shoes merely face us. How is it, Heidegger asks, that we find ourselves deeply moved by such an image? Don't we see shoes all the time? Who cares about shoes in the first place? For Heidegger these shoes belong to a peasant woman. Others have suggested that they may be the painter's own shoes. More recently, some have questioned our curious insistence in calling them a pair of shoes rather than two discrete ones.[36] This arguing, however, is rather moot, for once the shoes belong on the canvas, what inspired the artist in the first place is no longer important. The painter could have worked from memory or made up the shoes as he went along, what matters now is what was made of them. What may have been quite consequential for the creative process (a set of circumstances) has now given way to a single artifact facing the viewers.

The main point in Heidegger's argument is that the work of art creates strife between a "world" and the "earth." Both are simultaneously brought into being. Let us focus on the "world" first. Because the painting shows us the woman's shoes, it exemplifies "that already familiar horizon upon which everyday human existence confidently moves. . . ."[37] Now, most works establish a setting of some sort, often a group of characters, and a great deal of effort can be spent in making up actions of one type or another. Although we may construe the end result as a believable ensemble, it does not necessarily amount to a "world" as Heidegger describes it. Visualize, for instance, what a lesser artist than Van Gogh, someone schooled in academic realism, Jean-Pierre Antigna perhaps, would have done with the subject. He would have enlarged the view, showing us some quaint quarters. The brushed shoes would be neatly aligned on a bedroom's wood floor. Their owner, now in the picture, would be shown as a poor but honest young woman trying to make the best of her life in difficult circumstances. Clothes would be modest but clean, the pose agreeable, the mood sentimental. The nineteenth-century bourgeois looking at the painting would be moved by it, possibly even uttering some words of sympathy for the poor creature (today, think of *Pretty Woman* [Gary Marshall, 1990]). The painting, in short, would be filled with fanciful stereotypes in vogue at the time. The young girl would be picked from a gallery of stock characters, the room assembled from similar sets noted in other paintings, the details quite familiar to a habitué of galleries and salons. Constructed this way though, the scene would express what the German philosopher calls a "dissembling," when a masquerade takes the place of the real thing. Something would be suggested "which looks like, but 'in actuality' is not, what it gives itself out to be."[38] Because what we see is derivative, such painting would ultimately fail to supply a link to genuine entities anywhere. To the contrary, a "world" emerges when a work makes it possible for other things/beings to gather and show themselves in a definite historical moment.[39] When such an event takes place, "all things gain their lingering and hastening, their remoteness and nearness, their scope and limits."[40] In Heidegger's terms then, the principal role of a work of art is to provide a conduit, an umbilical cord if you wish, to everything else that is. A large scale enterprise such as the Pantheon is not necessary. Something quite modest can do the job. It is therefore indicative that Heidegger's example is a painting of shoes, footwear we use to function in the world but do not normally pay attention to. Now isolated, this prototypical equipment provides the needed channel to surrounding matter. Because the shoes are discovered for what they in fact are, shoes, they become the node around which other entities are now free to gather:

> From the dark opening of the worn insides of the shoes the toilsome tread of the worker stares forth. In the stiffly rugged heaviness of the shoes there is the accumulated tenacity of her slow trudge through the far-spreading and ever-uniform furrows of the field swept by a raw wind. On the leather lie the dampness and richness of the soil. Under the soles slides the loneliness of the field-path as evening falls. In the shoes vibrates the silent call of the earth, its quiet gift of the ripening grain and its unexplained self-refusal in the fallow desolation of the wintry field.[41]

Because the shoes are fully realized, they cannot be generalized or disposed of in a quick sketch. They bring in a platform where other entities at once make themselves known. Here the land, the wind, and the sky do not emerge from other texts but from this woman's share of our common ground. Moreover they arise on their own terms, as themselves, not as props ready to service our every whim.

But there is more, for the shoes' isolation also gnaws at us. Could it be that the woman recently died? They are thus not just someone's shoes anymore, they are also shoes by themselves, shoes left behind, shoes whose place in the world suddenly becomes insecure. Their usedness strikes us. Their nearness creeps up on us: it may even frighten us. After awhile, we feel like screaming. That is what Heidegger names the "earth": that which cannot be contained in the painting's "world." It is the possibility of life spent without redemption, of the meaninglessness of it all. Worse, the "earth" thrusts death upon us because the painted shoes remind us of the real ones we found in a closet after the passing away of a loved one. They anticipate as well the shoes we too will leave behind one day. By drawing out our own finitude, the painting also points to these other beings who once stood where we are, as comfortable in their surroundings as we are in ours, and those who will supplant us in turn: the individuals and environments change, the "earth" endures. For no single setting, however rich it may otherwise be, can actualize all possibilities of being.[42] The "earth," in other words, is everything *this* world could have been but is not.

Heidegger's view of what makes up a work of art is certainly unconventional. Far from extending to the viewer a sense of mastery over what is being depicted, it forces open a space where other entities are given a free hand as well as letting in a cold draught that prompts the spectator to remember his/her ultimate finitude. The impact is immediate and drastic. "In the nearness of the work," Heidegger reiterates, "we [are] suddenly somewhere else than we usually tend to be. . . ."[43] The work of art then tears down the cultural façade that protects us from experiencing existential fear. For a moment, for the viewer, something arises from the "world" of the painting that was sheltered before and will quickly disappear again. The work of art produces that fleeting moment of grace when someone can reexamine where he or she stands and make some adjustments as a result.

Let me summarize: the artist first works in the world, breathing, inhaling, absorbing the difficult material. After a moment, some strange forms appear, changed and reshaped by the artist's inner sensitivity. A transfiguration takes place. The artist is shaken. The work of art is now exhaled, opening up a space where viewers have momentary access to something not earlier part of their lives: the fullness of a factual "world" jutting out of the "earth," the latter being the reservoir of everything that once was or may one day be. At the same time that the precarious construct brings about a novel apprehension of the represented object in particular or life in general, it also draws out the limitations demarcating our access to these things. By and large, this is what culture or *cultura* is all about: the entire process through which art is planted, cultivated, and harvested. Its offshoot is a crop which, while sustaining, reminds us that plenitude cannot last and that the cycle will quickly resume. The work of art, itself a legacy of the resistance of the world's innermost being to the artist's *technē*, ends up reminding viewers that their own will to power, their grand desire to comprehend all things and dominate all creation, is bound to be but self-deluding aggrandizement.

## VII

I would like now to move to film and see how a work of art operates within the specificity of that medium. At the same time, rather than rehearsing the same argument, I would like to discuss examples that, in my view, broaden its scope. Let us start with a scene from Maya Deren's *Ritual in Transfigured Time* (1946). Halfway through the short film, a character walks into a salon full of people. The setting is quite familiar and so are the participants: guests enjoying a party. Immediately though, everything is other than normal. To start with, the film has no sound track, a choice which thoroughly defamiliarizes the social event. Deren also carefully choreographs the participants' moves, accentuating a gesture here, a turn of the head there. She uplifts extended arms as some party-goers reach out for others. She vamps up warm embraces followed by quick departures. Men and women seduce each other with the twirl of a body. A dance is initiated, then cut short as attractive newcomers make themselves known. Throughout the scene, the camera locks onto partic-ular gestures, freezing the image for a couple of seconds. By focusing on the party's exteriority, Deren brings out the superficiality of what is going on, the shallowness that engulfs the entire happening, the inauthenticity that mars much of social life. In her film, the party becomes a shell game, the encounters snares, people masks. Well, what of it? Surely this charac-terization offers nothing new: how many times have we followed a pro-tagonist to a social event, a dinner party, what have you, where the par-ticipants are shown to be pedantic or frivolous? In those cases, though, we are made to feel superior to the characters (we see *them* for what they are) whereas here the technique used steers us into accepting that *we* are no different from them. It is our gestures that are being depicted, our affec-tations, our mannerisms, our infatuation with our own self. This set is phony and so are the actions but, unlike the ones I attributed to Antigna, Deren dissects the event, calling attention to the phoniness at hand, pointing out its falseness. By so doing, she reminds us that much of life is spent in a state of *verfallen*, when we become so fascinated by the play we perform with others and so taken by the facticity of the moment that we lose ourselves in the process.[44] In this way her aesthetically beautiful arrangement is reclaimed as a grimacing mirror where we learn about ourselves. We realize something is missing in the distortion: a "world" then is raised in absentia.

Next, let us look at *Two Men and a Wardrobe* (Roman Polanski, 1958). I choose this particular film for several reasons: first, it was a student production shot in Lodz's film school in Poland by a very, very young director (he appears in the film and his youth is absolutely scary). Second, it was shot non sync, in black and white, without the expensive camera equipment now taken for granted by many students. Third, the entire project, a fifteen-minute film, could be shot today for less than a thousand dollars. I have seen the film many times through the years and my opinion of it has never wavered: the film "hangs" there, on the screen, solid as a rock, an undeniable masterpiece, an absolute work of art.

The film opens with two men emerging from the sea carrying an old-fashioned armoire. Happy to find themselves on dry land, they set forth for the city. There they are spurned by the local inhabitants. Because of their cumbersome piece of furniture, they are kept from boarding a tramway and denied entrance to a restaurant and a hotel. A sympathetic young girl also rejects their advances when she notices their unusual belonging. Later they are beaten up by thugs when inadvertently the wardrobe's mirror lets that same girl notice one of the hooligans ready to pounce on her. Dark motifs emerge behind the city's veneer: in full sunlight, a man embraces another while surreptitiously picking his pocket; later, having lost all sense of direction, a drunk goes up and down a staircase; finally a man is killed, his face bludgeoned by a rock. After being ejected, still carrying their armoire, from a dump full of barrels, the two men retrace their steps back to the beach. Walking through the dunes, they pass a boy who has covered the landscape with *patés de sable*, molds of upturned pails of sand. Crossing the field without walking on any of them, the two men return to the sea where they quickly disappear under the waves.

Technically speaking, the film is amazingly simple. Most shots are straightforward, photographed from an eye level position, possibly with just one lens. Most of the action takes place in the center of the frame. The camera hardly moves at all. Apart from a light and a reflector, which

add a little punch here and there, the exposure is plain. The editing is efficient but no more. And the sound track is minimal: a few sound effects,
a jazz score, no dialogue or voice-over. There is nothing fancy in the entire
film. In contrast to student filmmakers nowadays who believe they must
display technical brilliance and style, Polanski is satisfied with very little.
That little, however, concerns *physis* and *technē*. For the Greeks, if we follow Heidegger, *physis* does not mean nature for the latter can be domesticated, altered in some fashion. Rather the concept expresses "what flour-
ishes on its own, in no way compelled, what rises and comes forward, and
what goes back into itself and passes away."[45] And that is what we see in
the film: the sea, the sand dunes, the streets, the houses, the parks, the
people are just *there*. All display what could be called a Homeric clarity.
The locations, the events, the protagonists are deceptively ordinary yet
they mesmerize because of their elemental factuality. Unlike the shoes in
Van Gogh, which *express* a "world," the armoire and the other protagonists in the film almost seem to *institute* one, in the manner of the Greeks
before the birth of aesthetics.[46] As for *technē*, it has little to do with technology for its own sake (for instance, the morphing effects so popular in
film just a few years back). It refers instead to the way a human being nur-
tures the process of *physis*. *Technē* is thus a form of knowledge, "a disclos-
ing of beings [and things] as such, in the manner of a knowing guidance
of bringing-forth," a knowing that takes place "in the immediacy of
everyday existence."[47] *Technē* can thus be understood as a viewpoint on
the world within which the rest of the entities can display themselves.
Although an irruption into *physis,* the disruption can be minimized as
long as the artist lets "what is already coming to presence arrive."[48] Indeed,
in *Two Men and a Wardrobe*, the straightforward form does not take anything away from the "world" that shows itself. This originary "world," our
ground too, manifests itself with an evidence that blinds us. In a few
breathtaking minutes, something fundamental we had been forgetful of
arises. Polanski heaps upon us what was there all along but was no longer
showing itself any more to us. By and large this film is successful because
the reserve of its form matches the primeval simplicity of the material.

But what is the film really saying? To be sure, the wardrobe can be
said to represent one's heritage, the baggage of immigrants in a new land
after a long voyage at sea. Symbolically, the piece of furniture could stand
for the customs, the mores, all the "stuff" that turns people into outsiders
when they face a group with different traditions. More generally still, it
could connote issues of race or sexual preference (the two men dancing

together). There is no doubt that the ability of the film to speak universally of discrimination is part of its greatness. But how does the film manage such eloquence? "Truth," still according to Heidegger, "is never gathered from ordinary things that are at hand."[49] What the philosopher is saying here is that we pay little or no attention to what is familiar. Our daily actions and material things disappear in everyday employ; they become invisible to us. If the men, for instance, had been carrying bundles, suitcases, or trunks of one sort or another and had arrived at an airport or a train station somewhere, a believable background would have been set for the story. We would, however, have little or no access to that which daily life in fact conceals. By letting his protagonists arise from the sea and having them carry an incongruous wardrobe, Polanski departs from everyday circumstances. This choice, in turn, makes it possible for us to focus our attention directly onto the main idea. In other words, because the film transforms an ordinary event into a poetic metaphor, every episode thereafter can be seen and appreciated within the luminosity of a new landscape.

As with Deren, the unusual perspective also denies us the comfortable seats from which we normally witness and pass judgments on a series of events whose meaning is pre-given. We are not let in to identify with the two men against everyone else. We are in fact denied the cultural blinders which usually safeguard our world from any damage inflicted out there. Here the equation is actually reversed: the film's "world" puts us under scrutiny, moving us from the jury box into the dock. As our world becomes the subject of the investigation, we are made to realize that the society into which we fit so well has a dark side after all, and that we are more likely in our everyday life to behave like the burgers or the thugs in the film than the innocent wanderers who came from the sea. In a word, the film "brings the unsayable as such" into our world.[50]

Then again the film was produced in difficult circumstances. For Polanski was shooting in Poland in the late fifties and that environment was a lot more confusing than Cézanne's Mont Sainte Victoire. The Communism imposed on Poland by the Soviet Union at the end of World War II was more concerned with the Party's exclusive jurisdiction over the state's economic, social, and political apparatus than with the thinking of Karl Marx and Friedrich Engels. On the surface, the means of production were owned collectively, all aspects of life were managed in the name of the workers, and class struggles were a thing of the past. Everyone had a job. And the state took care of you and your family. In reality, the Party functioned like an arrogant new elite, the bureaucracy was choking off individual enterprise, and freedom of speech no longer existed. In particular, it was unthinkable to refer to the chasm between the official rosy ideology and the drab reality that was everyone's lot in daily life—the subject of Czeslaw Milosz's seminal book, *The Captive Mind.*[51] How do you find points of resistance in these circumstances? How do you speak the truth in a world devoid of moral certainty? How do you even articulate what cannot be mentioned? Every Polish filmmaker had to find ingenious tactics and crafty means to illuminate what was going on. Andrzej Wajda found his in *Ashes and Diamonds* (1958). Krzysztof Zanussi managed it with *Camouflage* (1977), Krzysztof Kieslowski with *Camera Buff* (1979), and Agnieszka Holland with *Fever* (1981).

Of them all, Polanski's solution was the most audacious. On the one hand, its use of metaphor kept the authorities at bay. How could anyone claim that the two men represented the Polish workers who had just rebelled against their government in 1956? By all means, no. And the wardrobe is just an armoire, not freedom. On the other hand, all those who saw the film were nevertheless certain that it was speaking about these other events and that it was in fact bringing the "unsayable" to the screen. Because finally that is the role of the artist: to find again and again the images (language) that make people confront and question what is being done in their name or what they themselves are in the midst of doing. *Two Men and a Wardrobe* is the kind of work that exposes the present by retrieving values repressed by the system. That it was able to do so in the midst of a cultural repression is little short of miraculous. Herbert Marcuse put it best, I think, when he wrote that

> fiction calls the facts by their name and their reign collapses; fiction subverts everyday experience and shows it to be mutilated and false. But art has this magic power only as the power of negation. It can speak its own language only as long as the images are alive which refuse and refute the established order.[52]

Polanski found these burning images. They call on a people not only to take back their life, but to change themselves. Through them, he claimed for the work of art the field of politics from which it is normally excluded. The "world" discovered by the two voyagers is shown to be corrupt and hypocritical to the core, a far cry from the human solidarity expounded by the daily propaganda. The "earth" at the end of the film (the nothingness of the ocean) though precludes us from imagining that all would be well were one political system to replace another. Democracy is no panacea. Think of Solidarity's disappointments once the Movement came into power. Maybe planning for the best and expecting the worst is really all we can do.

Today that forty-year-old student film begs us, with illuminating clarity, to look at our own society and carry on a similar investigation. Its modesty of means also puts to shame all those who, in film school, shoot 35mm productions with Dolby sound and spend in excess of $50,000 to do so. These films are produced in order to make their directors desirable in Hollywood's eyes. By doing so, these individuals have compromised their integrity before even being approached. Is that what they really want? In the 1780s, there were also many apprentices willing to work for the French court's pastry chefs. They pleased Marie-Antoinette no end and made a nice living overall. In fact they were so busy whipping up creams and puffing up their lovely creations that they remained oblivious to the fact the country was running out of bread. In contrast, the young Polanski and his film make clear that, for the artist, there is no alternative. Indeed to compromise on these issues leads to creative impotence, to suffocating the very spirit that animates you in the first place. Identity is not given, Jean-Paul Sartre reminds us, it is only through acting in the world that we discover what we are made of. By engaging ourselves in specific situations, by choosing this way over that one, we literally create ourselves, we become this person rather than that one. In the end, we either free ourselves or we get mired in "bad faith." [53] What kind of person do *you* want to be? The choice is yours.

# CHAPTER THREE

# *The Film School*

## I

Students enroll in film school because they want to make films and believe a college or university education is the most effective way to help them do just that. What most of them do not realize at that stage of the game is that cinema is far from a settled field of study, that filmmaking is a cultural battleground as well as an economic one. And even when students are vaguely aware of a fundamental difference between, say, a film by Jim Jarmush and one by Steven Spielberg, they do not suspect that a film department reflects these conflicts as well, that it too is an area of struggle between competing schools of thought. Jacques Derrida made this very clear when he stated that "everywhere where teaching takes place, there are influences representing the contending forces, the dominant as well as the subversive ones," and that consequently "there will be conflicts and contradictions . . . within its very walls."[1]

## II

On the most basic level, the different viewpoints fighting it out in film education today echo the nineteenth-century battle between the traditional humanists and the reformists for the soul of the American university. Then, the supporters of a liberal education believed that the curriculum should fashion itself after the German system of education. Certainly the selection of Wilhelm von Humboldt's Berlin University as a model was not without problems, for its founding principle was to use "culture" to create an administrative elite, a special class of model citizens who could carry-out the mandates of the new nation-state.[2] Specific features of the German program though had definite appeal on this side of the Atlantic. Most importantly, in James Morgan Hart's view, was the decision *not* to "attempt to train successful practical men, unless it be indirectly, by giving its students a profound insight into the principles of the science, and them turning them adrift to deduce the practice as well as they can from the carefully calculated theory."[3] "A German university," Hart concluded, "has only one object: to train thinkers." It is thus not a place "where any man can study anything. . . . It contents itself with the theoretical and leaves to other institutions the practical and the technical."[4] Through *Bildung* then, the student "learns the rules of thought, not a content of positive knowledge."[5] The classical curriculum that emerged in this country was therefore construed not as a direct preparation for any further occupation but as a training ground for the mind. Greek, Latin, and the classics were taught because these subjects were deemed to be particularly suited to build up "the discipline and the furniture" of the students' mind.[6] Such intellectual formation was especially needed, it was thought, in times of great social upheavals for it alone was capable of producing the first class minds, "theologians rather than pastors, jurists rather than lawyers," needed to see society through the changes.[7]

That argument did not sit well with reformists. John Dewey for one was quick to note that "there is implicit in every assertion of fixed and eternal first truths the necessity for some human authority to decide, in this world of conflicts, just what these truths are and how they shall be taught."[8] In other words, the ancient languages and the classics did not become exemplary standards by themselves, somebody declared them so. On a more practical level, the reformists were concerned that the core curriculum taught in the universities was frightfully out of tune with the reality of the times. Indeed, the industrial transformation of society had made it imperative in their view that the university respond by building up the scientific curriculum, the social sciences, and the study of modern languages. At the very least, Greek, Latin, and the Classics should be consolidated to provide room for the new disciplines. Students should also be allowed to specialize early on so as to be able to immerse themselves in their chosen area of concentration. "A well-instructed youth of eighteen," Charles William Eliot reasoned, "can select for himself—not for any other boy, or for the fictitious university boy, but for himself alone—a better course of study than any college faculty, or any wise man who does not know him and his ancestors and his previous life, can possibly select for him."[9]

Long after the proponents of the "elective system" won the day, it became clear that the departmentalization of knowledge it entailed was not free of consequences either. To put it briefly, the process was threatening the very independence of the university from business life. This led to what Robert M. Hutchins called a "service-station conception of the university."[10] Courses were now offered that directly "prepare[d] students to get better jobs and make more money" after leaving school.[11] For Hutchins and others, the enemy clearly was the notion of vocational education which had crept into the different curriculums. Discarding the idea of the university as an autonomous center of knowledge, such programs in effect emphasized its connection to business and turned students into mere trainees for the industry. We have no choice, Harry D. Gideonse countered, "we must meet the present on its own terms."[12] Expressing the thought of many, Gideonse scoffed at the thought that "participation in practice requires no special training, [that] a brief apprenticeship under technicians will suffice to make a superior practitioner of the theoretical product of the higher learning."[13] Modern society was so complex, so technically inclined, that it required immediate immersion in its works.

Through the years then, the argument had shifted from a debate regarding the merits of a universal classical education to one that focused exclusively on the degree of specialization to be given to the student. The Harvard Report on General Education of 1945 confronted this issue when it declared that "the problem is how to save general education and its values *within* a system where specialization is necessary."[14] In other words, the commission was trying to distinguish pragmatic learning in a humanistic environment from mere apprenticeship. The difficulty of such an operation is undoubtedly still with us today. Should the university serve merely as the job training facility of the business world or should it refract its practical teaching through a special prism, in effect wrapping up the immediate needs of commerce within a larger cultural perspective?

### III

Such querying cannot be detected in the 1929 founding charter of what would later become the School of Cinema-Television at the University of

Southern California, the first higher institution to enter the motion picture field. Quite the opposite, the document exhibits full confidence that the collaboration between industry and Academe will be a positive one.[15] What were the components of that program? Mainly, in alliance with the Academy of Motion Picture Arts and Sciences, USC's College of Liberal Arts introduced a series of specialized classes for juniors and seniors. In addition to a general cultural course "designed to give the average student a better appreciation of the pictures which constitute so large a part of his entertainment," there would be a series of classes on cinematography, writing, and art direction "for the limited number who may be found fitted to specialize in active preparation for definite work in the literary and technical branches of the industry."[16] Strengthened by the knowledge that these classes would involve the study of film chemistry, lens optics, the psychology of perception, the art of drama, etc., the dean of the college seemed to have had no second thoughts about the presence of moviemaking on campus. Indeed he declared the "school of motion picture sciences . . . comparable to schools of mining or civil engineering or architecture."[17] His endorsement, however, may have been clinched by the Academy's promise that it would "give [job] preference to those who have had the training in the courses outlined."[18]

What we have therefore, from the very first days of the film school as a center of learning, is a hodgepodge of sponsors and objectives. To start with, the program was initiated by the Academy. Why? What did the industry have to gain from such an association? It turns out that "the last few years the moving picture industry has been passing through a period of financial depression. Box-office receipts have fallen off alarmingly the world over, and in consequence the personnel of the industry has suffered. The talking picture has been a financial godsend to the industry, but it has not answered the cry for better films."[19] The films, in short, were no good, the audience had deserted them, and that in turn hurt guild members. Did that mean that Hollywood recognized itself as creatively exhausted, out of ideas? Some in the industry at least were voicing their concerns. In 1927 for instance, Milton Sills, a powerful executive, did not mince words when expressing what he felt was wrong with the movies. Addressing a group of business students at Harvard, he declared:

> It is unfortunate that the cheapness of the industry when it started has held over to some extent . . . [continually enlisting] mediocre men in its ranks. For the survival of the industry it is necessary today

to draft men of finer intelligence and cultural background, of greater energy, of greater business power, and of greater poetic creativeness. . . . Personally I look forward to the day when . . . schools of motion picture technique may be developed, from which we may draw our cameramen, our directors, our supervisors, our writers. . . .[20]

By 1929, however, a time of crisis, Hollywood was thinking twice about adding fresh competition to its ranks: "There are grave economic problems, too, in striking the fine balance between training sufficient new blood to keep the industry vigorous, and overrunning it with a horde of workers for whom there can be no work."[21] Hollywood's open-ended invitation to USC students was quickly rescinded as a result and the Academy's objectives were almost immediately narrowed down to the program's other emphasis: the film appreciation course whose broad goal was to help raise "the mental level of the audience."[22] Better films indeed would never get made "unless it can be surely known that there is an adequate market awaiting them. . . ."[23] Here the idea was to set up a model course that could be disseminated in other schools. And if that turned out to be impractical or too expensive, there was always the possibility for these schools to play back a "Vitaphoned reproduction" of the speakers' lectures at USC. In any event, it was expected that these students would eventually radiate outwards, infiltrating the public at large, pushing the demand for better films, possibly even attracting to movie theaters an entirely new audience. The film-educated college population would thus act as "the one small lump of leaven that can leaven the whole mass."[24] Faced with more demanding spectators, the industry would be put in a position to turn out better products, receive more monetary rewards, and thus improve the conditions of its workers.

For the Academy, the deal with USC turned out to be all profit and no loss. On the one hand, the film appreciation classes could in the long run become breeding grounds for a new class of customers. On the other, nothing was given away as the Great Depression served as an excuse to renege on the promise to hire "university men." What all of this meant was that, despite the good words of Milton Sills, Hollywood was not quite sincere about opening its ranks to a different kind of personnel. Nepotism continued as before and the unions remained closed to film students for another forty years. Cut off from the market place, the technical classes attracted few students, no more than ten a year. And, although sixteen millimeter film was eventually used to duplicate on a small scale what was happening in the studios, the program remained lecture-based, with almost no hands-on experience. This of course made little teaching sense. Back in 1922, Peter Milne, in a book on directing, had already warned that "to teach the craft through the printed page is just as impossible of accomplishment as instructing a steeplejack in his trade through correspondence school."[25] Not every student enrolled in the technical classes even completed a short film of his or her own. Mainly, one was lucky to rotate positions whenever any project was being shot. Afterwards, graduates found employment outside the industry, mainly in educational filmmaking, public relations films, and industrial films.

## IV

The film school phenomenon thus had to wait till the late fifties, early sixties to develop a full curriculum of courses. Three distinct circumstances were responsible for the advancement. First, there was at the time an influx of students who felt a special kinship toward motion pictures as a means of communication. Whereas the previous generation had remained connected to the power of the written word, this new group was entranced by the magic of the moving image. George Lucas is very clear about this:

> One of the things we tapped into—not just Steven [Spielberg] or I, but our whole '60s generation—is that we didn't come from an intellectual generation. We came from a visceral generation. We enjoyed the emotional highs we got from movies and realized that you could crank up the adrenaline to a level way beyond what people were doing when they treated film as a more literary medium.[26]

Second, the counterculture movement made it suddenly possible for these students to break away from the Hollywood model. Personal experimentation with images and sounds rather than conventional filmmaking became the thing to do. Public screenings of such films on campuses and at midnight shows in regular theaters were met with wild enthusiasm at a time when Hollywood was floundering badly. Third, this new approach to filmmaking was certainly helped by the arrival on the scene of super 8mm which made it financially feasible for students to produce a number of short films for a minimum amount of money. As all of this was taking place, professional moviemaking was losing some of its aura. It was found that directing, shooting, and editing did not, after all, require the kind of training enforced by the unions. Why spend years loading magazines before being able to get behind a camera? More generally, why shouldn't you be able to write and cut your own projects? Overnight almost, Hollywood was dismissed as an out-of-date factory producing goods nobody wanted. With good reason then, students could see themselves as genuine filmmakers who were going to take on the system. As for the film schools themselves, although their policies may have changed along the years, they never looked back, their continuing success with students allowing them to evolve into strong departments, even bona fide schools within their universities.

## V

Going back to the USC charter, we notice that it states that the lecturers for the technical courses are to be selected from among "the best brains in the industry and the University."[27] Thus, from the very outset, cinema courses were to be taught by two types of instructors, those who took a breather between two movie projects to relate their know-how to the young crowd, and academics who were progressive enough to be interested in the new area of study. The two types of instructors still share the podium today. Let us look first at the former group, which has not changed much along the years. They still consist of professionals who are regularly invited to teach whenever their schedule allows it or, if that is not possible, to make an appearance on campus as guests, perhaps when their latest movie is being released. Like stars, these Hollywood stalwarts carry the aura of the industry into the classroom, charging it for a while with the glamour of real moviemaking. In addition to this group, one finds semi-professionals, partially retired cameramen and editors, educational filmmakers, independents brutalized by the system, documentarians who need to supplement their income between projects, etc. Whether permanently hired or adjuncts, this second group carries in fact the brunt of the instructional process. Despite their generally being more open-minded than the true professionals, they nevertheless originate from film practice. Filmmaking, for the most part, is still what they are all about. Hence they cannot be said to represent truly the "university" or scholarly side of things suggested by the charter. They function as "academics" only in the sense that teaching is now their main occupation.

For someone like Mitchell W. Block, even that is not good enough. In his view, these instructors do not pass muster. If schools fail to effectively prepare students for actual careers in the field, he says, it is because "too little time is spent by faculty too underqualified in discussing an industry they are too removed from to understand."[28] The argument here is that these people are third stringers, that they are not up-to-date, that only top-notch professionals know the state of the art and, thus, they alone should be teaching students. Block is not being totally honest here, for he knows the difficulty (almost impossibility) of getting big-name professionals to commit themselves for fifteen weeks for what amounts to them as very little money. Furthermore, as evidenced in film schools that do manage to hire professionals from time to time, brilliance in the field does not necessarily translate into teaching competence. In complete disagreement with Block, I would say that if these semi-professionals can be faulted at all, it is because they do not promote vigorously enough alternatives to conventional filmmaking. Although their own taste is often refreshingly eclectic, in the end they usually come round and abide by Hollywood's norms. Far from offering a broader, manifold approach to filmmaking from a scholarly perspective, knowledge in their hands remains essentially defined by industry practice. As a result, the ideological imperative at the core of the American cinema remains largely unexamined. When all is said and done, there are no substantial differences between the two groups that teach production.

## VI

What is being taught in film school? What is the philosophy behind the teaching? What is its goal? As each school's curriculum is organized somewhat differently, the best way an aspiring filmmaker has to judge what a program actually emphasizes is to take a look at its student films. Not the exceptional films that shine through once in a while in each department but the run-of-the-mill films: What stories do they tell? How do they tell them? What techniques are they using, etc.? Thirty years ago, when both faculty and students believed they could change the system, the films tended to be daring in their subject matter, their filmic approach, their editing style, and the like. Remember: students at that time expected their work to become the norm eventually. As a result, they were not afraid to experiment, to push for an alternative cinema. The idea certainly was not to please the Establishment. And for a while, as pointed out by David Thomson, their hopes for a new industry seemed to be echoed by the high number of unusual films which met with public success as well as critical acclaim: *Bonnie and Clyde* (Arthur Penn, 1967), *The Wild Bunch* (Sam Peckinpah, 1969), *Five Easy Pieces* (Bob Rafelson, 1970), *McCabe and Mrs. Miller* (Robert Altman, 1971), *The Godfather* (Francis Ford Coppola, 1972), *The Conversation* (Francis Ford Coppola, 1973), *Chinatown* (Roman Polanski, 1974), *The Parallax View* (Alan J. Pakula, 1974), *Taxi Driver* (Martin Scorsese, 1975), *One Flew Over the Cuckoo's Nest* (Milos Forman, 1975), etc. Not only were these films deeply personal in terms of style, Thomson writes, they were also "adding to the discourse and ferment of the country."[29] For a while then, everything seemed possible. Then came *Star Wars* (George Lucas, 1977) and that was the end of it.

Bit by bit, the sixties teaching corps found itself out of tune not only with university administrations, which questioned the ever-rising costs of equipment and facilities, but also with a new generation of students who had discovered cinema through Messrs. Lucas and Spielberg and wanted to emulate their works.[30] Several years ago, at UCLA, the conflict erupted into a showdown and the last remaining radicals among the faculty were unceremoniously booted out. Immediately minions of the industry were invited to take their place. Less dramatically perhaps, many other schools followed suit. In exchange for their fund-raising abilities, the new department leaders were given carte blanche to align the curriculum more closely along current industry practices. Emulation of commercial requirements superseded artistic experimentation, the policy under the old guard. The 1929 Academy push to form recruits "in active preparation for definite work" in the field had finally come into being.[31] From now on, the major film schools were going to act as the training grounds of the industry, saving it, in the process, considerable moneys.

"Control instruction and you will control style."[32] The founding principle of academic painting in the nineteenth century remains valid in today's film schools. Here too a student's progress is measured against a rising scale of professional know-how. Students are pushed along a disciplining path that takes them from the pure joy of filmmaking at the beginning (when they can experiment with the medium), through the rote learning of how-to-do-things in the different crafts, to the production, at the end of their studies, of thirty-minute portfolio pieces that should demonstrate to producers, agents, etc., their capabilities as well as their willingness to work within the system. Most teachers agree wholeheartedly with this philosophy. Students generally are no longer perceived as artists in the making but as people who, like it or not, are going to have to work in the industry. Whatever their early disposition, most students end up agreeing with that notion as well. Surely paying back student loans comes into play. When you owe in excess of $70,000 for three years of instruction, it is quite understandable that many students find themselves under enormous pressure to find any high-paying job as quickly as possible regardless of what the work may entail. As for university departments, there is no doubt that the move to professionalism was exacerbated by the appearance of specialized mini-schools which have gotten into the business of teaching film. Because of these schools, universities must now compete for the student dollar on many fronts. There is the Maine Film Workshop with its wide smorgasbord of courses, the New York Film Academy, which travels across the country and offers "eight week total immersion programs for individuals with little or no prior filmmaking experience," and then there is the Dov S-S Simens' "Hollywood Film Institute," which advertises its no-nonsense, low-cost instruction as compared to the more conventional programs elsewhere.[33] "We teach facts. They teach theory. We're inexpensive. They're costly. We take just 2 days. They don't." And this too: "You learn in just one week-end the exact procedures for directing, producing, financing, shooting, selling and distributing feature films internationally. All in just 2 days."[34] Who could resist?

Film teaching is now very much vocational in spirit everywhere, even in graduate school.[35] This is the way it is done in the profession, these are the techniques students need to replicate. With every word, every gesture, the student incorporates not only professional techniques but also the ideology behind them. All the ingredients that are required to sell scripts in the industry need to be present in student written screenplays as well. "Strong" characters, eventful action, linearity, and clarity are a must if the project is eventually to "pay off," that is to say, if it is to secure the student a mythical job in the industry after graduation. And through shooting and editing, professional techniques must be adhered to for the same reason. All in all, the film should evidence the qualities the industry relies upon for its own shows: a well-managed drama, good direction of actors, and dynamic pacing. Experimentation, in fact any other approach to filmmaking, is frowned upon and discouraged, if not actively repressed. Extra bonus points go to students who are able to duplicate, on the cheap, Hollywood's special effects. A brochure from Florida State University's film school, for instance, extols a fifty-foot-high explosion in a student film, a train crashing into a car in another, a three-hundred-pound Bengal tiger sharing the screen with a boy in a third, etc. Once a year, each film school proudly invites agents, producers, and other studio representatives to take a look at its recent graduates. On their own, students also vie to show their films at Sundance, the student Academy Awards, on PBS, and on cable.

For critics of the system, such slavish rehearsal amounts to "machine-tooling the young" to the needs of a corporate sponsor.[36] Film students today are not unlike college athletes vying for employment in the National Football League. This much is evident. More ominously, today's programs can also be seen as furthering "the development of nonideological, technically oriented centers" where "an apolitical, value-free, non-activist achievement-oriented student body can be trained."[37] In film in particular, it is clear that the "general education" requirement the Harvard Report hoped to safeguard within specialized schooling has been given up without a fight. In Madan Sarup's words, it all boils down to: "the question now being asked by the student, the state or the university is no longer 'Is it true?' but 'What use is it?' In the context of the mercantilization of knowledge, more often than not this question is equivalent to: 'Is it saleable?'"[38] Alone in the industry, the great cinematographer, sometimes director, Haskell Wexler has condemned this utilitarian view of film education. Every idea for a script or a film, he suggests, is now measured against: "Will it help me get a job?" Even the choice of a film school may be decided by: "Will I meet the right people there?" Such calculated planning, however, keeps students from making the most of their years in film school. It impedes them from trying out "new ways of looking at things." In the final analysis, the operation is counterproductive even for the industry insofar as, ultimately, it needs unconventional talent to keep going. And Wexler to conclude: "If you can't experiment when you are a student, forget it, because for the rest of your life you're going to have to be practical. . . ."[39]

## VII

The best-known film schools would of course deny they favor a vocational mentality. We do not tell our students how to do things, their production chairs would respond, we help them find their own voices. But, in all sorts of ways, film schools are sending messages that are far from ambiguous. At USC, for instance, the production building is named after George Lucas and the sound mixing facilities bear the name of Steven Spielberg. The hallways are decorated with posters from successful Hollywood movies. Every incoming group is shown *Precious Images*, a compilation film by Chuck Workman of hundreds of memorable snippets from classic American movies. Even the motto of the department, which states "reality stops here," seems to reject the social and historical world—adopting essentially an antirealist, antidocumentary stance. To say in these conditions that all kinds of filmmaking are welcome is rather hypocritical.

And do the production chairs really believe that students show up one day unencumbered by the memory of thousands of scenarios and millions of (precious) images? To imagine that students are not influenced by all of that material is plainly ridiculous. To be in the world, to be exposed to its culture, means we incorporate its conventions and customs as we grow up. The inevitable result, insofar as film is concerned, is decried by many even from the industry. "Many kids from USC, UCLA or Columbia," Frank Pierson complains, "never had anything bad happen to them. They're 27 years old and all they know is what they've seen on 'Cheers' and in George Lucas films. They produce imitations of imitations of imitations of life. . . ."[40] Students, in other words, enter film school with too many movies in their head. They have no personal story to tell. Stereotypes fill the screen rather than human beings. Everything turns around providing a twist to an already exhausted genre. In contrast, listen to what Chris Hart has to say about what impelled him to write *Timeless* (1997):

> I was driving a delivery truck in Los Angeles. I witnessed a woman being beaten up unconscious in broad delight on a crowded LA street. I began honking my horn to get people's attention but did not get out of the truck to intervene on the woman's behalf—nor did anyone else.[41]

What motivated Hart, I presume, and I respect him tremendously for being open about this, is the fact he did nothing although the situation demanded that he take action. In other words, he failed the test. Surely it is painful to recognize one's momentary shortcomings, but that is also what makes one grow both as a human being and an artist. I therefore totally agree with Pierson: it makes little sense to enroll in film school before you have lived a little, gone through some relationships, experienced the world of work, lost a loved one, been punched hard more than a few times. These experiences are what give you both stories to tell and the inner voices to tell them with.

Beyond that, film schools should help nurture budding filmmakers by exposing them to contrasting styles of filmmaking. Take a look at *I Am Cuba* (Mikhail Kalatozov, 1964), *The Red and the White* (Miklós Jancsó, 1967), and *The Color of Pomegranates* (Sergei Parajanov, 1968), and you will discover narrative form liberated from the commercial constraints that usually keep it within generic bounds. Too often unfortunately, independent or foreign narrative approaches, documentaries, and filmic experimentations are excluded from mainstream film teaching. Nowhere, for instance, is there room for the kind of imaginative undertaking Peter Greenaway brings to his films. "There are ways other than linear narrative to organize material," he insists, and they include "the grid, numerical systems, color coding, all [of which] are capable of putting the chaos of existence into some kind of comprehensible pattern."[42] "The only given in cinema," he continues,

> is that the screen is a flat surface. It doesn't need to be a window on the world. We aren't obliged to tell stories—to manipulate space and time—the same way it's been done since D. W. Griffith. The dominant cinema illusion is that the materials and the creator of the film are not supposed to be artifacts themselves, that they should disappear behind some traditional story. A film is constructed. In my films I want you to notice the editing, the music, the drama.[43]

For many teachers, this is anathema. Even when a program allows a student to explore, he/she will probably be prevented from bringing back and integrating the values and processes encountered in radically distinct cinemas, documentaries, and experimental filmmaking within the "normal" filmmaking favored in film schools. What is marvelous about a film like *Irma Vep* (Olivier Assayas, 1996), for instance, is that it manages to incorporate all of these approaches into one package. In summation, all contending practices need be present once again within a school's curriculum. Such exposure is necessary for a student to realize that the impossibly conservative requirements of Hollywood filmmaking do not originate from solid filmic principles. These requirements express rather the fear of the unknown: what the "unassimilable" would do to all those who presently benefit from consensus filmmaking. To adopt such an inclusive view of cinema would, of course, require a radical change of direction for film schools, to some extent even a return to earlier days. But there is no alternative: one cannot simply sit back and expect fresh, uncommon perspectives to appear in students' minds as if by magic.

## VIII

Beyond this global acceptance of all forms of filmmaking, what would be required to further such an environment in the class room itself? It might be useful here to go back to some of John Dewey's ideas regarding education. Although his writing was for the most part directed toward primary and secondary schooling, it is in higher education, especially in film departments where the curriculum keeps students on a very short leash indeed, that his thinking can perhaps be most beneficial today.

Having witnessed the great social and economic changes at the turn of the century, Dewey was concerned about democracy's ability to survive. A real democracy, in his view, required an active citizenship to combat the natural tendency of society to harden itself and become static. This could be achieved only if the young were allowed not just to integrate prevailing values but also to test and eventually modify them for everybody's benefit. The key to the creation of socially concerned individuals was to be found in a different kind of education. Dewey certainly had little sympathy for traditional schooling. For him, to try to fit a child into a preexisting scholastic model made no sense whatever. This would almost certainly guarantee the production of conformist minds in the future. One had to use instead what was of immediate interest to the student, for each individual, he wrote, "has a certain primary equipment of impulse, of tendency forward, of innate urgency to do."[44]

Translated into film, this suggests that instructors should take advantage of the drive that brings the student to the classroom in the first place. That young man or woman wants to make films, be involved in the process, meet actors, understand light, see what happens when you play with sound, or move the cut around in editing. Dewey was formal about this: "As long as any topic makes an immediate appeal, it is not necessary to ask what it is good for."[45] The teacher should grab the opportune

MacGuffin and fly with it. The danger, for there is one, is to get stuck at this level of instruction. Dewey recalled visiting a painting class where an "air of cheerfulness, even of joy" permeated the classroom. Yet, he was quick to note, there was also an "absence of cumulative, progressive development of power and of actual achievement in results."[46] Excitement, fun and games, activities of one kind or another, were useful only to get the students' attention. Effective teaching, however, could not be achieved if one did not move from mere enjoyment of the material in its present state to a more abstract, more intellectual understanding of the issues connected to its use.

Let us take perspective as an example. In the traditional presentation, rejected by Dewey, the topic would appear one day as the teacher covers the properties of the lens: focal length, F/Stops, angle of view, depth of field, etc. The instructor might illustrate perspective by showing contrasting clips from *Citizen Kane* (Orson Welles, 1941) and *Hair* (Milos Forman, 1979). In the first film, the extremely wide angle lens visibly displays the social as well as personal isolation of the main character. In the second, the very long lens shows the Vietnam-bound troops being literally swallowed by the war machine, in this case the giant transport airplanes. Nonsense, a Dewey reformist would counter: you are introducing perspective out of context with the student's own development. Perhaps at that moment, this student is upset because he was not able to handle his actors well. Maybe that other student is thinking about her soundtrack. Showing exemplary moments of perspective distortion may not even get the students' attention as they are likely to get caught up in the story aspect of the scene. Finally, because students working with very modest equipment will have a hard time matching the effects seen on the screen, this lecture may set them up for a big disappointment later on.

According to reformists allied to Dewey, students would retain the material better if the teacher, instead of following a fixed program, introduced perspective when the topic emanates from the students' own films. See that shot over there? Well, if your story is about two men drifting apart, what if you had shot the rest of the scene with progressively wider lenses to emphasize what was taking place internally? And, in that other scene at the end of the film, when they have learned to accept each other, couldn't you have used longer lenses to bring the point home to the viewers? In other words, students would assimilate the importance of perspective through its direct impact on their own work. For the other students in the class too, the scene shot by a fellow student is not so professional looking that they might be distracted by the story or distanced by the superb, yet unachievable treatment.

That takes care of Dewey's first stage of the discussion. How do we get to the second one though? How do we access and understand perspective on a more conceptual level? Maybe it can go something like this. First, a distinction would have to be made between the lived experiential perspective of a human being and an artistic treatment that may or may not relate its outcome. Do we all, for instance, see the world the same way? What about past civilizations or people living in other cultures? What about the Romans? And the Aborigines? Although a certain amount of geographical and cultural coding pervades our view of the world, it seems that for the most part "we live with accurate perception the way a fish lives with water, relying on it, trusting it, rarely needing to think about it."[47] As a result, for M. H. Pirenne, "there is little reason to think that the main essential characteristics of human vision have changed in the course of history, or even prehistory."[48]

Artistic treatment though is an entirely different issue. Here one would have to explain radically dissimilar treatments of space. In murals from ancient Egypt, for instance, multiple points of view are incorporated within a single painting as bodies and objects are pictured from their most recognizable angle. At this point, one could evoke Nelson Goodman and suggest that pictures are but symbolic constructs that make a lot of sense to those who share that particular culture and have learned its code.[49] This said, how do *we* make sense of these other Egyptian images where inordinately large people share a fishing boat with tiny ones? The characteristic angles are still here but they do not explain the size difference. Nor can maturity since the small people are visibly all adults as well. What we discover here instead is a picture whose spatial representation is determined by that society's political stratification. The most important people in the group are the largest in the painting, the slaves the smallest, etc. All in all, it is clear that these pictures do not attempt to duplicate someone's vista. No one sees this. In fact it would be sacrilegious to make the Pharaoh a subject of anyone else's sight. The image rather is a statement, a communication about something. Better still, it is an affirmation, a proclamation of the way things are.

Looking at other paintings from China, Persia, and Japan, we notice different schemes operating in the images: the tiny size of travelers in Chinese landscapes, the fitting of human beings within flowery patterns in Persian paintings, and the curiously elevated, accented point of view that looks at interior spaces through missing ceilings in the famous *Genji Monogatari* illustrations of the Heian-Fujiwara age. In all of these examples, an actual visual impression of the world is not as important for the artist as the existing grid or schemata available to him or her at the time. "Between the subject and the world," Norman Bryson writes, "is inserted the entire sum of discourses which make up visuality, that cultural construct, and make visuality different from vision. . . ."[50] In fact, Ernst Gombrich concludes, "only the features for which schemata exist" will actually show up in images.[51]

Isn't our own perspective system, however, which is derived from the Quattrocento model, different in this respect? Doesn't it show the world as we actually *see* it? Indeed every line in a Renaissance painting is manipulated to duplicate the artist's actual experience from a unique point in space: the horizon line, the vanishing point, the transversals "growing closer and closer" giving the impression of "checkerboardlike squares receding in the distance," etc.[52] And when we belatedly stand in front of such a work, we too observe that the painted space fits before us just like it did earlier in front of its maker. The entire system is thus dependent on the presence on the spot of an individual: someone who sees this. That such a visual grid makes its appearance during the Renaissance is far from coincidental. In fact, it is but one manifestation of the profound social and intellectual upheaval that was rocking all vested authorities at the time, the Church in particular. Everything was being questioned, R. A. Sayce tells us, not just "science, medicine, law, but above all perhaps, the system of logical classifications and definitions which enable us to believe that we can make some sense of the world."[53] In other words, rules, precepts, decrees, as well as mediations of all kinds, which were mostly the lot of the world until this point, were rejected in favor of the direct, participatory involvement of the individual: *I'll* take a look at it, *I'll* see what is there.

Without going into all the details of an issue that has been debated thoroughly, let us just focus on two distinctive features of the Renaissance perspective scheme.[54] First, what happens when the scene shown by the painting has not in fact been experienced by the artist? More often than not, the view is nothing but a concocted extravaganza. A single example will suffice: in Sandro Botticelli's *Adoration of the Magi* (1475), we peer at a scene that appears to have been observed in situ by the artist: the presentation of baby Jesus to the traveling potentates. Plain common sense, however, immediately tells us that the depiction, far from being a documentary recording by the painter, is but an imaginary reenactment of Christ's birth based on the hundreds of other nativities that preceded this particular rendering. Problems abound: the costumes do not appear genuine, the participants lack Semitic features, and what on earth is Botticelli himself doing in the right corner of the picture? No less implausibly, Cosimo de Medici is recognized as the rich king who welcomes baby Jesus to this world.[55] One becomes even more befuddled when one is told that the prince also happens to be the painter's patron, the "producer" of the painting! In other words, whereas earlier (Medieval say) versions of the Nativity did not rely on any witness to substantiate the scene—being but assertions of the Christian story—the new scheme naturalizes the event as if it were really taking place in front of the viewer, turning him or her into an imaginary or false witness in the process. At the same time, paradoxically (to us anyway), the text appears to undermine its own effort by introducing inconsistencies at odds with the original narrative. There are no indications, however, that such incongruities bothered contemporary viewers. This is not as far-fetched as it seems if we recall that, just a couple of years ago, *Schindler's List* (Steven Spielberg, 1996) was offered to school children all around this country as a honest representation of the Holocaust. Even though the titles clearly acknowledged the presence of contemporary actors on the screen and Hollywood technicians behind it, the film was nevertheless portrayed by the organizers as history in the making. Even adults who should know better now end up imagining Auschwitz through the light of Hollywood moviemaking.

Second, regardless of what kind of picture is being shown, the Quattrocento perspective also helps confirm the spectator's own presence and his or her importance in the scheme of things. With all the signs pointing in the same direction—toward each viewer—the latter is under extreme pressure to take them in, to acknowledge, authenticate, and legitimize them. The subject's self-importance gets an immediate boost: the world does not only turn to me, nature makes itself meaningful in the process. Soon enough I believe myself the measure of all things. Unlike the other visual approaches which do not directly beckon viewers, the Renaissance perspective system instantly captures its viewers within a network of signs, producing them as the subjects they are.[56] In other words, the visual grid literally puts you in your place. This transaction is summarized by Philip Rosen in theoretical terms in the following manner: "It is not the subject who uses the signifying system, but the signifying system which defines the subject."[57]

When we use a lens that merely captures a scene, we thus contribute to the reification of the viewers. In shot after shot, the visual formation ministers to make them whole again. As a result, we become, to some extent at least, involved in the maintenance of today's social stratification. To question the links between lens optics, film equipment, and bourgeois society thus requires a profound investigation of the entire topic.[58] These issues, however, are not likely to be brought up by students unfamiliar with critical studies. "There is no spontaneous germination in the mental life," Dewey reminds us.[59] It is always the result of an outward cause. It is therefore up to the teacher to bring these points to the fore, giving students access to the larger intellectual debate that surrounds artistic rendition. All in all, effective film teaching should not consist of a pile of information presented by an instructor who is out of sync with his/her students' work. But neither should the subject be presented as if any figure of style were personal choice only, a matter unconnected to a historical, cultural, and political debate. For the curriculum, and Dewey is specific about this, needs to "arouse interest in the discovery of [the] causes, dynamic processes, [and] operating forces" that govern any topic.[60]

## IX

Another aspect of Dewey's educational philosophy is equally valuable for film teaching. Adapting ideas first developed by Johann Friedrich Herbart in Germany, Dewey rethought the relation between the past and the present. "The present," he wrote, "is not just something which comes after the past. . . . It is what life is in leaving the past behind." To study the past therefore "is of great significance when it enters into the present, but not otherwise."[61] To understand what is behind today's film staging for example, it would be useful to comprehend what led to it. How could we accomplish this? "When a pupil learns by doing," Dewey thought, "he is reliving both mentally and physically some experience which has proved important to the human race; he goes through the same mental processes as those who originally did these things."[62] So, instead of watching films by Griffith and being bored by what we perceive as primitive filmmaking, why not recreate with a video camera Griffith's original situation, inherited from the stage, and his creative solution to it? This is what Dewey had in mind when he advised his instructors to reconstruct the entire procedure that led to the making of a candle. "The whole process of getting illumination," he wrote, "stood revealed in its toilsome length, from the killing of the animal and the trying of the fat to the making of wicks and dipping of candles."[63] This was not nostalgia for an earlier form of light at a time when gas and electricity were already providing illumination in much simpler fashion; it was to make the young generation relive the cognitive thrust and the physical experimentation necessary to the progressive conquest of night by human beings. Similarly, to materialize Griffith's impatience with what was then the standard way of staging, is to confront the entire issue of what a representation is, maybe even perceive alternatives that were abandoned as impractical at the time for one reason or another. Such an exercise makes the history of cinema come alive, it makes it possible to revisit the past, not as a mausoleum but as a center of active research. What can be done with Griffith can of course also apply to Eisenstein, Welles, Godard, Janczo, Akerman, Greenaway, any director who became dissatisfied with staging as it was done in his/her days, producing a reformulation that expanded the limits of the medium as a result. In such a re-creation, the past is revisited as present, a novel insight is gained about the evolution of film, and the present way of staging can be experienced not as an acme of perfection but as a temporary construct that is bound to continue to evolve.

## X

A last point about Dewey's philosophy brings us back to the relation between film schools and the industry. As mentioned earlier, Dewey was concerned about the ability of the democratic state to renew itself. He therefore looked at schools as places where traditions, conventions, beliefs of all kinds could be explicated, then debated with a view toward their amelioration. To do the job, the school he had in mind needed to nurture a new kind of community, one in which the typical hierarchies operating in the outside world would not be mindlessly duplicated. In like manner, film schools should neither operate as little studios nor duplicate fixed industrial rules. There is nothing sacred indeed about the working arrangements that normally control Hollywood shooting. Most importantly, film schools should never, ever force students to compete against each other in order to get their projects produced by the department.[64] This destroys the chance to create a unique community of fellows who learn, share, and grow together. Second, there is no reason why someone working as a grip should not be able to turn to the director at any point during a shoot and offer some advice. After all, the beauty of being in film school is that no one really knows more than anyone else. Specialization has not yet locked anyone in. The boom person can comment on the lighting and the loader may have suggestions for the sound recordist. The lack of organizational discipline inherent in such a free-for-all is more than compensated for by everyone's genuine interest in the project. To shoot a film with your peers is truly exhilarating because the entire crew is composed of *amateurs*, people who love cinema and are doing what they can to help the creative process. Let us keep it this way. Likewise, the film school should always be a safe place, a place where it is okay to fail. Even if you fall flat on your face, people are not going to abandon you, you will still be their friend.

To the contrary, professionals, specialists, hired guns, dominate the industry. Technicians are brought in to do one thing only—their specialty—and they do it well, unquestionably. But their involvement is limited to their own work: the smoothness of the dolly, the sharpness of the focus, the exacting digital removal of wires, etc. They do not question whether the film, as a whole, is bad or that its message is deplorable. It says something about the industry that few of the grips, the electricians, the assistants, the below-the-line people who populate the sets, bother to see the film they worked on when it is finished. To shoot in the industrial mode means that you have bigger toys to play with, the job is more demanding, and you get paid very well. But the entire process is also repressive. Shooting is totally compartmentalized, it is done by the numbers. It becomes a mechanical operation that suppresses the feeling of brotherhood normally present in a communal creative environment. Regrettably, in film schools, chairs and instructors see nothing wrong in perpetuating these malignant values. Even when, in beginning classes, students are allowed to take chances and experiment, it is with the knowledge that, soon enough, they will be lassoed in by the system and forced to perform according to standard studio discipline. For Dewey, this would be all wrong. Indeed, to have any chance at revitalizing the profession, film schools need to rethink their role and come up with a strategy to help nurture an entirely different breed of filmmakers, encourage a brotherhood of minds capable of resisting the Hollywood lure.

## XI

Although Mitchell Block does not mention them by name, one suspects that the critical studies teaching corps is by definition included among those he considers "too removed from the industry."[65] Indeed, these university-bred instructors can be said to be the true academics envisioned in the USC film school charter. The problem in this case is that the scholars ended up divorced from production, unable to influence filmmaking in any shape or form. At the beginning, these instructors were few in number. They included mostly renowned historians of the medium (like Arthur Knight at USC) or generalists with an interest in film (Hugh Gray at UCLA would be a good example). For the most part, they taught the history of film or its aesthetics as a part of the general curriculum to be taken by all production students. In the sixties, however, the curriculum started to change. Following the sudden critical attention given directors, there was a push within the university to treat film much more seriously than before and to study filmmakers with the kind of breadth that had been reserved earlier for literary authors. "People," Rick Jewell said, "were looking for a way to convince college administrators that movies were worth studying at universities. They tried to argue that [film] was an art form, not a collaborative undertaking at all, and the work of a solitary artist—the director—who shaped everything."[66] Because these courses were generally well received on campuses, they became standard features in the curriculum. They were quickly followed by all the courses we now take for granted in a full-fledged department: the history of the silent and sound cinemas, American films, the international cinema, the different genres, etc. As the number of classes and instructors grew, it made sense to collect them all in a distinct discipline within the department.

At the time, neither production nor critical studies perceived the restructuring of the department as a split. The role of critical studies was still to service production students, to offer them an even larger menu of courses to choose from. Within ten years though, the situation changed radically. Under the influence of post-structuralism, film theory suddenly exploded in unpredictable fashion. Rather than taking its cues from film practice as it had done in the past, theory was now influenced by recent thinking in semiotics, literary studies, psychoanalysis, Marxism, radical feminism, etc. In the process, the old film generalists gave way to a new breed of instructors, more knowledgeable in these areas. As most of them came out of English departments, the new academics had little or no training in filmmaking. Quite logically, they preferred bypassing the idiosyncrasy of film practice, focusing rather on the signifying modulations of the texts. They generally showed little patience toward production teachers who tended to remain stubbornly impervious to what was happening in the cultural world. They endorsed the radical avant-garde at the expense of the more conventional type of filmmaking taught in production. And, if this were not enough, the language used in the new theoretical writing was so packed with jargon that the noninitiated were simply unable to access the material. Not surprisingly the two sides grew apart from one another. Teachers could no longer communicate with one another. Today, the production faculty snickers at the superciliousness of the critical studies corps while the latter continues to look at the former as a rather plebeian group. Even when coexisting under the same roof, the two divisions behave as if they had nothing, especially not cinema, in common.

This situation is troubling because it removed the one great advantage of American film education over the more typical systems found in Europe or Australia. There, film practice is regarded as an occupational activity whose place is in technical institutions in opposition to film theory, history, etc., which legitimately belong in university departments. This arbitrary division effectively puts film students in discrete programs, various buildings, separate schools, sometimes even different cities. In such a situation, students lack exposure either to the reality of the film process or to the critical thinking that questions its exercise. In the United States, where intramural coordination once was and still should be possible, the divorce between the two parties has made it equally difficult for students to benefit from what is happening on the other side. Each division, for instance, so overloads its students with its own requirements that critical studies majors are discouraged to take any production classes beyond super 8mm courses, and production students find it all but impossible to explore theory before the very end of their studies, that is to say, when it is too late to have any impact on their films. The specialization is enforced under the guise that there is so much to learn in the field. This argument is not unusual in academe and it fails to convince even a conservative critic of American education such as Allan Bloom. As he puts it, departmental saturation effectively "render[s] students immune to charms that might lead them out of the conventionally respectable."[67] In other words, each division operates as if it were fearful of the other's power to seduce "its" students.

This is ludicrous to say the least. Production students in particular get gypped in the process. Most of them (graduates as well as undergraduates) arrive at film school with little awareness of the cultural inroads of the last decades. What they get in the classroom at times can even smack of educational incompetence, for instance when montage is taught without a reference to Eisenstein. This is so because the professionals who teach editing today are not aware of his work, have not read his books, or dismiss his films and his thinking as irrelevant to our times. This is nonsense. What all of this means is that students are not given access to a challenging material that could prod them into making more demanding films. For film theory (adapting what Gerald Graff says of literary theory)

> is what is generated when some aspect of [the art], its nature, its history, its place in society, its conditions of production and reception, its meaning in general, or the meaning of particular works, ceases to be given and becomes a question to be argued in a general way. This is what inevitably arises when [film] conventions and critical definitions once taken for granted have become objects of generalized discussion and dispute.[68]

Broadly speaking then, to become aware of theory helps students question what it is they are doing as filmmakers as well as grow as active participants in the cultural debate of their times. In 1937, Harry D. Gideonse commented on the goal of liberal education. Such schooling, he wrote, "has always aimed at both theory and practice with the dominant concern of making the theoretical available for practice, and of correcting and fertilizing the theoretical by the practice."[69] Nowhere is this philosophy more urgently needed than in film schools today.

## XII

No director ever went to film school prior to the sixties. How did they do it? Well, there was that training ground called the studios where you could demonstrate your know-how in B movies. Generally speaking then, just to be around moviemaking seems to have been enough to get a sense of it all. To maintain a stable of would-be hopefuls, however, was an expensive proposition. Once the government forced the studios to sell their majority interest in theater circuits all around the country, they discovered they no longer could afford to pay people to learn their craft. Retrenchments became necessary. Hence, it is no coincidence that film schools became palatable to Hollywood at the exact moment the studios stopped being a home for prospective talents. A sort of privatization before the letter eventually took hold, with the universities now in charge of winnow-ing the chaff from the wheat and grooming the best of their recruits for future employment in the industry.

Today, film schools appear to be the only way into the movie busi-ness for those without connections. But are they really? What do they in fact provide? On the surface, students are being taught the different skills necessary for making a movie: directing actors, loading cameras, lighting a set, editing pictures, recording sound, etc. In reality, the only thing film schools give you is time to hone your talent. Time indeed is necessary for anyone to figure out what works and what does not work in a script. It takes time to recognize who will be the right actor for the part. It takes time to understand where to put the camera. It takes time to become sen-sitive to the subtle change of mood provided by a different lighting scheme. It takes time to get the right sounds to accompany specific images, etc. All a film school really does is to put in front of students, again and again, a canvas on which they can discover and develop their craft.

The rest is far less important. You probably already know that col-lege degrees mean nothing in the film business. Although they are no longer disparaged by the unions, as they used to be, they still do nothing for you. Not to have to worry about a degree means that you are free to leave film school whenever you believe you have exhausted what it has to offer. Cut your stay there to the minimum. *Never* run up a huge debt. If you absolutely think school will help, take an extension class somewhere, spend a few weeks at the Maine workshop, or (God forbid!) even attend a Dov S-S Simens seminar. On another front, do not think for a minute that equipment is important. It is easy when you speak with profession-als to be impressed by the jargon—HMI lights, Avid editing systems, DAT recorders, what have you—and think that this equipment is a pre-requisite before you can go ahead and shoot your film. The highfalutin' rig, however, is not necessary at all. "The best movies," Greenaway makes clear, "are made cheaply. . . . When it's cheap, it knocks the shit right out of the process."[70] The point is: you can make a very good film with out-of-date equipment.

Once you understand that what the film schools (and the studios before them) really supply is practice, you can start thinking of alterna-tives. One learns from doing, one learns from making mistakes. If you have any sensitivity at all, you will in time notice what does not work in a scene and make sure you do not fall into the same trap again. The more you shoot, the more you accumulate this kind of know-how. It follows that you will learn all there is to know by making a few films (shorts to start, fifty-minute pieces later, features last). Today, thanks to video, you can complete a feature for, say, less than $5,000. Read what low-budget specialists, like Rick Schmidt, have to say about cutting expenses down to the minimum.[71] But make real films, not exploitation pictures. You want to try your best, push yourself as far as you can in each project. Also, forget about releasing what you shot: these are sketches to be shown to friends only. Take your time. Do not jump the gun before you are ready.

The Latin root of education, Roberto Rossellini once wryly observed, entails the notion of castration.[72] If you decide after all to register in a film school, be careful of what you ask for! Sure, it isn't easy to become a filmmaker but, by working on the process yourself, at least you are your own master. That alone makes the journey worth taking.

# CHAPTER FOUR

●

# *Writing*

## I

Films originate from written words. Words here, now; images there, later. The question that has plagued the motion pictures almost from the beginning is how best to proceed from one medium to the next. Should the film be devised in minute details during the early process of writing or should the screenplay represent only a first draft toward the major creative effort that is to take place during the production phase? Should the people involved be the same ones throughout or should each job be left to specialists? Today no one questions the well-entrenched system ruling Hollywood. Yet its methods and guidelines are not necessarily neutral and would benefit from an open discussion. For instance, it is my contention that the working arrangement between writers and directors is not disinterested in nature, for it helps the system define film as a commodity to be packaged, manufactured, and distributed worldwide. This gentlemen's agreement is not likely, to say the least, to bring about the individual, innovative film that expands our idea of narrativity or furthers our understanding of life, culture, and history. In this essay, I will thus concentrate on three obstacles that, in my view, are largely responsible for blocking the development of such cinema: (1) the repressive and inhibiting division of labor between writers and directors, (2) the compulsory format which writers must use, and (3) the stereotypical dramatic structure now peddled everywhere by Hollywood proselytizers as "the" way to a successful project.

## II

Storytelling for film developed mostly out of necessity. As the movies lengthened and the stories grew in complexity, it no longer made sense to leave storytelling to the "momentary inspiration of directors, camera men, players, or workers of the office staff."[1] As a result, each studio quickly developed its own scenario department to help crank out the large number of shows required by the ever-expanding market. Soon afterwards though, it became clear that, by themselves, in-house writers were unable to prevent the kind of problems that arose from carelessness in shooting. For example, critics at the time complained a lot about sloppy continuity. One such case involved "a lost child who wandered away bareheaded, with nothing in his hands, yet later when he is shown among the hills he has a hat which plays quite an important part in his being found."[2] As Janet Staiger puts it, it became obviously "cheaper to pay a few workers to prepare scripts and solve continuity problems at [an early] stage than it was to let a whole crew of laborers work it out on the set or by retakes later."[3] Thomas Harper Ince, Hollywood's answer to Henry Ford, went to work and successfully managed to codify and standardize the entire practice of filmmaking under the aegis of a central producer. At "Inceville," in the Santa Monica mountains, writing for films became truly efficient for the first time. It developed into the indispensable core in a systematic operation. For instance, to counter the problem of directors improvising at the last minute and coming up with shots that either did not cut well or failed to bring out the "punch" of a scene, the latter was carefully broken down and parceled out in specific shots at the time of the writing. The drama was thus articulated visually ahead of time and the role of the camera limited to the duplication of these shots. One such scenario editor explained: "Under our system a script goes to a director in perfect form. He can immediately go to work on it. Four or five experts of our staff have read and discussed every phase of the script and every effort has been made to eliminate any flaws of structure."[4] The screenplay of *The Big Parade* (King Vidor, 1925) is exemplary in this domain. It mandates, early on in the film, that a street parade with flags and band be photographed in a long shot. This scene is followed by a close-up of the main protagonist, Jim, looking to the left. Then there is a close shot of his feet as they move to the beat of the music, a close-up of his face as he now turns to the right, and a medium shot of the base drum as it passes on the street. Then we cut back to Jim's face as he smiles. And back to his feet moving to the beat of the music, etc. Screenplays in fact became detailed shooting scripts that were given to the director for implementation.

The idea here was not that writers were necessarily better than directors at visualizing a scene but that, in general, a practical method could be systematically applied to preordain the action into "thrilling and telling" material.[5] Ince himself was known as "an expert plot builder" who was not only extremely good at condensing the scripts submitted for his approval but also at segmenting them into an appropriate series of shots.[6] For Tom Stempel, the result spoke for itself: "the scripts, the notes on the scripts, and the cutting of the films all add up to films that told stories clearly and cleanly."[7] As the film was undergoing this process, other specialists would go over the script to determine what would be required by the production team in terms of sets, props, titles, stock footage, and the like. All in all, the detailed continuity script became the engineering blueprint of the entire film project. As inefficiencies in the making of films were significantly reduced, films could be shot more profitably than ever before. Pointing out similarities with other industries involved in mass production, Staiger describes the continuity script as the necessary tool that provided "the uniformity and regularity that guides multiple workers in their filmmaking."[8] In effect, an industrial "quality" control could be maintained on the entire output regardless of the specific projects or the individuals involved. What did directors think of this system? According to Peter Milne, "individualists oppose Mr. Ince and belittle his methods. He doesn't bother about them often as he employs directors who are willing to work into his scheme of production and these for the most part have been richly rewarded."[9] As for the studios, needless to say, they benefited the most from the introduction of a detailed writing format.

### III

This situation came to an end as the silent cinema gave way to the talkies. The problem faced by the writers and the studios was a vexing one: how to adapt the existing screenplay format to the unique demands of the new sound movies. Previously, the bulk of the writing concerned the actions of the characters: what the protagonists actually did in the shot, how they reacted to one another. It made their gazes clear, it spoke of their emotions. As early as 1911, Epes Winthrop Sargent had suggested that these descriptions be kept simple. The story, he wrote, should seem "to tell itself, rather than to be told. It is more like a happening than a narrative of past events."[10] Actions thus formed the core material of the screenplays, interrupted only by the segmentation into shots and the intermittent titles that were to appear on the screen. Typically these titles were indented on the page. They could be descriptive or explanatory ("Where the mountains bend to the desert's whispering") but, more and more throughout the twenties, they became substitutes for the missing voices of the players, telling us in effect what the characters were saying to each other, e.g., "Mary, this is the end for me."[11]

As the synchronized voice of the actors became the draw of the early sound movies, dialogue emerged as the dominant element in the screenplay, forcing a readjustment of the writing format. Dialogue specialists were called in, often from New York, to help screenwriters in the novel undertaking. And, to make room for the dialogues (now indented as the titles used to be), the description of the protagonists' actions was progressively reduced to the absolute minimum. In the screenplay of *Men Must Fight* (1932), for example, C. Gardner Sullivan, one of Ince's top men, starts the script in his usual manner by assigning close-ups, medium shots, and the like to describe sets and characters. By Scene 5, however, the master shot of a room carries nine exchanges of dialogue between characters without any additional description or change of camera position. Two scenes later, a hotel bedroom scene covers seventeen repartees. Scene 12 (a "hospital office" assumedly in a master shot) has sixteen such lines and Scene 47 ( "a library" with no shot description) carries no less than forty-four exchanges occupying several pages of the script.

This displacement from action descriptions to mainly dialogue lines did not take place overnight, for the writers had to find their way through the changes in technology. What made the situation untenable for them was the fact that neither set of writers (the new dialogue specialists no more than the original story tellers from Hollywood) clearly understood the requirements mandated by the sound technicians, imported from broadcasting, who were suddenly ordering everyone around. Among their recommendations for staging a scene: actors should remain at a constant distance from a hidden microphone, they should speak one at a time, they should never turn away from the microphone, etc. Confronted with such limitations, directors clearly had their hands full, but the writers were now entirely out of the loop. Should spoken scenes still be broken down into shots or left to run all the way? Was it all right to interrupt a character's speech and move the camera to a new position? As a consequence of the general confusion surrounding the introduction of sound, writers were forced to leave out of their screenplays what Ince had made them add: the very detailed breakdown of scenes into shots. Jean-Paul Torok is thus absolutely right when he designates the changeover as most important for the practice of cinema.[12] From this point on, film continuity was redefined away from the shot, toward the nonstop rush of the dialogue, with only minimal description of actions and very few if any camera directions: "instead of a flurry of fragmented images, one broad all-encompassing view of the setting."[13] Meaning therefore was no longer conveyed by the image and the linking of images through editing but by dialogue-driven scenes. By the early thirties, a film script consisted essentially of a series of scenes involving people talking to one another. Today the professionals who read scripts for a living scan the dialogue lines with but a wink toward the rest of the information.

## IV

Whereas Ince's system located the essence of the movies inside the screenplay, the new format, superficially at least, split it between two distinct moments, two discrete labors, the writing and its execution. Once again, superficially, it was up to the director to decide how to stage the action and where to place the camera. Yet, even though screenplays were no longer the exact blueprints of films, deep down, nothing much had changed. It was still essentially a cinema dominated by the story. The visualization process remained entirely subservient to the drama described by the script. The core of Ince's contribution which, as Stempel puts it, was to "catch the audience up in a story and propel the viewer through it," had not been overturned.[14] Neither mode of writing concerned itself in the least with the specificity of the visuals: the particular way in which light, composition, staging, motion, even the grain of the film can speak to us each in its own way. For the most part then, the directors' work remained interchangeable, very much like a nonessential, transparent veneer on top of the story material. To borrow the words of François Truffaut, a comfortable, predictable, unimaginative "tradition of quality" resulted from this state of affairs.[15]

To counter the drabness of such cinema, critical attention was given in the fifties to little details through which a director could give vibrancy and flair to otherwise conventional material. Following Truffaut, the critics of the *Cahiers du Cinéma* were now consistently isolating and praising "certain recurring characteristics" displayed by American directors. Andrew Sarris, their proselytizer in the United States, summarized their thinking this way:

> The way a film looks and moves should have some relationship to the way a director thinks and feels. This is an area where American directors are generally superior to foreign directors. Because so much of the American cinema is commissioned, a director is forced to express his personality through the visual treatment of material rather than through the literary content of the material.[16]

What kind of treatment is Sarris talking about? Let us take an example from the ending of *Naked Spur* (Anthony Mann, 1952). In the last scene of the film, the writers Sam Rolfe and Harold Jack Bloom have Kemp, the bounty hunter, carry a fugitive's body to his horse. The dead man means a lot of money to the protagonist, his chance to start anew in California. The writers convey the action in the following way: "He hefts the body into his arms and walks toward the clearing." As Lina, his girlfriend, is repelled by Kemp's fixation on bringing back the dead body, he defends himself by saying: "I'm goin' to take him back, I swear it. I'm goin' to sell him for money. I'm goin' to. . . ." Then:

> His voice breaks as tears well up in his eyes. He turns away from her violently and stands facing the body, staring at it as if seeing it for the first time. The hates and tensions slowly drain out of him. Then as Lina watches fearfully, Kemp, almost gently lifts Ben's body from the horse and lays it [on the ground]. He pulls a shovel out of the burro's pack. . . .

The way the scene unfolds in the script suggests that the camera is showing Kemp's face at all times, first from Lina's point of view, then from the opposite direction as he turns away from her. We thus become aware of the changes the character is going through by watching his facial features. But instead, Mann shoots both the pulling of the body toward the horse and the moment of intense introspection after it from *behind* Kemp's back. In other words, in the film we do not have access to the man's face. We can only witness his desperation through the way his body struggles

with the emotions that traverse his entire being. We must imagine what
is going on, we cannot see it. Although this is the only area where Mann
improves on the screenplay's final scene, it is decisive in terms of giving
viewers access to a more subtle descriptive style. Indeed, what Mann actualizes here is a departure from a narrative mode that assumes that everything is accessible to viewers at all times. Instead, a mediating space is
inserted between the action and the spectators. The unexpected camera
angle, therefore, is far from gratuitous and it is not surprising that the
*Cahiers du Cinéma* critics rejoiced when they witnessed achievements
such as this. Such moments of bravura in effect broke down the routine
of the commercial cinema, its repetitive dullness, its bureaucratic programming. It is, however, uncanny to think that, had Ince's format managed to live on, Truffaut and company would have had to pin authorship
on gifted writers instead.[17]

## V

To the surprise and resentment of writers in this country, directors were
now recognized everywhere as the auteurs of the films they directed. The
furor reached its apex "when Otto Preminger had the temerity to advertise *The Man with the Golden Arm* as a film 'by Otto Preminger.' Novelist Nelson Algren and the Screenwriters' Guild raised such an outcry that
the offending preposition was deleted."[18] The situation has not gotten any
better since. Witness for instance the recent vicious attack against writers
by John Carpenter in the Directors' Guild magazine: "As a director, I am
the author of my movies. If the writer thinks he's an auteur, then let him
thread up his screenplay in a projector and we'll take a look at it."[19] As for
writers, Harry Brown didn't mince his words either when he complained
that "most directors have about as much story-sense as a sick mink. . . .
I've met damned few who didn't have a top-sergeant's mentality combined
with the sensitivity of a Port Said whore."[20]

Humor aside, the rise of the director as a bankable author of the
film had unexpected consequences of its own. Although outwardly the
script is still conceived with a movie in mind, in practice, with the help
of the Writers Guild of America, the dialogue-driven narrative is now
being peddled as a distinct, concrete "property" to be auctioned by agents
to the highest bidder. Although this has benefited many writers who can
now command a high price for their work, it is not clear that the end

result of the bickering between writers and directors has necessarily been beneficial to cinema. In fact, I would argue that our modern charged-up screenplays have their own best interests in mind instead of those of the film. The fundamental concern of writers is for the script to catch the interest of agents, readers, and producers during the pitch session. It is the "here" and the "now" that is affirmed. The goal of writers is to come up with a *screenplay* that flies, material that pitches well. Ignored, unloved, and resentful, writers have given up on the very medium they work for. They no longer care what happens on the screen. They have taken refuge in their own neck of the woods. Whatever happens after the contract is signed is no longer their responsibility. It is up to the directors, if they can, to do something with the product. Even in commercial Hollywood terms, what we are witnessing here is an abject withdrawal, a complete turn around, from Ince's basic philosophy. No longer conceived for the long run, as a helper to the production process, the script now serves the sole and immediate needs of writers, their financial goal. [21] Today the Writers Guild could advertise a new motto: "Each screenplay for itself."

## VI

To counteract such hostile and, in the long run, self-destructive tactics, I would like to take a second look at the entire procedure of writing for the film. In *The Art of Photoplay Making*, published in 1918, Victor O. Free-burg publicized the steps through which a narrative would become a film. He saw the operation as taking place in three distinctive steps: the selection of the materials, their arrangement in some order, and finally their performance or execution during the shooting of the film. [22] In my view, these premises are as good as any to open the discussion. As just mentioned, the trend today is to keep the writer in charge of the first two stages of the production and to assign the director only the last stage. I believe this arbitrary division of labor to be a fundamental mistake because it undermines the chance of producing a more varied kind of cinema. To start with, it once again demotes the director to the level of a mere technician: someone who deals with the actors and coordinates the different technical fields. Second, more insidiously, it establishes the screenplay-property at the core of the film project, meaning that the story as written is complete and that it needs only visualization to become a gratifying film. This system thus locks in a drama whose essence is expressed mostly through the actions and the dialogue. Third, the necessity to sell single-handedly blockbuster scripts foreordains a heavily plotted film with energetic action, dramatic surprises, and vivid characters. In such scripts, buttons are pushed every two minutes to keep the pace from ever languishing. Because today's writers do not concern themselves with the finished product, their souped-up screenplays are neither suggestive nor eloquent. By this I mean they are not conceived as open texts to be interpreted and given thoughtful amplification by an innovative director. Instead, the work embeds a whole set of regressive assumptions, values, and solutions.

How different is Godard's method! Jean-Claude Carrière, the celebrated French film writer, recalls the director's approach: "He would collect some images that for some reasons mean something to him, obsess him: a landscape, the face of an actor, a photograph cut out from a newspaper. Then he would show these to me and he would ask me, as for example with a painting by Bonnard: ' Is there a scene in that?'"[23] It is not important in my view whether it is Godard who suggests an image to Carrière or Carrière to Godard, what matters is the coming together of two people with complementary skills, two individuals who love cinema, two talents whose aspiration is that maybe a good film will come out of their joining forces. What primarily interests the two men is the harmonious crafting of a film from the initial idea to its final completion. Typically, Buñuel would also ask Carrière to come and see the rough cut and make comments about it.[24] So we are not talking just about a director helping in the writing of the screenplay but also of a writer aiding the director in the cutting. How do a screenwriter and a filmmaker work together? Screenwriter Jean-Loup Dabadie recalls his own encounters with director Claude Sautet:

> First, we kind of get to know each other. What I mean is that, the director and I, we meet, we talk on the phone, we have lunch or dinner together. We drink, we laugh. We are getting comfortable with one another. One day we bring up our idea. . . . We talk a lot, we walk back and forth, we say all kinds of things, without any order, almost on automatic. . . . Quickly though I need to know something definite that we both agree on: what is the meaning we want to give to our story.[25]

It could be argued that the situation I am describing is very French. But is it really? In 1917 in this country, Jesse Lasky had exactly the same idea when he announced that in his studios "each director will have his

own writing staff and the [writer] will continue active work on every production until its conclusion, staying by the side of the director even when
the film is cut and assembled."[26] Today, since the writer's "property" is
going to be packaged anyway by an agency with a director, major stars,
etc., why not encourage an earlier rapprochement between the two creative forces? Why not also move across agencies and present a fait accom-
pli to the respective agents? With the director present at the time of the
writing, the plot may suddenly become less paramount. Why not initiate
the story from an accident one has just witnessed? What about the strong
mood that emanates from a tenement? And why not think of a character
first? Ozu and his screenwriter, for instance, often reread old scripts to
extract from them a secondary character, to see what they could do with
him or her. Images may be jotted down, gestures and camera movements
as well. And, as ideas are thrown all around, there may already be some
definite ideas about the use of sound. Mainly, the script would advance
on two fronts simultaneously—through audio *and* images. All the film's
potential would thus be engaged from the very beginning of the project.

## VII

The writing format too may be of help. In France and a number of other
countries, it is not paramount to present a screenplay in a specific form.
It is best left to the taste and custom of the individual writer. In the
United States, unfortunately, everyone must submit scripts in the sanctioned format or it will not be considered. This does not mean, however,
that screenplays must be written that way. If other models prove more
fruitful for developing the work, they should be used; at a later stage, the
script can be translated back into the conventional model for the sake of
agents and producers. What would be gained from such an arrangement
is the rediscovery that words and images can interact creatively in all sorts
of ways. One illustrious example of alternative format (one which film
students could seriously benefit from) is Carl Mayer's screenplay for *Sun-
rise* (Friedrich Murnau, 1927). One excerpt goes like this:

> Now:
> The Vamp walks into picture
> In very short negligee, with limbs exposed.
> A typical creature from a big city.

Beautiful.
Racy.
Coquettish?
Just lighting a cigarette at the burning candle.
Now smiling and looking around.
What should she wear?

The very short sentences, the poetic feel, the unexpected questions, all call for the staging to go beyond mere illustration. Another excerpt, at the end of the film, when the protagonist is searching the waters for his wife who has been shipwrecked, reads like this:

Trying to locate Indre.
Slowly tilting up and down
For some time.
But no results.
No signs.
But now:
In the far distance: a body?
Floating on top of the water.
Gradually coming nearer and nearer
Towards camera.
And now! Indeed!
Indre!
Seemingly unconscious.
She floats along
Wrapped in the bulrushes.
A pathetic figure
Racked by the waves.
Fog.
Lights.
Boats.
Yells across the water.

What is radical about Mayer's approach is that he somehow found a form that reads like poetry while simultaneously suggesting specific actions. In his hands, the screenplay truly became a magnificent instrument.

Other formats have dominated international film practice. In one, the page is divided vertically into two columns. On the left side, one finds the separation into shots, the description of actions and anything else that can be seen on the screen. To the right, there is the audio: not only the dialogue but also specific sound effects required by the scene, maybe even the name of a piece of music. Peter Greenaway goes even further: "my scripts," he told an interviewer, "are very full, often containing information that might seem unusable, such as the smell of the air or a person."[27] At first sight, the two columns may appear to be just another way of arranging the same information. In practice though, the side by side arrangement helps the writer think of the project differently, away from the absolute dominance of plot and dialogue. Put in simple terms, the juxtaposition of the two tracks offers a choice: is the information going to be delivered through this mode or that one? Tonino Guerra, who wrote for Fellini and Antonioni, describes his own creative process in the following manner: "At first, the scene is totally made up of dialogues. . . . Then, little by little, words are dropped in favor of gestures and movements by the characters. That is to say: the story becomes what can be seen visually. At the end of the work, even the best lines are being dropped, those that initially I felt so strongly about."[28] Another way of expressing what Guerra is telling us is to see the creative process as a movement from the right to the left side of the page. This progressive condensation of the writing in favor of gestures or body language can be observed in the last scene of *Bicycle Thief* (Vittorio de Sica, 1949), when the boy witnesses his father's desperate attempt to steal a bike so as to get back the job he lost when someone else stole his own bike. As the father is handed by the crowd to a policeman, the boy places his hand in his father's. The man's humiliation and the boy's pain eventually soften the mob and they are let go. The crowd disperses and father and son, holding hands, disappear within the multitude. During this most dramatic scene, the two do not exchange a word. The emotion of the scene originates exclusively from the action and what we imagine is going on inside each character. This is the kind of moment that can be imagined when a director and writer join forces to come up with what is best for the film. Even Torok, a screenwriter who passionately defends his craft against the abuses of pretentious but inept directors, agrees that "to collaborate with a [good] director is enriching because it fuses on a daily basis the written text and its representation in images. There is a reciprocal fertilization between the literary imagination of one partner and the formal concerns of the other."[29] To conceive the film from the beginning along both the visual and audio tracks must become once again the goal of the film's creators if cinema is to find anew its way out of plot and dialogue-driven material.

A third method involves Alexandre Astruc's concept of the *caméra stylo*. In his seminal essay written some forty years ago, the French writer/director opened up his discussion with an observation that is still pertinent today. "Our sensibilities," he wrote, "are in danger of getting blunted by those everyday films which, year in year out, show their tired and conventional faces to the world."[30] Yet film language had shown itself capable of overrunning the prosaic system through which most movies were still being conceived. Rather than originate images from words, it was now possible to *initiate* thoughts using the film itself. And Astruc went on:

> We have come to realize that the symbolic associations which the silent cinema tried to give birth to exist in fact within the image itself, in the development of the narrative, in every gesture of the characters, in every line of dialogue, in those camera movements which relate objects to objects and characters to objects. All thought, like all feeling, is a relationship between one human being and another human being or certain objects which are part of his universe. By clarifying these relationships, by making constant references to them, the cinema can really make itself the vehicle of thought.[31]

What Astruc has told us here—a message learned then, but long forgotten—is that cinema speaks on its own terms (through rhythm, camera angles, light, the grain of the film, etc.), that to continue to see it only as a mere illustration of prefigured elements is not to take full advantage of its power. For him, it became essential "that the scriptwriter directs his own scripts; or rather, that the scriptwriter ceases to exist, for in this kind of film-making the distinction between writer and director loses all meaning. Direction is no longer a means of illustrating or presenting a scene, but a true act of writing."[32]

To understand the extent of Astruc's proposal, it may be useful to relate Freeburg's subdivision of the film process (the selection of the materials, their arrangement in some order, and their performance during the shooting) to what the Russian Formalists called *fabula*, *syuzhet*, and style.[33] The *fabula* consists of the linear, chronological story, reconstructed after the fact and involving everything that happens to the characters from the first event in the tale to the very last. The *syuzhet* on the other hand is the actual unrolling of the film, the chosen order of the scenes, possibly also their manipulation through point of view techniques. Think, for instance, of the first moments of *Citizen Kane* (Orson Welles, 1941): they show us Kane's death rather than the snowball scene from his childhood. Clearly the decision to use a complex flashback structure to recount Kane's life is momentous for the film's potency. As for perspectival views, they too can radically alter our grasp of the story, vide *Rashomon* (Akira Kurosawa, 1950). Finally, style can be construed as that which "actualizes" the *syuzhet,* its transformation into a film, e.g., high angles, long shots, low key lighting, the number of cuts, etc.[34]

Many commentators have focused on the *syuzhet* as the most important of the three phases because, through it, countless formless events are shaped into a story that makes sense and speaks to the viewers. The role of the *fabula* thus comes to an end as soon as the *syuzhet* has made the most of what was available in the material. The same people also generally consider style to be no more than "the film's systematic use of cinematic devices."[35] In this case, once again, the director's job is construed as applying mere visual technique to a text already complete in itself. My contention, however, is that one should never refrain from engaging any of the three constructs at any time during the film's creation, from its conception to its finalization during post-production. Far from imagining the *fabula* as forbidden territory once the script is finished, one could think of it instead as a *terrain vague,* some abandoned field in which unexpected people may suddenly show up. In *Shoot the Piano Player* (1960), for example, Truffaut's camera accompanies the main protagonist as he goes to see his agent. As he approaches the office, we hear a violin performing solo. Just a moment later, a young woman comes out of the office carrying a violin. Then, instead of staying with the protagonist as he enters the room, the camera dollies back with the woman and even follows her outside while we hear the protagonist playing the piano. In this little interlude, Truffaut follows Balzac's counsel not to shy away from describing in full even secondary characters. What is important here is that the accompanying camera movements transformed an extra into a full human being with a potential history of her own. Also, this addition to the *fabula* probably originated at the time of the shoot. Similarly, using the beginning of *Once Upon a Time in the West* (Sergio Leone, 1967) as an example, would we be taken seriously if we were to argue that it is the *syuzhet* alone that keeps us riveted to our seats, that we really want to know who the men are, what they want, etc.? Isn't it obvious to everyone that it is Leone's restrained pace, his breathtaking wide screen compositions, and his provocative use of sound that do the job instead? What Astruc makes clear, in other words, is that film creativity cannot be parceled out into neat little boxes, jobs, or moments, but that a film's entire resources must be available at all times to its creators. Understood this way, *fabula*, *syuzhet*, and style are components of a single creative potential, they are elements capable of cross-pollinating each other at any time.

Certainly, there were many excesses during the New Wave (the school of filmmaking most in tune with Astruc's thinking). Astruc had opened the door for a new kind of movie, one based on images in preference to words. Ten years of film practice demonstrated, however, that one could not bypass words entirely. The hubris of some directors eventually put an end to a very exciting movement in film history. Hierarchies and egos therefore should not come into play if one is to avoid such mistakes in the future. That films would benefit from directors working with writers is clear. For directors, the encounter would be an eye-opener into *all* the possibilities of a story. For writers, they should be thrilled to be able to present their material differently. Carrière for instance has suggested that "by necessity if not because of personal taste, the screenwriter is much more a filmmaker than a writer."[36] The key point here is that writers would once again have to care for the finished film instead of their limited assignment. Such a rethinking I believe is necessary if cinema is to move beyond the current system of screenwriting which keeps harking back to film as a mere illustration of a preexisting story, and if the creative process is to be realigned away from the arbitrary as well as nefarious division of labor between writers and directors.

## VIII

Long before there were film schools, screenwriting was taught in all sorts of venues so as to feed an industry already desperate for new products. Sixty-one courses in film writing were offered as early as 1915, including one at Columbia University, and by 1920 no less than ninety books on the subject had been written.[37] There were the Home Correspondence School, the Photoplay Clearing House, the Fox Photoplay Institute, the Palmer Institute of Authorship, the Irving System, the Eleanor Glyn System of Writing, etc. What was actually taught in these courses is far from clear and what influence they may have had on actual screenwriting is difficult to evaluate. At one time, however, in the early twenties, the studios were receiving between two hundred and four hundred unsolicited scripts a day.[38] Some of them were bought by the studios for their story potential. A more seasoned screenwriter would then take over, shaping the script up Ince-style into material suitable for filming. This was necessary because, as someone familiar with the system wrote in 1922, "continuity [should be] written only by those on the inside, who were trained to write it—and the outsider can't do it. It is virtually impossible for the plot builder unacquainted with the inner rules and regulations of a motion picture studio to prepare a motion picture in continuity."[39]

Other, important books, were published later, for instance John Howard Lawson's *Theory and Technique of Playwriting and Screenwriting*, but it is with Syd Field that screenwriting took a definite turn for the worse.[40] Timing was critical: *Screenplay: The Foundations of Screenwriting* was published in 1979. By 1977, the global success of *Star Wars* (George Lucas) had reestablished the dominance of the American cinema on international screens after quite a long draught. More importantly maybe, the fact that *Star Wars* had been directed by a former film student boosted the enrollment in colleges and universities offering training in motion pictures. The new recruits, however, saw things very differently from their predecessors, the sixties generation. Far from rebelling against the system, they were glad to embrace it. Field simply happened to be preaching the right message at the right time. His method told Hollywood hopefuls that commercial success could be duplicated, that writing for film could be simplified to one easy-to-use formula with trite characters and a prototypical dramatic structure. Many imitators have since followed in his footsteps: Linda Seger, Richard Walter, Robert McKee, Dwight V. Swain, John Truby, and others. Est-style weekend seminars became the favorite arena to disseminate the goods. These weekends proved to have enormous appeal and, of course, for the performers, the medium was not without advantages. As hundreds of people could be jammed in a large auditorium at one time, the writing gurus could easily gross a million dollars a year while working only so many weekends. Field, McKee, Walter, and others have since branched out beyond the United States. As the Green Berets of American cultural imperialism, the dedicated missionaries of Hollywood culture, they now preach the good word everywhere, even at the very core of the enemy's territory: the Sorbonne in Paris.

More recently still, a different kind of tutoring has been made possible through computer software. *Blockbuster* promises to deliver "the secret weapon of successful Hollywood writers." Even if you lose your way, "Truby's Story Coach is only a click away . . . for tips and tools that radically improve the commercial potential of your script."[41] And programs like *Dramatica* profess to guide the novice writer through all the necessary steps leading to a great screenplay. The software, so the ad goes, "focuses a writer on the underlying dramatics of their [sic] story, or 'deep structure.' By helping writers clarify their intent and underlying argument, *Dramatica* can help fix story problems and strengthen character and theme."[42] Carrière has bitterly, but correctly in my view, summarized this mechanistic approach: "It expresses the American desire to codify everything, not only the screenplay, but cinema as a whole: to take its measure by reducing it to a number of little drawers, with a label on each classifying the contents. . . ."[43] Had writing gurus and *Dramatica* been around when Ince was alive, he not only would have embraced them but also would have made them standard fixtures on his lot.

## IX

What is this classical model incessantly preached about by Field and company? Someone wants something. Obstacles (people, situations, whatever) stand in the way of the objective. Struggles ensue. Most often, the protagonist triumphs in the end, possibly learning something about him/herself in the process. There are three acts to the journey: the set-up, the confrontation, and the conclusion. And plot points (at least in Field's version) pepper specific pages of the screenplay. This paradigm, to use the fashionable jargon, is now so wellknown that even someone like Arnold Schwarzenegger has no problem explaining its fine points to the viewers of *Entertainment Tonight*.

The central ingredient taken for granted by the formula is that characters are men and women who know themselves fully and transparently. Let us talk about this. Are protagonists in films truly lifelike? Are they human beings who have matured under the twin influence of genes and the environment? Movie characters show few signs of this dual heritage. Once upon a time, Emile Zola wrote no less than twenty volumes tracing the negative impact of a sexual union on the following generations. The interest in Francis Galton's eugenics, however, faded quickly as other writers felt it was too reductionist in nature and too restrictive for good literature. Today, even though most scientists agree that genes do play a part in the formation of our character, such influence is almost never activated in moviewriting, probably because it is wholly foreign to the notion of autonomous individuals. As for the influence of place or *milieu*, we can do no better than turn to Honoré de Balzac, who was known to open a novel with thorough descriptions of a neighborhood, a local street, and a particular house, before moving inside, outlining every detail in a room, homing in at last on the apparel and the countenance of one character, then another, and another. For the French writer indeed, in Henry James's words, "the place in which an event occurred was . . . of equal moment with the event itself."[44] For Balzac then, a human being is defined by the totality of one's environment, the narrowness of the street, the wallpaper in the room, the view from the window, the style and age of the furniture, the material and the color of one's clothing, etc. This emphasis too has been de-emphasized in movies, maybe in response to the globalization of films, fashion, and products. Rather than contributing to the characters' formation, film *milieux* tend to provide eye-catching scenery (the Italian-American neighborhood in *The Godfather* [Francis Ford Coppola, 1972]).

With ancestral heritage and social order out of the way, we are left with individual psychology. Film writers today favor the accidental in one's growing up, or circumstances that shaped this individual alone. Caleb resents his father's preference for his brother in *East of Eden* [Elia Kazan, 1955]). John is bitter because he sacrificed his boxing career for the sake of his brother's racketeering scheme in *On the Waterfront* (Elia Kazan, 1954). More often than not, a character's salient traits can be brought out in a few images without explanation of any kind. *Cool Hand Luke* (Stuart Rosenberg, 1967) is typical in this regard. The film opens with the drunk protagonist methodically taking apart one parking meter after the other. This brief sequence summarizes Luke as the sixties anti-hero, the young man who rebels against the establishment. From this point on, nothing is added. We never really find out why Luke is this way. To be a maverick is deemed enough to understand the man and motivate all his actions.

Whatever we discover about the characters should arise from the action itself. Richard Walter, for example, insists it is not important to signal any character trait or problem in a screenplay apart from sex and gender.[45] Put another way, this means that, in the great literary debate between showing and telling, the movies have followed the lead of the theater. There, as Percy Lubbock puts it, "a character must bear his part unaided; if he is required to be a desperate man, harboring thoughts of crime, he cannot look to the author to appear at the side of the stage and inform the audience of the fact; he must express it for himself through his words and deeds, his looks and tones."[46] Simplified for the movies, the idea is expressed as follows by Walter: the "characters' physical and emotional traits ought to grow from what they say and do. Their actions and dialogue define them. What they do and say *is* their character."[47] This type of presentation, however, insinuates a rational link between self-made men and women and the actions they generate, a connection that becomes meaningful as well as explicit for the viewers. Nothing new here? After all, didn't Aristotle already associate tragedy with "men in action"? Didn't he also say that an "action is brought about by agents who necessarily display certain distinctive qualities both of character and of thought"?[48] The *Poetics* have been marshaled many times to grant validity to today's strong movie characters, people who make things happen. As a result, we have learned to interpret in the movies "someone's actions by reference to his intentions, beliefs, desires, etc."[49] In my view, these forceful, self-determined, yet knowable characters sound more like *Übermenschen* than regular human beings. As for the direct line that connects a person's will and an outcome of some kind, it too deserves more querying.

X

Working from different premises, a number of contemporary theorists have suggested that, far from originating from a stable, secure point of origin, personal identity is inevitably marred by loss, fragmentation, and the influence of culture. Certainly, one is aware of occupying the same body day after day and it is easy as a result to posit a distinct, autonomous, and constant self. Self-consciousness, however, should not automatically imply a rational, coherent, or permanent identity. Instead, the self may be marked by what exceeds it: the unknown in one's very core (the unconscious), the assumption of symbolic identity through the learning of language, and the endless influence of ideology insofar as it socially produces us through the regimes of gender, race, class, etc.[50]

To start with, that which escapes us, the unconscious, is often represented, in popular culture in general and Hollywood movies in particular, as some kind of missing package that somehow failed to be delivered at the proper moment. Because of the lack of information contained in the brief, the character is in flux. With the help of the proper authorities however, an effort can be made to retrieve the missing information and complete the subject, thus letting him or her be just like anyone else. *Ordinary People* (Robert Redford, 1980) perfectly illustrates this almost magical transformation of an individual. For the American psychoanalytical establishment then, "no true mystery, no essential unknown transcending the ego's capacity for comprehension exists."[51]

Through the years, this simplistic version of the unconscious has been revised or supplemented in various ways. Georges Bataille, for one, does not believe that the unconscious is in fact accessible through therapy. "There remains within us," he writes, "a part that is dumb, withheld, impenetrable."[52] Like the foundations of a building, they remain underground, out of view, inaccessible for perusal when visiting or standing in an edifice. As for Jacques Lacan, he too questions the very idea of a Graal, of a single object or component available in one specific place. He sees the unconscious more like a mirage, appearing somewhere then vanishing from view, only to reappear moments later somewhere else. As explicated by Terry Eagleton,

> the unconscious is, so to speak, "outside" rather than "within" us— or rather exists "between" us, as our relationships do. It is elusive not so much because it is buried deep within our minds, but because it is a vast, tangled network which surrounds us and weaves itself through us, and which can therefore never be pinned down.[53]

Here the unconscious is theorized as impersonal or transpersonal, which makes it impossible to grab through individual therapy. In still another view of things, Heideggerian this time, one could argue that our unconscious resides not in our humanity but our beingness, that is to say, the more fundamental, ontological background that surrounds all existence.

Beyond these views, the query has also shifted to the compartmentalization of the mind and the working organization of its parts. Are some sections dead to the world? Have all components equal access to the balcony of consciousness? For Donald Davidson, for instance, the Freudian legacy implies that the rational mind does not own the entire territory, that there remain wild areas beyond its sovereignty. Beyond the "personal [Freudian] unconscious" that is possibly redeemable through therapy, he writes, we find "quasi-independent structures that intersect in ways the [rational mind] cannot accept or explain."[54] If I interpret him correctly, this means that some dormant structures nevertheless remain alive and capable of impacting the subject from time to time. For instance, some formations may have developed without entirely erasing the earlier models. Is there really no trace of the child's mind inside ourselves? Isn't it capable of reappearing in special circumstances? And, beyond normal subject growth, should not one also consider Henri Laborit's argument, at the beginning of Alain Resnais' *My Uncle from America* (1980), that the evolving brains of our ancestors did not simply replace one another along the evolutionary cycle but simply added themselves on top of one another, thus leaving open the possibility for the less "human" forces—say, the reptilian brain inside of us—to snap back in time of crises. For Davidson, all of this changes the way we should look at ourselves and others. "What was once a single mind is turned into a battlefield where opposed forces contend, deceive one another, conceal information, devise strategies."[55] Far from an *Übermensch,* the human being is now redefined as fundamentally fragmented with the rational element not always fully in charge. Thus to project characters as wonderfully well behaved, may not just miss the mark but also contribute to perpetuating humanistic illusions about ourselves. Puerile reactions or bizarre behavior may thus be very much a part of someone's "normal" train of thoughts and everyday actions.

Second, taking his cues from Ferdinand de Saussure's work in linguistics, Jacques Lacan brilliantly reconfigured the entrance of the subject into language. Some time after birth, following a moment of bliss during which one is incapable of distinguishing the self from one's immediate environment, each human being is necessarily introduced into what Lacan calls the "symbolic." In his configuration, what I truly experience and wish to translate to others must necessarily go through the sieve of words. And words are far from stable. It always comes down to a choice between this word or that one, a preference for one nuance at the expense of another, more attention to the sentence's flow than to its grammatical clarity, etc. Words may also carry secondary or latent meanings that imperil what in truth we wish to say. Repressed personal links may sneak in at any time. Because our speech is fundamentally slippery and ambiguous . . . we can never mean precisely what we say and never say precisely what we mean."[56] Far from being a neutral tool allowing "me" to communicate transparently with others, language becomes a preexisting grid which conditions what it is I am saying.

It is also through this symbolic field that we learn to develop our sense of self. And here too we learn to distinguish ourselves from others through prearranged mental categories. Who "I" really am as a result cannot ever be securely recognized. What matters instead is how "I" fit within a set of preexisting cultural possibilities: for instance, that I am male, the third boy of a middle-class family, that I come from a small town in Nebraska, that my father is white and my mother American Indian, that I am a Baptist, that a sport's scholarship landed me in Stanford, that I am studying to become a doctor, that I am gay but discreetly so, etc. Seen in this light, the individual, far from being the expression of a unique distinguishable self, is recast along preexisting categories or types.

Philip Rosen was able to rehearse the consequences of all of this in two nice pithy sentences: "It is not the subject who uses the signifying system [language], but the signifying system which defines the subject. It is not the subject who 'speaks' the signified, but the signifier which 'speaks' the subject." Human beings are thus produced by language every step of the way. And language is not so much something we use to express ourselves, but the blueprinted path our subconscious intentions take in order to surface in our consciousness. We access the world through the conditioning of language. Even our identity is but a series of options that are available to us at the time rather than a pinpointing of something deeply personal or unique. Anything we say, who we are, cannot be unfastened from the system that permeates and organizes speech. All in all, society stands behind us and everyone of our words.

Third, Louis Althusser spelled out for us the means taken by society to reproduce itself. First, through schools, families, unions, television, and the rest of the mass media, we are given a systematic template of the world. Later on, each time we see things happening the way they were presented to us early on, we recognize the fact, exclaiming: "Yes! That's how it is, that's really true!"[58] Once the basic model is ingrained inside of us, it becomes extremely difficult even to imagine the possibility of alternative viewpoints. At the same time, these venues also teach us the basic "know-how" necessary for economic survival: solid work, self-discipline, obedience, and respect for others and their property. Reaching adulthood (assuming no misstep of the system) means having taken in and ingested a level of programming so systematic that it is entirely invisible to the subjects themselves.[59] "It is indeed a peculiarity of ideology," Althusser writes, "that it imposes (without appearing to do so, since these are 'obviousnesses') obviousnesses as obviousnesses, which we cannot *fail to recognize*. . . ."[60] Hence we are far from capable of addressing our real conditions of existence so caught up are we in imaginary representations. Again and again one is "interpellated" as a citizen who votes, drives, consumes, pays taxes, gets married, watches television, etc. It is these incessant reminders that confirm "our" understanding of where we stand in society. "Identity," Samuel Weber sums up, "depends upon repetition, which, however, in turn presupposes something like [a social] identity."[61] And through it all, we pay little or no attention to the way the "political unconscious" determines many aspects of our life, for instance, family law, property arrangements, etc.[62]

Finally, there is a difference between what someone wishes to accomplish and what effectively comes out of that action. Henri Bergson, who investigated this topic with much care, distinguished different kinds of cause and effect situations: a billiard cue striking a ball, a sparkle exploding gun powder, the spring of an old gramophone that lets us listen to a melody. In the first example, the path and the impact of the ball are determined by the special handling of the player. In the second, the explosion always takes place, but what exactly will be destroyed cannot be determined in advance with total accuracy. In the third, how long we hear the voice will depend on the winding, yet the quality of the melody remains independent of it. Inconsistencies and variability may also at any time alter the expected output. In summing up, the French philosopher asks us to think about what happens when an arm enters a box full of tiny steel balls. As the arm forces its way through the mass, the displacement of each ball of steel alters the position of all those surrounding it. Although the overall outcome might somehow be predicted, there is no way anyone could accurately imagine every single reaction that takes place as a result of the original action. What all of this means is that "while succeeding in carrying a person's intention, the action itself, new and in the present time, differs from the intention which aimed at renewing or rearranging something already past."[63] So, although we may focus our attention on the *expected* consequences of what we just did, taking note of the success or failure of the operation, our action "has all kinds of outcomes that could not be predicted," effects that will remain largely unnoticed at the time.[64] What a character does therefore and what happens as a result of his/her action cannot be represented as a regulated, perfectly controlled situation. Unpredictable outcomes are likely to arise, consequences capable of affecting not only the character but those around him or her, possibly even the rest of the world in all sorts of ways. Whereas movie stories generally focus on what is foreseeable in an action, history (a more interesting and possibly more valid portrayal of human attempts to carry out their objectives) often evidences what happens when "things go wrong."

To keep manufacturing characters untouched by internal malfunctions, unmarked by cultural codification, free of ideological inference, independent of all legal, social, and economic structures, and to make them the originators of likely outcomes, is just a little too expedient. On the contrary, characters do not have to be of one mold. Some aspects of one's personality may contradict others. Multiple internal voices may be present, not all of them contemporary or agreeable. Characters can be undermined by the heterogeneity of language, the identity of others revealed as socially constructed. Finally all kinds of unplanned consequences may ripple out of anyone's actions, effects that may ricochet or hit back like a boomerang while one's back is turned. A human being can thus be conceived, and a character represented, in Bergson's elegant metaphor, as "the thread that holds the pearls together."[65] Or, to use Feyerabend's language, it should be possible to see characters as "loosely connected parts . . . [functioning] as transit stations for equally loosely connected events, such as dreams, thoughts, emotions, [even] divine interventions."[66] In other words, more effort than before must be directed toward ascertaining the real conditions of existence which modulate how we in fact live. And we need to make clear the gaps, the deficiencies, and the profound contradictions in the personalities of the men and women who populate our films. In the end, this would provides us with richer characters and a larger, more complex canvas.

## XI

Character is behavior, we are told, and "behavior is action."[67] Although all kinds of actions are theoretically possible, the screenplay model focuses on conflict. "The action story," we are told, "is about engaging in combat."[68] Protagonists in other words battle it out with opponents. We are so used to this presentation of events by now that it takes an outsider like Raoul Ruiz to point out that the paradigm posits a state of "constant hostility" between people and that "the criteria according to which most of the characters behave in today's movies are drawn from one particular culture (that of the USA)."[69] Ruiz reminds us therefore that there are cultural presumptions at work underneath the claimed universality of the model. Aggressivity, competition, and pushing aside those who stand in your way may be taken for granted as the usual way of doing business in this country, but it is not necessarily how one acts in Sweden, Singapore, or Mali. Certainly, there is something inherently visual, dramatic, and ultimately liberating in identifying with someone who gets things done like Schwarzenegger in *Terminator 2: Judgment Day* (James Cameron, 1991), but one easily forgets that, in reality, one is much more likely to be the victim of such a rampage than its author. Furthermore, for other cultures, the wild individualism portrayed in American films is totally at odds with the way these societies handle conflict. Not only does it go against local customs and mores, it is potentially damaging to them insofar as it provides a thrill that may be difficult to contain after the show is over. For Ruiz then, the American screenplay paradigm is a dangerous, even a "predatory theory," for it makes manifest "a system of ideas which devours and enslaves any other ideas that might restrain its activity."[70] In other words, left behind are different kinds of characters, concerns, behaviors, and goals, an entire world we could discover again.

## XII

Finally the model also tells us that a narrative has a beginning, a middle, and an end. And that the story, as already quoted from Sargent, "seems to tell itself, rather than to be told, [that it should be] more like a happening than a narrative of past events."[71] This basic narrative choice thus aligns classical screenwriting alongside what Plato and Aristotle called mimesis (when the poet speaks through the characters) in opposition to diegesis (when the poet speaks in his or her name). It also forms the distinction between story and discourse. In the former, the French linguist Emile Benveniste tells us: "Truly, there is no longer a 'narrator.' The events are chronologically recorded as they appear on the horizon of the story. No one speaks. The events seem to tell themselves."[72] The words used by Benveniste, one cannot fail to notice, are almost an exact match for Sargent's. In this mode of writing, the plot also often overdetermines the freedom of the characters and the latitude of their actions. In discourse, on the contrary, a real or implied narrator is present, someone whose mediation cannot be ignored. In contrast to the standard model, such an approach can produce alternative narratives which, paradoxically, release the autonomy of the characters and the scope of their actions.

Let us listen, for instance, to Hayden White who has called our attention to different modes of narration in the writing of history. First, he questioned the very assumptions of the standard historical narrative, doubting that "the world really present(s) itself to perception in the form of well-made stories, with central subjects, proper beginnings, middles, and ends, and a coherence that permits us to see 'the end' in every beginning."[73] In opposition to such transparent writing, he offers two alternatives, annals and chronicles. The former is characterized by mere lists of events, ordered chronologically, but containing "no central subject, no well-marked beginning, middle, and end, no peripeteia, and no identifiable narrative voice."[74] In one of White's examples, the year 732 is characterized by the following sentence: "Charles fought against the Saracens at Poitiers on Saturday."[75] An event important enough to write down took place, but the historian does not let us know how the battle fits in the grander scheme of things: what led to the invasion, what was at stake, who was Charles's opponent, etc. And, more curiously still, the bit of news that the battle took place on a Saturday was somehow more important for the writer than mentioning who won the contest. In a chronicle, on the other hand, the material is more coherently organized around a "central subject," and may include "some great undertaking," thus acknowledging a consistent purpose in historical events. A chronicle has a clear beginning and "the work appears to be unfolding a plot but then belies its own appearance by merely stopping *in medias res.* . . ."[76] In other words, the narrative functions more like a regular story but stops in the middle of the action, without offering a permanent or, at least, a satisfactory ending to the story.

I spent some time describing White's argument because I believe that the concept of annals and chronicles can help us undermine the formulaic presentation of action by Field and company. "What's the best way to open your screenplay?" Field asks, "Know your ending!"[77] In other words, the plot tells you your characters' moves. In opposition to this, let us take a look at *Paisà's* fourth segment (Roberto Rossellini, 1946). In that piece, the Germans and their Fascist allies are fighting a rear guard action against the Allied forces in the streets of Florence. A nurse working for the Americans goes looking for her boyfriend—a partisan leader who may have been wounded during the battle. She teams up with an acquaintance who wants to rejoin his own family. They go through the city, meeting different people on the way. As they get close to their destination, her companion's sudden rush across a street causes a partisan to be shot. She helps the wounded man while those responsible, three Fascists, are summarily executed. As this is going on, she learns from the wounded partisan that the man she is looking for died some time ago.

As a matter of fact, my summary of this sequence encapsulates more narrative continuity than is present in the text. We know literally nothing about the two main characters except that they think it important to risk their lives to get where they want to go. Other characters appear and disappear, never to be heard of again. A British officer, for instance, shows up for a brief moment. Quirkily, he uses his binoculars to survey the highlights of Florentine architecture rather than pinning down the German positions. Even what happens to the principals is eventually left unsaid. For example, her companion is not seen again after crossing the street. It is not known whether he was able to reach his family after all, whether they were unharmed or not, nor whether he felt any guilt for having caused the partisan's death. As for the "heroine," the film stops, *in medias res*, when she finds out about her friend's death (the whole effort therefore was for naught). Nor is there a clear resolution to the battle for Florence. Although events (historical as well as fictional) do take place, they are recounted in a manner reminiscent of annals and chronicles. Armies are on the march but on the field of battle the characters' experiences have nothing to do with the liberation of Italy. Their goals are very limited and the extreme volatility of the situation makes it clear that, at any street corner, anything can happen. The allied strategy for the liberation of Italy disappears behind incidental but personally important encounters (the "Saturday" of the annals). Death happens without rhyme or reason: people die because they are hit by gun fire not because it is mandated by the plot. In other words, the camera is far from omniscient. It is as if the writer/director too were discovering the events as they unfolded, in complete ignorance of a final, satisfactory resolution. This segment of *Paisa* thus demonstrates another kind of film writing, a narrative where "the events truly tell themselves" at the very moment they are happening, without anyone capable of reframing what is going on within a larger context. At the same time though, the dislocations are also experienced as style, the mark of an exceptional narrator.

## XIII

In view of all of this, I would like to suggest that the Hollywood paradigm functions in fact as a super genre. It is a genre insofar as anyone easily recognizes any material organized under its regime. The key point here, according to Derrida, is that "as soon as genre announces itself, one must respect a norm, one must not cross a line of demarcation, one must not risk impurity, anomaly or monstrosity."[78] And today, indeed, a norm, admitting few exceptions or variations, marks off the boundaries of American screenwriting. For writers laboring within the system, to be read at all, to have a chance at being produced, there is no alternative, you must write as you are told, the format must be respected, the formula applied. For producers and studio executives, the norm allows them to measure the worth of a screenplay against a false standard of quality. "That's the evil part," Jim Wedaa complains, it makes these people "think they know what they're doing when they actually don't."[79] They end up discussing the work of writers and making suggestions because they believe they know what writing is all about.

The paradigm is also a super genre because it supersedes all previous genres. It does not matter at all whether the film is a Western, a thriller, a love story, or a science-fiction epic, the scripts essentially conform to the invisible lay out. As all the films end up following the same model, the concoction makes for very dull cinema. For example, as noted by Godard, in these films everything always arrives right on schedule whereas, in his own films, he found it interesting to arrive a bit early or late."[80] And with one master narrative being produced time and time again, the audience can only look to special effects to help differentiate one product from another. "To copy something is just plain dull," Godard goes on, "thus to fight the abysmal monotony of the project, one veils it under millions of dollars of mere gloss."[81]

The super genre dominates all other ingredients. As a result, characters cannot escape the clothes they are forced to wear. They sound alike because they are cut from the same mold (compare this with what characters say in the early films of John Cassavetes). And the plot rather than the participants dictates what the characters actually do. In this kind of narrative, the story—what happens to the protagonists—does not evolve from within, from the encounter of the characters with each other, from the way they engage one another. Their meetings instead are predetermined by the overriding structure of the script. In this model of screenwriting, Olivier Assayas suggests, the plot is so overpowering that "it leaves no room for anything else."[82] Far from an exciting dialogic, polyphonic, Galilean exchange between different individuals, the show forces the characters to go again and again on the same journey, to relive well-worn actions, to utter the same lines, etc.[83] What is missing in all of this? In *Technique of the Photoplay*, published in the early teens, Epes Winthrop Sargent relates an anecdote that remains significant for today's cinema: "Perhaps you have attended some dramatic performance where the theater cat has strolled upon the stage. Perhaps the big scene of the play has been hurt if not ruined. The moment is tense and dramatic, but the cat is a novel surprise and for the moment stronger than the acting of the star."[84] Sargent is right: the cat is a success because it does not know its place. Failing to recognize the conventions of the play, the cat simply goes about its business. And the spectators love the fact that, with incredible ease, the cat breaks their suspension of disbelief. Sargent's solution is radical: to save the show, "the cat has no place in the scene."[85] It is my view that the cat must be let out of the bag, in screenplays as well as in films, so as to breathe fresh life into a dying art form.

# CHAPTER FIVE

## *Staging*

### I

To shoot a film is not easy. Even a dedicated professional like Ingmar Bergman can experience the vicious aspect of the process. "For me," he writes, "shooting a film represents days of inhumanly restless work, stiffness of the joints, eyes full of dust, the odors of makeup, sweat and lamps, an indefinite series of tensions and relaxations, an uninterrupted battle between volition and duty, between visions and reality, conscience and laziness."[1] Day after day, a director must move the film along. Actors need cajoling. Crew members need to be instructed so as to produce the desired effect. Thousands of details, some very important, some mere routine, have to be addressed. Decisions must be taken quickly and, inevitably, there are times when the wrong choices are made, when one decides to compromise rather than fight for something, when the body and the mind are simply too exhausted to see clearly and one falls back on automatic for a while. In these conditions, any success at all is taken as a great achievement, a personal triumph one need not be modest about. In any event—victory or defeat—shooting is more than simply another moment in the construction of a film. It is its very life, its heartbeat, its sculpting. It is a performance that gives birth to an entirely new set of figures. Sergei Eisenstein expressed this very well when he suggested that the screenwriter and the director should not duplicate each other's work, that when "the scriptwriter puts: 'Deathly silence.' The director uses: still close-ups; the dark and silent pitching of the battleship's bows; the unfurling of the St. Andrew's ensign; perhaps a dolphin's leap; and the low flight of seagulls."[2] To stage a film therefore is to reimagine the screenplay, to make people and objects speak anew. It means to require this movement, this gesture, this color, this light, this shadow, this camera position, this perspective from the lens. It means proposing ideas and instructions that transform one's immediate surroundings. Beyond this, one must also remember that the director works with human beings, not signifiers. To stage a film goes beyond language, it is to act in the world, to find, transform, and animate people and things in a certain way. As Maurice Merleau-Ponty put it so well, in the world words are said "not by a mind to a mind, but by a being who has body and language to a being who has body and language, each drawing the other by invisible threads like those which hold the marionettes—making the other speak, think, and become what he is but never would have been by himself."[3] Hence, to direct a film is not just to act upon the world. It also means understanding and accepting that the world talks back, continuously addressing, changing the director through countless recoils. On the set then, the director is placed in a distinct environment whose thickness, materiality, and resistance simultaneously arise and provoke him or her. To direct is to inhale as well as to exhale. To direct is to be promiscuous with everything and everyone around. To shoot means to fornicate with the world in order to procreate.

## II

Enter a studio, strike a few lights, look around, listen. The place is magical. The cavernous size, the high ceilings, the catwalks, the unused equipment, all contribute to the impression. Think of *The Bad and the Beautiful* (Vincente Minnelli, 1953), *Sunset Boulevard* (Billy Wilder, 1950), or *Peeping Tom* (Michael Powell, 1959): these films were made in places like this. Alfred Hitchcock, Max Ophüls, and William Wyler worked here or could have. What you see and hear is what they responded to as well: the emptiness, the silence, the stillness that is the mark of sound stages the world over. Marcel Carné in France and Fritz Lang in Germany experienced them also. It is a place where you can let your imagination soar, your mind dream for a while. In the empty stage indeed, nothing stands in the way. It is but an empty container. You can fill it up with your own creation. Overnight, sets can be built to duplicate any location whatsoever and time itself is at your mercy: this morning, snow will fall in North Dakota, this afternoon, it will be a balmy 1930s California night. The studio contains all these images. Their echoes resonate in its hall. The studio then is like the inside of a large pyramid, a dark place out of time with its tomblike silence, where the dead are buried surrounded by the icons that made them famous. For the directors, actors, and technicians who once made the place so alive are still around. Their ghosts still haunt the place. In the old days, a light was even kept burning through the night in their honor. Listen! Pay attention! They are here! And it is here also that the living assemble once more to perform the rituals initiated by the pioneers. Like them we conjure up the spirits with the magic words: "Camera!" "Action!" "Cut!" Like them, we form a procession, walking grimly and silently alongside a dolly as if it were a hearse carrying a loved one. Like them, we solemnly go over and over the same action until finally "It's a take!," which means that something quite numinous has finally been captured on film.

As a tomb, a cenotaph, the studio is the great repository of our film culture. It is the formidable graveyard of all film practices. It is the place where the past dominates, where symbolic structures overwhelm the visiting filmmaker. In front of the dead, the tone is grave, heads are bowed, bodies stand still. We give respect. We censor ourselves. To shoot films then, *our* films, we must go elsewhere, find places where we can be free to move as we want, do what we like, create in an environment that does not conjure up the past. To make films today we must go on location.

### III

This is what Roberto Rossellini, Vittorio de Sica, Giuseppe de Santis did in Italy just after World War II. This is where François Truffaut, Jean-Luc Godard, and Agnès Varda chose to go to during the early days of the French New Wave. To be sure, historical circumstances forced them to go on location, but there are other reasons as well. In a studio, a set may look like the real thing but, quickly, the eye realizes the artificiality of it all. Alfred Hitchcock referred to this when he suggested that a set dresser needed to think more like a screenwriter. By this he meant that a set dresser should make a special effort to avoid generic furnishings, imagining instead how the actual human beings living in this room would furnish it, make it theirs. Unfortunately, he concluded, "he doesn't, and that's why you see so many films that have an artificial look."[4] One gets lazy in a studio too. Because the space is large, the rooms that are created there are generally much too big for those who are supposed to live in the environment. Look at the spacious living room in *How Green Was My Valley* (John Ford, 1941): it makes no sense for the poor miners nor does it fit the size of the real house we see from the outside. Finally, the light that falls from the catwalks prettifies everything and everyone. And the coifed and preened actors who show up in front of the camera resemble no one but other actors in other films. They never work at anything. They never eat either. They look great "waking up" in the morning. And their lines are so inane they often require background music to make us care. Yet, studios have no trouble attracting filmmakers by playing on their hubris, their desire for total control over their project. You are made to believe that, in a studio, the world has no limit, that technology can supply whatever it is that is needed. If you call for it, you will get it. The studio thus exemplifies what Martin Heidegger called *Bestand*, a standing reserve, a repository where "everything is ordered to stand by, to be immediately on hand," where objects, separated from the real environment that produced them, now "lose their distinguishing traits and become stock-in-trade against which orders can be placed."[5] What emerges, as a result, is a cinema of routine where professionals perform without passion or imagination. A cinema where nothing is real anymore.

For there lies the greatness of a location. Blaise Cendrars reflected on this when he compared a scene from a film actually shot on Mont Blanc to another in which the actors stood in front of a painted scenery of the mountain in a studio. For Cendrars, shooting on the real mountain brought in "emanations, luminous or otherwise, which have worked on the film and given it a soul."[6] Even when an audience cannot tell the difference, a location invades the substratum of the film by providing a living, concrete environment that cannot be ignored. Actors feel in their bones the coldness of the wind that sweeps down from the summit. And the crew must adjust for this as well. Even in mundane locations, the everyday world resists the creative endeavor of the filmmakers: the walls that simply cannot be torn down to make room for the camera, the sun that is being "lost" as it slowly makes its way to the other side of the building, and the sound of the traffic down below that keeps drowning out the voices of the actors. Ermanno Olmi explains what these circumstances mean to a director:

When you shoot in the studio, you've set the lighting in advance; the lights are the same from beginning to end. You can shoot the same shot a hundred times and it will be the same. The real tree, on the other hand, is in continual evolution, modifying itself inside the situation, so much so you become anxious lest you not be able to capture a particular moment when the light is changing. This too is beautiful, because between the first take and the fourth and the fifth there are variations—it is continually palpitating.[7]

For any location you have chosen is unique: the room is in a building in a certain part of town, it has a texture and a smell that come with the neighborhood. Certainly, it can be repainted or propped to fit the characters and the story, but its core element—its situation, its context—cannot be magically erased during the shoot. This is not to say that Hollywood does not try when it ventures into the great outdoors. What happens then is more like a conquering army on the march as Richard Rush wittily observed in *The Stunt Man* (1980). There are the trucks and the trailers, the huge equipment, the arc lights, the cranes, and the generators. The stars with their own quarters on wheels. The directors' chairs for the above-the-line talent. The costume department. The green people. The stunt personnel. The explosive specialists. The food services. More than using a location, Hollywood invades it for a day. It covers up what gives it its distinction, prettifying it, bringing it up to "its" own standard. And, of course, in the context of a studio picture, this must be done, for a location left to itself would give the lie to everything else in that kind of film: the story, the actors, the technique.

Henry Jaglom, on the other hand, has made the most out of real places, working sometimes even without a permit. If asked about one, he would send an assistant looking for a nonexistent piece of paper back in the motel. In the meantime he would get the shots he needed, then move quickly somewhere else—a practical approach so long as you work with a very small crew. Jaglom is also quite aware of the dissonances brought about by other components of professional filmmaking. Extras, for instance, belong in Hollywood. On location you cannot use them: "Extras act like extras, you know?" To use them would contaminate everyone else. Soon enough, "the actors start thinking that they're actors and they're not people any more. The cameraman thinks he's got time to light and suddenly you're making a 'movie.' . . ."[8] There is a domino effect in all of this: if you are not careful and let a single Hollywood component slip by you, the rest will resurface in no time at all. In his view then, to shoot on location involves a full package of techniques that includes abandoning the script once you are shooting, not allowing makeup for the actors, permitting very little artificial lighting, etc. Such filmmaking, needless to say, keeps you on your toes: you must adjust the screenplay to reflect the changes experienced by the actors/characters as they confront the resistance of the real world, and you must be able to move quickly. You shoot fast and you go. You are always on the move. Contrary to general belief, to shoot in a studio or on location is not a mere matter of choice. The decision can reflect one's philosophy. More than questions of convenience or budget, one shoots in the former to avoid contamination by the real world, in the latter when one embraces it.

## IV

Whether on a set or location, there are different ways of shooting a film. Each approach carries specific baggage—advantages and inconveniences—that one must be aware of. These methods, however, should not be viewed as exclusive of one another and it is perfectly all right to take a little of one and a little of another. The best approach is to stay flexible and do what works for you. Let us imagine a crowded auditorium. A man enters, looks around, locates a friend; he then goes and sits next to her. A conversation follows. To start with, the director has to decide on the kind of room and get the right people to fill it. Actors have been selected to play the parts and lighting is built up so as to duplicate the kind normally found in large meeting halls. In the coverage method, which we will look at first, a master is shot as well as a series of closer shots covering the key moments of the scene. This can be accomplished by simultaneous shooting by several cameras equipped with different lenses.[9] In this case, either the close-up cameras stay far back with longer lenses or they "are 'blinded' behind convenient pieces of scenery" placed somewhere in the shot.[10] Almost from the start, the limitations of this approach became clear to all. It was felt that the close-up lacked clarity, expressing nothing new, showing only what had already been observed in the master. In the words of a critic, "nothing is carried forward."[11] The scene was felt to stagnate dramatically.

The other coverage approach—asking the actors to keep repeating their performance to satisfy the multiple angles—was no panacea either and it too found early critics. Beyond being time-consuming and expensive, the clinching factor for William de Mille was that "the actors can repeat the physical actions but they cannot repeat the psychology of a former scene. Once the mood has gone by, once the emotion has been allowed to cool, the [truth of the scene] cannot be recaptured."[12] Whereas, in the theater, actors benefit from the entire buildup of the play to maintain themselves "in character" throughout an entire night, in film they are asked to produce repeatedly specific emotions without the help of a proper buildup. In such situation, actors need to be exceptionally responsible to turn out performances that are more than mechanical. With coverage then, the essence of a scene, like a Hegelian spirit, is expected to show up at different times and places, yet be ever the same, always identical to itself.

More assumptions about the nature of cinema are embodied in scene coverage. The most important one, I think, is that the action is conceived as preexisting its capture by the camera. Because a director using coverage acknowledges the prior reality of a continuous action, the latter becomes the dominant component of the shooting process. The only thing left for such a director is to provide the audience with good vantage points that make it easy to understand what is going on so. As a result, stylistic form is demoted to the status of a fancy wrapper without intrinsic value. Second, coverage also refers to a cluster of views: a master generally too loose to be used in its entirety and miscellaneous singles where segments of the whole are enlarged for the audience's information or pleasure. Nestor Almendros compared this habit of shooting every action from every angle to blanket bombardment where the hope is that at least some of the bombs will hit the target.[13] It follows that, despite the apparent weight given to the performance during the rehearsal, the exact meaning and importance of a scene, its buildup, its rhythm, its truth really, is postponed until the editing stage. Only then, depending upon the actual strength of each shot, will it be decided to construct this scene from these four angles. Third, coverage is also a way of protecting yourself in case something goes wrong with the acting dynamics, the continuity of a scene, or the safekeeping of the film itself as it travels in the camera and is manipulated in the lab. André Téchiné is quick to see the danger in this: "Once you start covering 'for safety,' you'll never stop."[14] Fourth, there will be a lot of pressure to shoot close-ups of actors' faces even though you know you will never use them or do a second take albeit the first one was perfectly good. Taking all of this into account, it becomes clear that coverage is a concern of management rather than a useful creative requirement. Although it is absurdly expensive to shoot the same material from different angles, it makes sense within an industrial mode of production that is skeptical of a more personal type of filmmaking. Coverage can thus be characterized as standard language, corporate patter, the only kind our culture industry feels comfortable with.

Absolutely essential to coverage are the ideas of continuity and objectivity. As already mentioned, the story we see on the screen has to be understood by the audience as happening independently of its recording. To do so, the shot-to-shot progression of the action must evolve without a false move. Not only should there be no gap between successive moments of an action, all the elements present in the scene must remain consistent throughout the multiple viewpoints. This includes sets, props, and costumes details, body positions, speed of gestures, etc. Matching cigarette lengths, for instance, used to be a full-time occupation for the people hired to watch such details. Taken to the extreme, continuity can become a nightmare on the set, ordering everyone's moves. This is how Dennis Hopper recounts that kind of situation:

> Let's say for example there's a script girl writing this down. I just take a drag off this cigarette and I'm talking to you. She just wrote down that I took a drag off this cigarette. That means when they come around and do my over-the-shoulder shot, uh-oh, I just put my hand over here, so not only am I going to have to watch my cigarette, I'm going to have to watch my hand too. Meanwhile, I'm talking to you and saying, "Do you know what the weather is like outside? It's snowing. The plane's not going to be able to come in. The deal's off. Now, you know what that means, doncha? Doncha?" and as I say that I'm pointing at you. The script girl just wrote down that I'm pointing.[15]

It is not difficult to imagine how all these details can end up asphyxiating the making of a film. Yet, in Hollywood moviemaking, the fear of discontinuity is taken very seriously indeed and the battle against it is fought relentlessly. A simple solution: if you shoot so you never duplicate an action on the screen, none of this is relevant.

Let us now move to the role of objectivity in Hollywood filmmaking. During the early days of the system, specific techniques were devised to help facilitate the audience's access to the show from the 180-degree line to eyeline matches. The camera work was rationalized so as to provide plain but efficient positions from which to observe what was happening. When the job is done well, the question of who is watching the scene is never raised. For there is a dangerous paradox at work in classical film language, one that could possibly unbalance the entire system. On the one hand, the photographic image is optically constructed to resemble human perception so that viewers feel at home watching it. On the other hand, it is imperative for the system that, in the spectators' mind, the same image should not actually imply the presence of anyone watching the scene. Hence the use of two techniques which have proved quite effective at keeping audiences from assigning the shots to another human being. First, again, by multiplying the viewpoints, coverage made it almost impossible to ascribe the fast-changing views to a single human consciousness. Second, if we follow an argument developed by Nietzsche, although every view is necessary perspectival in nature, the connection to an interpretative observer can be loosened or even severed in time. What is left then are sites offering common places, sights construed as common views.[16] In the same manner, in the cinema, by carefully stripping shots of all that could suggest a unique human perspective, the views they provided were made generic in tone. To reinforce the difference, so called "POV shots" often go beyond accessing the mere geographical position of a character. If the protagonist is walking, for example, the shot can be loaded with easily recognizable markers: a slightly shaky camera view, out-of-focus foreground objects standing in the way of the gaze, etc. A character's hallucinogenic state too has produced potent imagery in many films. All in all, by highlighting what makes a shot belong to someone—putting it in isolation so to speak—the system in fact protects those that belong to no one from unwanted contamination.

In summary, two classes of images populate standard moviemaking. To illustrate the difference between them, one could refer to Merleau-Ponty's observation that in real life the world "is not arrayed before me as if I were God, it is lived by me from a certain point of view."[17] Correspondingly, POV shots endeavor to subjectivize a character's finite, limited viewpoint. In opposition to this, the "objective" images which make up most of the shots in Hollywood movies suggest that no one but God is watching and that we, the viewers, are privileged to share the Lord's ubiquitous perception. As for the protagonists, they remain ignorant of this Faustian deal. They go on with their lives unaware that all—even their most intimate moments—are observed by camera and voyeurs alike.[18] They therefore do not gaze at the lens, etc. All in all, coverage works with continuity and objectivity as a total package. It is difficult to use the former without the other two.

V

In contrast to coverage, stands *découpage*. *Découpage*, in French, suggests turning a piece of material, paper for instance, into a shape that can be identified: a cut out. The paper itself remains blank; it says nothing. It is the resultant shapes alone that connote a fish, a tree, a human being. In film, the technique implies that the director, working alone or with the screenwriter, has previewed the action in direct relation to specific camera positions. That movement is seen from that angle. There is a close-up of the antagonist at this junction. Then we place the camera outside the window to see this. Emphasis is on distinct views in place of random or customary standpoints. Instead of so-called "objective" shots, what we see expresses the subjectivity of the filmic narrator, the intention of the storyteller.[19] When preparing a script this way, "the description of each scene, each image, of the future film involves not only its action and dialogue but also the sounds and the music that will accompany them, even the technical means expected to be used at given moments. . . . By providing an exact shot list, [the arrangement] also envisions the duration of the film, its rhythm."[20] *Découpage* could thus be described as dividing the scene into a series of independent shots, rejecting in effect the fundamental premise of coverage (shooting the same action through different angles). But even this definition is not quite right for, when a *découpage* originates during the writing of the picture, the scene does not in fact precede its viewing through a camera point of view. The two are imagined, constructed, and designed simultaneously. They are co-present from the very beginning of the project. This scene is included in the script only because a camera sees what is happening from a certain angle. As a Marxian superstructure, the scene's existence is now contingent on the presence of an extrinsic reality: the camera as the absolute base of all operations.

Although d*écoupage* does not guarantee good filmmaking (mediocre cinema was produced that way), it is an indispensable tool for the serious filmmaker. In opposition to coverage where all options are left open until the editing process, the technique makes it possible to engender a viewpoint from the very inception of the story. *Découpage* can also be said to modify our understanding of a director's work. Far from merely embellishing a self-sufficient text, the technique overturns the traditional relation between form and content. Here instead, in Susan Sontag's words, "the matter, the subject is on the outside; the style is on the inside."[21] More precisely perhaps, the two are so enmeshed that it becomes impossible to disentangle them. Luis Buñuel, for example, always conceived and shot *découpage*, refusing any coverage whatever. "If I shoot two hundred and fifty shots," he said, "there will be two hundred and fifty shots in my finished film: no waste, no luxury."[22] In this kind of approach, the director knows what he or she wants, possibly from the very beginning of the project. It is filmed that way and that is very much the way the shots end up in the film. The technique also happens to be very economical for the production.

But now comes the difficulty. As Michelangelo Antonioni puts it, "there are more than a thousand ways an actor can enter a room and [do something]. But there is only one right way; the other fifty thousand are all wrong. It's a matter of finding the right way."[23] Remember: in *découpage* you have no coverage to go back to in case your intuition failed you. So which is the "right way"? Going back to our earlier example of a man entering a meeting hall, should the camera survey the scene from a high angle position or should it be attached to a Steadicam and follow the actor from his entrance all the way to his sitting down (an approach David Mamet wittily called the Uzi technique in reference to the nonstop firing of the Israeli machine gun)?[24] What is the difference? Of course, each setup will achieve a unique feel for the action, the former maintaining a certain distance toward the character, the latter forcing a closer identificatory contact on us (even if we do not care about the man, we nevertheless will viscerally respond to his physical progress in space). So the key question becomes: what is the scene really about, what is happening here, what does the director want the audience to get from it? In other words, things do not just happen indifferently in a film, they happen in a way that positions viewers in relationship to the action, thus influencing their reading of the event.

Let us take a sequence from *The 400 Blows* (François Truffaut, 1959). In the first scene, the young protagonist is sitting in the living room, concentrating on duplicating his mother's handwriting in a letter designed to explain his absence from school that afternoon. Next the boy welcomes his father in the hallway. We hear they will be eating alone tonight. While they cook some eggs in the kitchen, we find out that the mother and her son are not getting along very well. The next scene is in another section of the living room where father and son bicker about a missing book. Finally, later at night, we find the boy trying to sleep on a cot in the hallway. As the father goes to the bathroom, a car is heard stopping in front of the house and, soon enough, the mother comes in, climbing over the cot to enter the small apartment. She goes to the bedroom where the father accuses her of having an affair with her boss. The argument quickly spreads beyond the affair: the missing book, the mother accusing the boy of being a liar, the father reminding her that he is her son, not his, the possibility of sending him to a boarding school, etc.

Each setup consists of a single angle, generally in a medium shot. There is no coverage whatever, no close-ups or cut aways. One angle, no more. As a bonus, because each scene takes place in a different room, there are no continuity bits to worry about (apart from the clothing the characters are wearing). No matching of motions, gestures, or positions. Finally, if the first four scenes show what is happening quite conventionally, the last scene is exemplary of the power of *découpage*. Instead of following the mother to the bedroom and shooting the couple's fight in a full shot or in a series of shots/reverse shots, Truffaut's camera stays on the boy's face as he listens to it all: the realization that he is a bastard, that his mother does not love him, that his future may involve a disciplinary school, etc. To play it this way was not an editing decision. Rather, Truffaut understood from the beginning that the heart of the scene was there, on the boy's face, and that there was no point in putting the camera anywhere else. In *découpage* then, you know what you are doing *before* you stage a scene.

There are indeed a thousand ways to shoot any action, but it is possible, with some effort, to find one solution you can feel comfortable with. It is really a question of imagining a flow of images, one that will bring to the spectators the filmic narrator's feel, take, his or her viewpoint on the action. For that, finally, is the job of the director: to grope with a developing action and sense its potential, complexity, and truth in relation to a series of specific camera angles.

## VI

*Découpage* is relatively easy to execute in a studio, but what happens when the reality of a location clashes with one's pre-visualization of a scene. Talking about the work of Paul Cézanne, Merleau-Ponty suggested that "'conception' cannot precede 'execution,'" that, to bring about his project, the painter had "to forget all he had ever learned from science."[25] Leaving behind the landscape schemata, those formal patterns passed on by generations of painters, the French artist was desperately trying to bring to his canvas what his eyes actually saw of the world.[26] He was concerned with the actual shape of these trees, not how he had been taught to render them, the actual shadow of that house at four o'clock, not a conventional form learned at the Academy. In a similar manner, a number of directors have made it clear that they too need to see and feel the actual set or location before deciding what to do with the actors or the camera. For instance, when a "'collision' takes place between the environment in which the scene is to be shot and my own particular state of mind at that specific moment," Antonioni confesses, "I feel as though I were in front of a blank page—I have no idea where to begin."[27] To handle the situation, he would muddle things on his own. Only after a while would he come back ready to tell his actors and crew what to do. Jean Renoir could not agree more: "[At the moment of filming] a terrifying phenomenon occurs: in the presence of the actors and the settings I realize that all I've done and written is worthless; I realize that a bit of dialogue I thought full of vitality, once said by an actor who brings it to his own personality, [becomes] meaningless."[28] Ermanno Olmi's reaction to a specific environment is even more pronounced: "I think about the ambiance and all the events that are to be presented: place, lighting, people, color. I construct the fiction I need. When I feel this fiction corresponds to my needs, then I go to the camera and let myself be dragged along by the event without establishing beforehand that 'here' I'll do a close-up, a long shot, a camera movement."[29] What these directors are telling us is that the multifarious aspects of the world often affect the response of great filmmakers. In such case, the best plans bow before the reality of the situation. This does not mean that coverage takes over, only that the reality of the environment is not ignored, producing either some adjustments or a complete rethinking in the selection of shots.

What is happening in location shooting is that everyday life carries forward all kinds of unexpected details that make the planned fiction less believable. Danielle Huillet once observed that "the hardest thing to bring into a film is what people do all the time in public: awkward gestures, little movements that mean nothing."[30] It is also this actor's unusual gait, this other actor's facial mannerism. It is the crack in the stucco that runs through the wall: a character may now be imagined tracing it with her fingers. It is the breathtaking view of the church's spire one did not expect from the window: suddenly, one decides to move actors and camera around so as to include it in the shot. However well prepared a director may be, there is always so much more one did not expect. Directors who thrive on the unexpected *take a shot at it*, hoping for the best. Talking about the New Wave, Peter Brook expertly pinpointed the difference between that movement and the time-worn cinema that preceded it. "What the French have begun to do . . . ," he wrote, "is to introduce into the direct narrative all sorts of other elements—outside references, surreal behavior, like those odd things in *Jules and Jim*, bits of theatre and so on, which by breaking through the conventions increase the opportunity for a denser expression of reality."[31]

These odd bits were certainly not particular to the French in 1960. Rather François Truffaut and company, by shooting on location with very little equipment and unknown actors, became aware of all kinds of discontinuities between the flux of contemporary life and the restrictive operations of moviemaking. Instead of rejecting out of hand the "awkward gestures," the chance encounters, the unforeseeable happenings as their predecessors did, they welcomed them in their narratives. Following his master Renoir, Truffaut in his philosophy went even further than that. "One must," he declared, "shoot against one's screenplay."[32] By this he meant that the shooting of a film should not just actualize what had been pre-visualized in the *découpage*. No: other forces necessarily came to play during the filmmaking phase of a project and it was the job of the director to seize upon them and make them work for the film. Needless to say, most directors have avoided being put on the spot, for the situation could show them to be without clothes after all. Talking about D. W. Griffith, Peter Milne expressed these differences between directors very well when he wrote:

> The usual director is like a motorist who has carefully studied his road map before setting out on a journey and who refers to it time and time again during the trip, specially when he comes to a cross roads. Mr. Griffith never studies a road map. He just jumps into his car and starts going. When he comes to the crossing he takes the road that seems best to him. Sometimes this road is the wrong one. Most often it is right.[33]

All of this implies a third approach to staging: directors who trust their own abilities to respond impulsively but effectively to the concreteness of their immediate work environment. A *découpage* created hour by hour as the film progresses.

## VII

Regardless of the staging method chosen, a director must be able to handle crew and actors. Somehow they should become a team, molding themselves to the needs of the director. That is not always the case unfortunately. Some directors of photography, for instance, unfortunately insist on using cumbersome equipment which can undermine the director's control over the film. Godard once diagrammed the consequences for the shoot brought about by the choice of a camera.[34] In his drawings, the large Panaflex is shown as producing enormous traffic on the set (all sorts of assistants, grips, etc.), activity that makes it difficult for the director to concentrate on the scene at hand. In contrast, the Aaton 35mm, which Godard expected to be even smaller than the actual camera eventually marketed by the company, leaves a clear line of sight between the director and the actors. In the first example the director must manage an army of employees, in the second he/she is surrounded by a group of friends.

To choose a camera is thus not without consequences. A large camera implies more crew and goes hand in hand with these other excesses that happen once people realize you are making a "movie" (to recall Jaglom's pertinent remark). Two examples involving directors who graduated from smaller independent films to bigger Hollywood productions show what is involved here. Martin Scorsese, ever the most vocal and lucid of all American directors, once complained about the size of the equipment he was suddenly forced to use and the number of people buzzing around it. "It gets to the point," he said, "where you can't even fucking turn [around on the set]."[35] As for Arthur Penn, he had additional problems on *The Chase* (1966):

I was dealing with a cameraman and I remember Marlon [Brando] coming to me and saying, 'Why? What's this about not getting our first shot at night until one o'clock in the morning?' And I said, 'That's this guy.' He looked at me in a leery fashion. He was implying: 'Get rid of him!' It never occurred to me. I bought into the whole system when I bought into that picture."[36]

In such cases the bulky equipment and the large professional crew simply get in the way of the project. They become handicaps rather than tools to make the job easier. Martin Heidegger made an important distinction in one's use of equipment. A hammer, for instance, is ready-to-hand when it is used to nail something and one's attention is on the job itself. In that case, the tool "disappears" in the project to nail something on the wall. On the contrary, that same hammer becomes present-at-hand when its handle is wobbly and one's attention is on avoiding hitting a finger rather than on the task itself.[37] If one cares to keep control over what is going on, it is thus important to work with crews and equipment of the ready-to-hand type. Big crews operating with huge vans full of everything one could possibly ever need often also turn out to be the most conservative in their thinking. Both Godard and Jaglom have had to deal with reluctant crew members. Godard's solution was most poetic. He recalled that on the set of *Everyman for Himself* (1980):

> When nothing was happening I would tell [the camera crew] to go out in the sun, stay there and rest for a while, listen to some music, bring a friend, whatever. The production would pay for it. Just pay attention to the way the light changes and tell me about it afterwards, for instance, that during the day, in full sun, there were four different types of light and "that" one was particularly nice. This was not so bizarre, but their reaction to it was rather violent, they were taken aback.[38]

As for Jaglom, he got good advice from Orson Welles: "whenever a crew tells you 'It won't cut, it doesn't work, it doesn't make sense, you can't find it in the pages [of the script],' you just say to them, 'It's a dream sequence.' Suddenly [the director of photography] didn't need his rules about what cuts and what's logical and so on."[39] If large crews require the constant attention of the director, small crews—less than ten people—allow the director to concentrate on the scene at hand. The film comes out the winner.

## VIII

More intractable yet is the problem of the actors. Once upon a time Cecil B. De Mille could "explain" acting with the following anecdote:

"The scene may call for an actor to be seated at a desk thoughtfully smoking a pipe. Perhaps the actor may handle the pipe like an amateur. Inquiry may uncover the fact that he is far more at home smoking a cigar. Thereupon a cigar is supplied and the scene proceeds smoothly."[40] If only all the problems encountered on the set could be solved as easily! To initiate the discussion, let us consider the relation between internal and external in one's daily life. One of the key tenets in Merleau-Ponty's philosophy is that:

> We must abandon the fundamental prejudice according to which the psyche is that which is accessible only to myself and cannot be seen from outside. My "psyche" is not a series of "states of consciousness" that are rigorously closed in on themselves and inaccessible to anyone but me. My consciousness is turned primarily toward the world, turned toward things; it is above all a relation to the world.[41]

This being the case, "love, hate, or anger . . . are not psychic facts hidden at the bottom of another's consciousness: they are types of behavior or styles of conduct which are visible from the outside. They exist *on* this face, *in* these gestures, not hidden behind them."[42] So it is not just looks or accents that determine what Jean-Paul Sartre called the "signifying humus" of language, but also facial expressions, gestures, and body language (how we stand, walk, turn our head around, etc.) that bring to the surface of the individual another level of communication. What we see, feel, and respond to can go hand in hand, enhance, or contradict the words expressed by someone. Sometimes the words seem more important, at other times it is the whole person we trust. Occasionally we may experience a dissonance between the two modes of expression and keep our distance as a result.

On the written page of a novel, a play, or a script, characters live by their words alone. They do not have to perform. Unless the writer tells us more about what is going on, we believe what they say. On the stage or in film, however, words originate with the actors speaking for the characters. A lot therefore depends on their performance. Diderot once remarked that on the stage, "it is not the expression, 'I love you,' which prevails upon the resistance of a prude, the vanity of a coquette, or the virtue of a righteous woman. It is rather the trembling of the voice that accompanies the words; it is the tears and the looks that go with them."[43]

The text then only goes so far. What makes one character convincing to another, what really gets the audience hooked, is the wrapping that goes with the words, the theatrics of the body. Sartre put it well when he remarked that "to be present at a theatrical performance is to apprehend the characters *on* the actors. . . ."[44] For actors to convince viewers of the sincerity of their words, it is thus not enough to memorize lines, the body has to articulate them convincingly. A human being has to come alive on the stage or on film. Someone has to inhabit that body and say such things.

To act thus implicates the other. From the Greek Thespian to the No performer to the modern actor, the fundamental question turns around the impersonation of an other in public. The occasion is solemn, the situation portentous. One need be careful about such an operation lest the soul of the being or a god be awakened and initiate vengeance. It makes sense then that distance be kept at first: maybe a mask to hide the identity of the player, then a pattern of stylized gestures and a distinctive declamatory style that no one could possibly take as the normal behavior or the voice of a real individual. Later on, when the fears of punishment subsided, actors were able to approach characters more directly. Edmund Burke for instance, reflected that it was not especially difficult to imitate others. He wrote: "I have often observed, that, on mimicking the looks and gestures of angry, or placid, or frightened, or daring men, I have involuntarily found my mind turned to that passion whose appearance I endeavored to imitate."[45] In other words, if you strive to replicate someone else's body language, you will probably take in that person's overall character as well. The idea in this case is to draw from another human being. He or she is going to provide you, the actor, with the breadth and the fire you need to make your character believable. Listen to Hamlet, pay attention to Antigone. To get into them, or others, some initial questions about character and action have to be answered: Who is this person? What circumstances does he find himself in? How does she react? What does he want? What stands in her way? Once these questions are answered, the actor can move in, giving the character flesh and voice, all the time imagining what it would be like to be that other human being. Lawrence Olivier has admitted working in this manner, fully researching the part and assembling all kinds of details gathered exclusively on the outside, not only in real life but also in the closeanalysis of other performances of the part. "I usually collect a lot of details," he explains, "a lot of characteristics and find a creature swimming about somewhere in the middle of this. . . ."[46] For Richard III, he did not hesitate to enhance his performance by modeling some bits after Hitler. All in all, the goal here is to acquire what Jerzy Grotowski called an "arsenal:" enough ammunitions to carry the character through the play.[47] It is not that actors working in this fashion actually disappear behind their characters—after all we see *them* on the stage or on the screen—but that they see their job as constructing as well as possible this other human being, someone who, in the final analysis, has little or nothing to do with their own selves. For it is the impersonated others who must move the audience through their doubts or ambitions, it is the characters who must scream or cry. The goal of the traditional actor then is to externalize the protagonist, to flesh out the words, to bring a believable voice and a consistent body to what would otherwise remain but a literary construct.

## IX

Early in the century, a Russian theatre director rebelled against this manner of acting, thinking it phony, much too mechanical, not real enough. The words spoken on the stage did not seem to him to originate with the people speaking there, they did not feel spontaneous enough. Actors were merely pretending to be someone else. They had nothing at stake really. Things were done in general rather than by this person experiencing tonight these particular circumstances. Confronted with a specific situation, as Jean Renoir observed, "the actress pulls a little drawer, a symbolic drawer, and she finds four, five expressions she's used already a hundred times and other actors in the world used millions of times."[48] Worse, actors had also become too dependent on conventional ideas for the interpretation of their role: what this character is supposed to be like, what this play is reputed to be about. In view of these failures, Konstantin Stanislavski proposed a radical alteration to the typical relation between the actor and the part. His key idea was to "go from yourself."[49] It consisted in using the self rather than others (real or imagined) as the source of details, emotions, and characterizations for the part. The actor, he insisted, "can't expel his soul from his body and hire another to replace it."[50] In other words, the actor needed to use his or her own soul to get at the core of a situation. When successful, the technique allows the actor to escape the trap of trying to imitate someone who will always remain an other. To achieve this, Stanislavski suggested that actors use "what if" as a technique to connect the part to their own subconscious: how would *you* behave if you had the power of that character, what would *you* do if you found yourself in that situation, how would *you* feel if that person did that to you, etc. The actor in that case merely tries to find in him/herself a conviction that parallels that of a character. The initial questions about a scene are thus modified: What do I use from *my* self to create this character? How do I personalize the circumstances that surround my character, actions, goals, etc.? Most dramatically, an actor may use his or her personal emotional memory bank to key in a reaction experienced by the character.

At this point, however, we move from the purely Russian system of Stanislavski to the American Method of Lee Strasberg.[51] Mark Rydell, I think, summarized quite well the tenets of the Method in its American application. He said: "[The situation] has to relate to you as a human being, in some way you can understand and identify with, then you can move to any area. . . . Something has to be real. If an actor walks on stage sobbing, you'll believe any line he speaks. You'll believe, 'My father is dead,' you'll believe, 'I lost my comb.'"[52] In other words, because "real" tears suddenly take the place of "fake" ones, everything else about the character appears truthful as well at that moment. Spectators have no choice but react as fellow human beings to the suffering of an other, to the reality of that pain in that person. A subtle but effective sleight of hand has thus taken place: something absent, out of sight, not available to the viewers (whatever the actor is using in his/her own past) is immediately connected by the audience to the present situation faced by the fictional character. By fusing two beings—one who offers us his/her body but whose soul is out of sight (the actor), the other, absent really but whose persona dominates the play (the character)—the Method was able to produce electrifying moments on stage and in film.

Acting though is a cultural activity. Hence it is subject to the dominant ideas that suffuse any historical period. And Strasberg's approach has in time been criticized as being unrealistic as well as an intrusion of American overcharged individualism into the domain of the theater. The attack focused on the exclusivity given by the Method to internal motivation. For instance, in one of her very influential books expounding on the Method, Uta Hagen recommends six steps for actors preparing for their role: Who am I? What circumstances am I facing (time, place, immediate surroundings)? How do I feel about those whom I come in contact with? What do I want? What is my obstacle and what do I do to get what I want?[53] While this preparation makes sense in a play where characters run the show, it may be out of place in a film shot on location, one that stays open to the actual environment and the depth of reality surrounding the actor.

Let us imagine a young man driving to his girlfriend's apartment to tell her that their relationship is over. Putting Hagen to work—and that will be the tendency of many directors and actors—the focus would be entirely on the upcoming confrontation. The director would emphasize the tension of the moment. And the actor's motivation would impregnate his driving, his going up the elevator, his ringing of the bell, etc. In another kind of film, however, the character distracted by his grumbling stomach could be looking for something to eat on the way. Later, applying the brakes for a stray dog that rushed across the street, a flow of childhood memories involving Brutus the family pet may unexpectedly take over. In front of her building, he is both frightened and moved by the sight of an old woman shuddering in the cold. Finally, as his girlfriend opens the door, our protagonist is so taken by her genuine welcome that he decides not to bring up the issue that brought him to her in the first place. As we see, it is not that Hagen is wrong (she indeed suggests that the character connect to places, objects, people) but that, in her way of thinking (taken from Stanislavski), a single objective dominates all others. Most films, alas, will not veer away from the line in the script that says, "He drives to her apartment," keeping the protagonist internally focused on the goal at hand. For directors willing to improvise, however, the reality of the driving may change the character or at least open him up to casual encounters. In such a scheme, whether planned in the script or not, the stomach, the dog, the homeless woman truly exist for the character to react to. In contrast, by sticking with a super-objective for the entire scene or play, the Method does not allow for any false note: everything inside and outside, in the acting as well as the staging, must move in unison toward a single end, point, or message to be impressed on the audience. By doing so, Strasberg's Method dismisses the actuality of the surrounding world which normally affects people as well. The Method may have produced outstanding acting moments but, when all is said and done, it may be that Strasberg's blueprint is as close to daily life as Curnonsky's rich cuisine is to most people's meals.

## X

Under the influence of post-structuralist studies, the notion of characters as real people and a play as an actual event also came under review. This naturalization process—the hiding of both the discourse and the means of production within the play—is taken for granted by bourgeois art. Other theories of acting, however, have provided us with a wide range of alternatives. There is Jacques Copeau who compelled each actor to start from zero, to become a complete *tabula rasa* before entering a character. There is Antonin Artaud who went a little further and prodded his players till they achieved trancelike performances. And there is Vsevolod Meyerhold, who forced his company to perform a variety of jerky acrobatics throughout a play. As for Bertolt Brecht, he not only revolutionized the technique of acting, he also questioned the role and function of the actor on the stage. In short, compared to traditional or method acting styles whose efforts are directed toward making the characters and the actuality of a situation come alive, these other models all suggested different purposes for a play and a distinct conditioning or motivating force for the actors.

Without going into the details, one could generalize such theories by saying that they all radicalize in some way the distance between character and actor as well as rethink the relation between representation and audience. A modern way of conceptualizing acting therefore requires a rethinking of the actor's role: not as someone who incarnates another human being so convincingly that one loses track of the differences between them, but as a performer whose job it is to communicate or, rather, to signify. "The actor's task," Phillip B. Zarrilli persuasively argues, "is creating signs through voice and body."[54] Seen in this light, the actor becomes a signifier in charge of a signified. Brecht for one felt very strongly that actors not get lost in their parts. Indeed, when method actors go inside the self to find emotional equivalents to what troubles the character, the original predicament is uncritically internalized. In other words, they accept everything that happens to the characters as "natural and unavoidable."[55] Not only are the events justified, but spectators are also invited to identify emotionally with the plight of the individuals on the stage. Brecht wanted none of this. First, he advocated moving the emphasis of the play from the individuals themselves to what happened between them. A typical ploy here involves the substitution of a social *gestus* for the mere motion of an individual human being. The *gestus* is a recognizable social comportment that is made extreme in order to retrieve the original meaning of the act. For example, to bow before someone was quite common in Europe in previous centuries. If shown naturalistically, audiences take it as a hello, a custom just like a handshake. Accentuating the bow, however, can expose the social domination of one class over another. In the larger scheme of things too, Brecht insisted that actors study not only their lines, but also their meaning, their context, so as to be able to produce the larger picture for the audience's examination—the famous *Verfremdung* or alienation effect. The idea, the German playwright tells us, is to present to the audience not a Richard III that one could empathize with, but an English monarch working his way through the social and political reality of his times. For instance, the actor should not spurn the idea of making clear the many contradictions consuming the character, for they are likely to reveal the larger ideological conflicts at work in that society. Indeed, the Brechtian actor should strive to reveal "the determinants under which (these contradictions) develop."[56] By witnessing a situation whose meaning can be debated instead of a slice of life that is accepted as the character's destiny, viewers in turn can become more aware of the fact that society's structure is after all always up for grabs, a revelation of possible significance for their own immediate lives.

Hence, in the Brechtian system, the actors are not stuck in their characters. They use them rather to point to the larger reality outside the theatre then and now, in the fiction as well as in real life. "Without opinions and objectives," Brecht sums up his thinking, "one can represent nothing at all. . . ."[57] This view is of course totally opposed to the tenet shared by all partisans of the American method, which states that "in both rehearsals and in performance [actors should] avoid commenting on the play, or the character, or the circumstances, or the symbols, or the message [of the text]."[58] Certainly, the portrayal in this country of Brecht's political approach as dry, boring, pedagogical theater and the *Verfremdung* effect as an annoyance that keeps you from enjoying the play has kept many from wanting to emulate the playwright. Yet this characterization does not truly reflect all of Brecht's intentions. He insisted, for instance, that his actors approach characters in successive circles of understanding. First, they had to find out about their characters and their historical circumstances, then, in a second phase, they could move in and experience what it felt like from within. This is the moment when the actor could "identify with the character, search for the character's truth in the subjective sense."[59] Only afterward, would they be ready to step back and see again the larger picture, how individuals get stuck within the social and political determinants of the time. In his directing too, Brecht was very much concerned about giving spectators pleasure: *theatrical* pleasure. Far from being unilaterally pedantic, he saw his staging as an exciting seesaw alternation between diegetic action and non-diegetic commentary often in the guise of a song. Even the distancing moments in a play were meant to engender a distinct pleasure for the audience, one, however, that stands radically opposed to the traditional enjoyment provided by identification with the emotions experienced by the individual characters.

It is difficult to find in commercial features the kind of acting/directing approach suggested by Brecht. At best we encounter some disagreements with the dominant techniques. Antonioni, for instance, maintains that "the director owes no explanation to the actor except those of a very general nature about the people in the film."[60] In *The Cry* (1957), this approach brought him in constant conflict with Steve Cochran, an actor accustomed to more conventional directing methods and who complained loudly about being treated as a puppet. But then again Antonioni also found himself in trouble with Jeanne Moreau, a well-educated and eclectic actress, on the set of *La Notte* (1960). Understandably, actors may feel abandoned when they are supposed to do and say things without knowing really where these words and gestures come from. The Italian director's refusal to discuss his views of the characters with the actors is perhaps more in line with David Mamet's teaching than Bertolt Brecht's philosophy. At a now famous seminar at Columbia University, Mamet told his students not to rely on acting but on editing to tell the story.[61] To put it briefly, actors should not be asked to inflect every moment of the film with their overall understanding of the play. They must never go beyond their immediate objective (walking toward the class room, looking at the clock) while performing the physical actions required by a shot.

More to the point, we can look at Robert Bresson and Jean-Luc Godard as the directors who have most consistently demonstrated in their films a radically different view of acting. Bresson to be sure goes against everything acting is normally about. To start with, he does not use actors but real people he encounters by chance in the streets. In his *Notes on Cinematography*, he explains his choice: "Beings (models) instead of seeming (actors). Human models: movement from the exterior to the interior. (Actors: movement from the interior to the exterior). The thing that matters is not what they show me but what they hide from me and, above all, what they do not suspect is in them."[62] By calling his players "models," Bresson unfortunately muddles things up for, in French as well as in English, the term also suggests an ideal worthy of imitation. Bresson's "model" in fact refers back to the unfinished quality present in the plaster figure that precedes the making of an actual sculpture. His "models" thus suggest human prototypes rather than accomplished actors. But this too does not tell the entire story, for his "models" are not behaving like normal human beings either. They move in unison; they never laugh; they deploy but a narrow range of human emotions. Their speech is contained as well. "Speak as if you were speaking to yourselves," Bresson advises them, "monologues instead of dialogue. . . . Don't think about what you are saying, don't think about what you're doing."[63] Typically, the actors are not to make use of the basic informations granted most actors: who am I, what am I doing here, what do I want, what stands in my way, etc. Instead of working toward the creation on the screen of ordinary people, Bresson wants to see "beings and things in their separate parts." He thus eliminates from his models all conventional human characteristics until each one "has brought home to him all of him that was outside."[64] Bresson's idea then is to wrench the "signifying humus" from the being in front of him, rendering him impenetrable to our gaze. In siphoning off the life of the character, a different kind of alienation effect is produced. To some extent, we experience his "models" in the same way we stand next to Alzheimer patients. They stay incommunicado in a world we know nothing about. They are absolute others. And we, in turn, fear for our life, not knowing anymore what makes us human. All in all, Bresson's "models" behave as souls rather than human beings. The experience can be illuminating or deadening depending on where one stands on the subject.

More radically still, Jean-Luc Godard pushed acting beyond the boundaries of the character in a film. Using Anna Karina, his wife at the time, in *A Woman Is a Woman* (1961), Godard left in the finished film a recorded moment when Karina moved from the character to herself. This shift had nothing to do with the internalization of the part in Method acting since, there, audiences cannot tell actor from character. Having flubbed a line, Karina retraced herself, now speaking as the actress to the director, then did the line a second time in character. For the audience, the impact is enormous. We suddenly access a second reality (the actress's real life), a second world of meaning at work during the making of a film. Although the woman on the screen did not change, her signifying status shifted in the middle of a line. She became truly "herself." By keeping the line in the film, by bringing in the actress in addition to the character, Godard galvanized the text, doubling its semiotic richness. Documentary material suddenly fuses with fiction and the film now moves eerily from one realm to the other. Navigating between two worlds, the French director was able to use one to echo, question, and radicalize the other in a most Brechtian fashion. With the expansion of the signifying status of the actress/character also comes the doubling of the world—represented and real. In Godard's films also, the flow of the "film," of the screenplay, of the story, is often interrupted so as to introduce external viewpoints that comment on the action from a different angle or context. His films eventually became notoriously complex essays where the core story was no more important than the digressions scattered throughout the texts. Some say he ventured so far in uncharted territory that he got lost and never found his way back. More problematically, I think, Godard no longer offered the audience the pleasure of "smoking a good cigar," something Brecht knew was necessary for his kind of theatre to be successful. However, Godard's ultimate failure should not discourage anyone to explore again the terrain scouted by the director. In the spirit of Henry Jaglom, one could explain to the producers that to use the actor as the actor as well as the character is to get two for the price of one. Or that to mix the real with the fiction of the film is like getting entire new sets without having to pay for them. In a more serious vein, the sudden presence of Karina as herself on the screen put an end to the charade that cinema must depict a single unified world. Direct discourse was let in, supplying the director with entirely new tools and tactics to think out the film.

One final word about acting. Although it may be extremely difficult to avoid using actors/stars in feature films, this is not the case in student films. And it is here that Haskell Wexler's advice comes in handy. Instead of using fellow students or, at best, "Dramalogue" actors who dream of becoming celebrities, students "should not close their eyes to the people not seen on television, those we don't see in our everyday life."[65] Go out of your way therefore to find ordinary men and women with interesting faces. Pay attention to the working people you come in contact with: the cashier at the market, the waitress at the coffee shop, the clerk at the DMV, the mailman, the ninety-nine percent of the population that casting agencies ignore. Sure it is difficult because the media are regulating the way people speak, look, and behave in daily life, but it is still possible to discover out there strong individuals who have resisted such influence. Their presence alone will electrify your project. It may even force you to reevaluate not only your direction but your entire filmmaking practice.

## XI

Staging involves not only the actors in a space but the view from the camera, the light that shines on the scene, the sounds we hear, etc. The conventional manner of conceptualizing this grand ensemble is to assume that all these elements build on each other. The camera's job is to support the actors' confrontation from that angle and that height. The light's purpose is to reveal the protagonist's expression, to tell us what kind of day it is and the general mood of the scene. The sound's goal is to make sure we hear what is being said over the noises of the world and the music. In effect, this way of directing the film adopts what Richard Wagner called *Gesamtkunstwerk*, the working together of the different components of the work.[66] Staging a performance of the *Walküre*, Eisenstein described what it was like: "Men, music, light, landscape, color, and motion brought into one integral whole by a single piercing emotion."[67] Despite their belonging to entirely different aesthetic domains, the realms combine in providing a single overall tone to the piece. One could say that they relate to one another as different voices in a harmonic composition. The work as a result achieves formal unity.

There is another way, however, of imagining the overall operation of staging, and that is to construe it dialogically. Mikhail Bakhtin, a Russian formalist thinker, introduced the notion of dialogism as an alternative to the usual situation present in the novel wherein the author conveniently dominates his characters as God its creation. In such texts, individuals are allowed only so much independence. Their entrances and exits from the narrative, what they do or say, all is carefully orchestrated so as not to upset the overall balance of the text. These characters then are not really on their own. They have little opportunity to air their full views or let out their complete personality. Although they act and talk in the narrative, their comportment and conversation are let in only insofar as they do not do damage to the main thesis expounded by the author. Using the work of Dostoevski as an example, Bakhtin presented an entirely different way of handling things. In Dostoevski, he said, each character is given the entire stage to present his or her views so that it becomes more difficult for the reader to ascertain moral superiority over them. With the Russian novelist, Bakhtin insisted, characters are "not voiceless slaves . . . but free people, capable of standing alongside their creator, capable of not agreeing with him and even of rebelling against him."[68] Applied to film, truly independent characters would do a lot more than simply advance the plot, make others look good, or relieve a sequence through humor.

John Cassavetes' work brings us an inkling of what dialogism would mean in practice. In his movies, characters are given a lot more freedom to explore the reality of their situation than in conventional movies. Whether this deepening is accomplished in rehearsals or during shooting (improvisation) is finally of little importance: the bottom line is to unshackle characters by letting actors live their parts more fully. Even more striking is the approach developed by Mike Leigh, who literally asks his actors to discover their characters in the most minute detail before any script is written around them. This "fleshing out" goes way beyond the kind of backstory many actors generally imagine for themselves when they are hired for a film. Here, as actress Katrin Cartlidge tells it, "you build up memories, experiences, a whole life that becomes almost as real to you as the one you live yourself; it infiltrates the fabric of your subconscious."[69] You must be able to answer any question about your character, even questions that may have nothing to do with the content of the screenplay: from what she thinks about pre-marital sex to what presents he gave his family for Christmas.[70] In addition to this, actors working for Leigh are supposed to experience the life of their character on a day-to-day basis as well: to work at *their* job for months on end so as to understand how they feel there and how their overall view of life is shaped by it. In contrast, each actor is kept from even thinking about the other personages so that, when "rehearsals" start, fully developed personalities clash with each other, literally creating the story through a series of deeplyfelt improvisations. With Leigh then, characters come first, plot second. While radical, this strategy simply constitutes a novel challenge for the artist. For Bakhtin indeed, "Dostoevski creates a new kind of unity in his novels, not the familiar unity based on the pervasiveness of a single idea or theme, but the familiar expressive unity inherent in the dialogic relations between several opposed ideas or voices."[71] The same can be said of Leigh's films.

Dialogism, however, can be pushed beyond a world of independent characters. If, as Bakhtin writes, the dialogic author "does not express himself in [the speeches of the character]—rather, he exhibits them,"[72] what happens to the author's own speech? Let us be general here. In conventional nineteenth-century novels, the author's speech is often never noticed by the readers. The reason for this is that whereas the speeches of the characters are placed within inverted commas, that of the author is not. The author's speech merely fills in the space between these other speeches as if it itself were not one as well. Colin MacCabe called the author's speech the metalanguage of the text.[73] In film, that speech consists mainly of camera angles, lighting choices, and editing decisions. Although this particular speech generally guides us through the action and tells us how to interpret the characters' words, it itself remains transparent. No one specifically seems to be speaking. It comes from nowhere in particular. Something is happening on its own accord out there. The technique (coverage) supports the action. There is no false note anywhere.

To apply Bakhtin's idea to staging would force a change in the usual harmonious orchestration between speech, gestures, and motions by the actors on the one hand, and camera position and lighting style on the other. Let us take a look at the strategy used by Lars von Trier in *Breaking the Waves* (1996). In scene after scene, the director of photography would preset a space, lighting it all minimally with practicals and pushing the film to its limits in the lab. Actors who had rehearsed elsewhere would then show up on the set and the shooting would start immediately. In effect, the actors were discovering the space for the first time and thus were not bound to say their lines or do certain actions in specific areas: they moved as they saw fit at that moment. In turn, it also meant that the camera operator had no idea of what to expect during the shot. Hand-holding the camera, the operator merely attempted to respond the best he could to what was going on. As the director of photography, Robby Müller, put it, "we would shoot the whole scene in one shot. It was the choice of the camera operator or me when to look where. None of the actors knew beforehand what time they would be in the shot, or if they would be in the shot."[74] Perfect focusing or harmonious compositions were thus rejected in favor of the authenticity of the moment. For von Trier, this made sense: "If *Breaking the Waves* had been rendered with a conventional technique, I don't think you could have tolerated the story. One normally chooses a style for a film in order to highlight a story. We've done exactly the opposite; we've chosen a style that works against the story."[75] In other words, the quasi-documentary approach contrasted with the highly melodramatic situation experienced by the characters. *Gesamtkunstwerk* can thus give way to full dialogism, not just of characters but also of technique. What has to be clear here is that polyphony does not have to end up in chaos or cacophony. This is certainly not the case with *Breaking the Waves*, quite the contrary. To apply dialogism to film thus permits directors to stimulate characters and discover new ways of organizing the relation between them and other storytelling techniques.

## XII

In comparison to the incredibly complex, ever-fluctuating operations of the narrative process, Jean-Paul Torok once declared the core operations of directing as contributing little that is new to the film. "There are not," he noticed, "thirty-six thousand ways of staging a given scene or situation, but only a few, always the same ones. . . ."[76] If you think of shooting a conversation between two people in a car or in a hallway, it is indeed difficult to imagine a novel way of positioning the two actors or the camera. The car and the shape of the hallway "tell" you where the occupants are going to sit or where they will walk. Unless the project—a rock video for example—allows for radically different behaviors or camera angles, all directors will stage such scenes within the same general parameters.

But is this observation really significant? Torok's argument would have been stronger in my view had he attacked our reified view of the world rather than its architectonics. To explain the situation, let us recall the work of Viktor Shklovski and his notion of *ostranenie* or "making strange." Working in the years 1910–19, the Russian critic had noticed that the very process of daily life slowly but inevitably moves us beyond our first impression of an object, landscape, or person. Soon enough, however thrilled we once were with it, we end up taking it for granted. Think for a moment of an object you really coveted. Once in your possession, that object slowly became part of the furniture. Because it is always at your disposal, you pay less and less attention to it. After a while you no longer experience the powerful longing you originally had toward it. It is still the same object but it has now definitely lost its shine. In opposite fashion, recall your shock when, after an absence of some years, you suddenly rediscover the face of someone you knew very well: a parent, a friend, a former lover. Yes, it is still Dad, Mary Jo, or Clint, but somehow their faces do not match your memory of them. Whereas in earlier years, you saw "Dad," "Mary Jo," or "Clint" as familiar, constant characters in your life, now the changes brought about by their aging force you to pay full attention to their features once again. Everyone and everything then, through accessibility and daily encounters, becomes familiar and unnoticed.

Recognizing this deadening of experience, Shklovski proposed *ostranenie* as a countermeasure. *Ostranenie* is the tool of the poet, the technique of making things strange again, of defamiliarizing what would otherwise be recognized too quickly by the viewer. "The technique of art," he wrote, "is to make objects 'unfamiliar,' to make forms difficult, to increase the difficulty and length of perception, because the process of perception is an aesthetic end in itself and must be prolonged."[77] Practically speaking, it means to jolt mundane representations by using unexpected words or a surprising visual approach. Shklovski's point is even more pertinent today because of the omnipresence of the mass media. Whether we want to or not, we are being bombarded week after week by thousands of images depicting every possible dramatic situation. All together, these scenes which form the shared cultural tapestry of our life, have numbed us to the emotions or activities themselves or their potential as dramatic material. Worse, it is not clear that poets, artists, and filmmakers have remained immune to this textual accumulation, for they too live in the world and, maybe even more than the general audience, they tend to study and analyze normative images. Their creative insights as a result cannot help but be deadened by these images. Hasn't everything been shown? Hasn't every approach been explored? Isn't our aesthetic choice limited to trite rendering or parody? In peril is artistic imagination. At stake is art's survival. This is where *ostranenie* can still be of help.

Let us take an example: the close-up. Think back to the scandal of having someone's face suddenly occupy the entire surface of the screen. For some of D. W. Griffith's contemporaries, the incredible magnification of the face was too much, almost obscene, and they attacked it accordingly. Today the situation has reversed itself: we see so many faces in close-ups and medium close-ups (especially on television) that we pay no further attention to them or the technique. There are two reasons for this: one, visual practice along the years has accustomed us to going to faces for reactions to whatever is happening in the scene and, two, the faces themselves have been neutered so that they no longer impress or scare us through their differences. Today indeed the faces we see on the screen are so preened, made up, coifed, domesticated that, when we look at them, we no longer see the incongruity of particular arrangements of skin and bones but respond only to the conventional emotions displayed by the actors. These faces, in other words, have been made to shed their distinctness, their scars, they have been made to look innocent, banal, not very different from our own after all. This should not surprise us for, as pointed out by Emmanuel Levinas, the reduction of the other to the same is a consistent feature of Western ideology.[78] His own philosophy opposes this weakening or devitalization of the other. In his view, our faces express our difference, they invoke the absolute alterity between us. It is by showing his or her face, a face that is different from mine, that the other approaches me as a vulnerable being and delivers itself into my hands. The face, in other words, is a radical reminder of one's finitude, it implies the presence of someone else in a world we must now share. Furthermore, to see someone as an other is to accept that I myself am an other for that being as well. The heterogeneity you see on the other's face is on yours as well. The face—theirs, yours—then is what is always on the other side, what makes you other even to yourself. Surely at times, the nudity I recognize on someone's face makes me want to dominate or even destroy this absolute other which makes demands on me. At other times though, that nakedness elicits a sense of responsibility and compassion toward that being. All in all, the face is what ultimately defines us as human beings.[79]

To encounter a face, with Levinas, is to open the world to the presence of the other and, through it, to see oneself as never before. Surprisingly, not many filmmakers have availed themselves of this most formidable weapon. Márta Mészáros in fact stands almost alone in making the most of the technique. In all of her films, but in *Adoption* (1975) especially, her camera consistently offers an unusual view of her characters' faces. To describe what is going on, it might be useful to distinguish the way she handles the camera from what we discover on her actors' faces. First, her camerawork is very unlike that which we encounter in most films. For the most part, the gaze fails to reveal anything significant in the person we are looking at. By the same token the technique is not showy or flaunting of itself. And it is not active or probing as in some documentary work where the camera prowls the subject, looking for a flaw, and is quick to condemn. The best way I can describe it is to say that her use of the camera is gentle, almost affectionate. It is like the hand of a loved one placed on your shoulder or your waist: it feels good and you trust it so fully that you accept it as another part of yourself. You don't have to think twice about it or question what it is doing there. It becomes part of you. Clearly there is a different sensibility at work here, a gentleness one does not find too often in a cinema dominated by male directors. Second, Mészáros has the uncanny ability to make us interested in mundane faces. Her actresses indeed (her protagonists are primarily female) are not exceptionally beautiful. They wear little makeup. They portray working women with ordinary problems. Nothing terribly exciting happens to them. They do not have great lines to articulate. Yet for ninety minutes we are mesmerized by their presence on the screen. The key thing, I believe, is that the women (the actresses and the nonprofessionals the director also uses) are not trying to project as much emotion as is usually the case with actors. Rather they appear to be lost in thought or absorbed in their work. Left on their own, by themselves, the naked faces become ciphers. Instead of theatrics, we access someone's soul, we contact her humanity. With Mészáros' films, we end up rediscovering what is closest to us: the poignancy of another human being.

Another notable exception can be found in Carl Dreyer's *Passion of Joan of Arc* (1928). What makes this particular film so compelling are the visages per se, what in fact they are made of, their features. Shot without makeup, we see skin, pores, ridges, and wrinkles rather than "Joan" or "Cauchon." It is not surprising therefore that when Béla Balázs, the only film theoretician to investigate close-ups in the cinema, lyricizes about a "microphysiognomy of the faces," he uses *Joan* as one of his examples.[80] The point though is that the approach reawakens our interest in the subject. For Shklovski indeed, "art exists [so] that one may recover the sensation of life; it exists to make one feel things, to make the stone *stony*."[81] Here it is the materiality of the face, its physicality, that demands our full attention. Whom do I see on the screen when I watch Dreyer's film? Is it Joan? A historical character I identify with? Not quite, for I know that an actress (Renée Falconetti) is portraying her. Then is it Falconetti that I am connecting with? But I do not know anything at all about her as a person. Did the actress even think of Joan while acting, did she make use of someone else from her own past, or was she merely reacting physically to the commands of her Danish director's unusual highhanded style? One will never know. What makes the close-ups in *Joan* so eloquent is neither the character nor the star but the naked face of this woman, especially her transfixed eyes which become even more dominant after the cutting of her hair. And the same can be said for all the men around her: the thick lips here, the furry eyebrows there, one judge's strong chin, another's large ears, ordinary features which here become extraordinary and acquire a life of their own. The faces stand before us with the vividness and the texture normally exhibited by age-old trees and formidable craters. Whereas in other films the faces refer us back to the soul of the characters, here the drama of the film is located exclusively on the surface of the skin. And the person that elsewhere I would call "Joan" or "Renée" fades behind the dramatic intensity of her features which cry, suffer, and beg for mercy. They are the ones that call upon me to intervene and help. They force me to pay attention. I see and respond to them as I see and respond to the "stoniness" of the stone.

In contrast, in most films as well as in everyday life, masks are worn. "Those we encounter" in normal circumstances, Levinas writes, "are clothed beings. . . . [They have] washed away the night and the traces of its instinctual permanence from [their] face. . . . What does not enter into the forms [of propriety] is banished from the world. Scandal takes cover in the night, in private buildings, in one's home—places which enjoy a sort of extra-territoriality in the world."[82] Everyday movie faces hence do not let on that which makes them truly human: the "scandals" they perpetrate in the middle of the night when no one is watching. They do not allow themselves to become the mirrors in front of which we too would recognize our own "scandalous" existence. Contrariwise, *ostranenie* rips conventionality from someone's safe presentation. It lets faces be faces. And it can do the same for every body or object on the face of the earth. When we fail to see things then, it is not because the world has nothing more to offer us or we have exhausted their dramatic potential, it is because we do not take enough of a long look. We have become lazy. *Ostranenie* can help us fight our lethargy.


## XIII


To shoot a film is to go to battle. The real war that is taking place is not between the director and the crew, the actors, or the location, it is rather an internal struggle for the soul of the director, a clash between the rational and the unconscious. In the Laser disc version of *El Mariachi* (1992), Robert Rodriguez provides a nonstop commentary on the shooting of the film. The monologue tells us about the practical and aesthetic problems he encountered during the shooting and how he solved them. Truly, Rodriguez must be thanked for being candid about his work and what he says cannot but benefit aspiring filmmakers. Especially important is that he demonstrates it is not necessary to spend thirty million dollars to shoot a film: if I can make a feature film for $7,000, he says, so can you. And he goes about demystifying the whole process of filmmaking. Look at the difficulties I encountered and witness how they were dealt with. I cannot get two actors to appear together? Just shoot them at different times, making sure their gazes cross the camera correctly. That location is no longer available? Shoot in another one, and even if the lighting does not match perfectly, no one will notice. And we must agree with what he says, for the film playing under the audio proves him right—no one would ever pay attention to the small discrepancies. Young filmmakers can certainly learn from all of this.

Yet, when all is said and done, there is something almost superhuman about Rodriguez's lesson of cinema. He knows it all. He is on top of it. You just need to understand film language (editing, shot/reverse shot, the 180-degree line, the 30-degree line, etc.) to solve any problem that may show up. It is not just the process of shooting that Rodriguez successfully demystifies in his commentary, it is the entire idea of cinema as a poetic medium. Cinema, for Rodriguez, is a terribly rational activity dominated by the Hollywood practice where the filmmaker "operates on the assumption that no true mystery, no essential unknown transcending the ego's capacity for comprehension, exists. . . ."[83] In such a view of filmmaking, the director is totally in control of the project and nothing can possibly go awry as long as he or she keeps referring back to the instruction manual. That is not, however, the experience of film communicated by other, moreseasoned directors, men like Ingmar Bergman who do not mind acknowledging he did not have all the answers regarding the transference between the two characters in *Persona* (1966), or Luis Buñuel who commented that "a film takes form outside your will," very much like "a nocturnal voyage into the unconscious."[84]

Surely, one needs to make oneself familiar with the rules that govern the usual syntax of film but, when all is said and done, these rules amount to nothing more than what Roland Barthes called a *studium*. *Studium* belongs to culture. It is the sum of all the codes that control a signifying practice, all that can be learned about it. It is, Barthes writes, "a contract arrived at between creators and consumers."[85] To know the *studium* then is to remain within familiar themes, characters, and techniques, which is exactly what Rodriguez does. First of all, knowing that this track was recorded long after the film got picked up and distributed worldwide by Paramount, I question the timing of his cockiness. Was Rodriguez really that confident during the actual shoot? And what about editing when most directors must face the reality of what they shot: the weaknesses in the performances, the rhythm of the action that just doesn't play well, etc. It is certainly a time when one's original intentions come into question and one's ability as a filmmaker is in jeopardy. And was the original mix such a pleasure for him? For everyone else, it is a humbling experience to realize that most scenes require the sweetening of the sound effects tracks to become at all believable. Let us not pretend then that we are in control. Let us be truthful and acknowledge our shortcomings. Buñuel is right. To a large extent, a film drives itself: a director can only hope to keep it from crashing! At the same time (Buñuel's second point), it is also clear that all kinds of unexpected forces enter the camera from all sides. Rather than foolishly attempting to restrict their entry or, later, claiming authorship over them, let us admit that at times we do not necessarily know why we do certain things in a film. This is, for instance, what Basil Wright said about his documentary film *Song of Ceylon* (1934):

> While I was doing it, I had these extraordinary, inexplicable impulses, which made me shoot sequences and things that I couldn't have logically explained. . . . [Later] they all fell into their places, like the birds flying up, that sort of thing. I had no reason to shoot them; in fact, they were shot at a time when I'd finished for the day and was very tired, but something forced me to shoot a number of shots. . . .[86]

Although unplanned, the birds section is quite lyrical, almost mystical in the film. How refreshing this is compared to Rodriguez! But these moments are never going to appear if directors shut themselves off from the poetic, the irrational, the unknown, the unconscious, the "nocturnal voyage"—for these experiences alone bring magic to the cinema. To make a film the Rodriguez way is to think of movie making as an infinitely controllable assembly line, where every gesture, every move, every technique is planned to the last detail. Certainly *a film is being shot* but the meaning of the sentence has shifted: it is cinema that is being shot. Rather than submit to this, take cover and run. Or, better still, regroup guerrilla-style and resurface when you are ready to take on the world.

When the shooting ends, reality reasserts itself. Max Ophüls once mused about leaving a film behind: "There are no last words," he said, "no apotheosis, no baton to lower. The film instead disintegrates progressively, it slowly founders in a sand pit. For a few days already, the break down has made its mark. People disappear one by one. . . . Suddenly one gets a peek behind the set of the black hole of the studio. . . . The waitress in the food services brings up your bill and the hairdresser wants your autograph. . . . What am I going to do with my afternoon?"[87]

# CHAPTER SIX

# *Lighting*

I

Sun: the world slowly emerges from darkness and displays itself in its manifold diversity. The body wakes up, vivified by the light, and every other living thing responds as well. Temperature rises and the body reaches out, expands, ready to spend its reserve of energy. It is time to go out, make things happen, partake in the life of the entities. Everywhere light strikes, it reveals forms and shapes and provides assurance that everything is as should be. Shadows appear too: they stretch ever so far at first, get reduced to almost nothing at noon, then expand again at the end of the day. Shadows: doubles made of nothing that nevertheless confirm that something is there. Yet, sadly, as the eyes tire of the extraordinary performance that is taking place, light and shadows are quickly taken for granted. It is rather the objects at hand that mesmerize our gaze. In a world of light indeed, Emmanuel Levinas observes, "all is given but everything is at a distance."[1] Our response to light thus conditions our apprehension of space. We do not just see objects as distinct entities, we simultaneously locate them in space. This leads Maurice Merleau-Ponty to muse that "the idea we have of the world would be overturned if we could succeed in seeing the intervals between things (for example, the space between the trees on the boulevard) as objects and, inversely, if we saw the things themselves—the trees— as the ground."[2] In the light of day, however, our eyes remain glued to the entities: they constitute the world of everyday life.

Moon: darkness has set, visibility has shrunken to one's immediate surroundings, uneasy shadows quiver with a life of their own, activities have quieted down, the temperature has dropped, and the body is tired. One feels vulnerable and alone as the surrounding darkness "squeezes you inside yourself."[3] Sounds make you pay attention, suggesting that something is going on over which you have no control. But that is not all: soon the body must give itself to even a darker night, that of sleep when the self may have to face unpleasant dreams and frightening nightmares. And so, against its will, the body surrenders itself to the unknown, to what the Egyptians called the domain of the dead. Night therefore marks a time when the self is forced to renounce any claim of mastery over the world. It is night now that calls the shots, changing the very look of things. Maurice Blanchot described how night takes over in the following terms: "The darkness immersed everything; there was no hope of passing through its shadows, but one penetrated its reality in a relationship of overwhelming intimacy."[4] At night, space is flattened and light and objects fuse, merge, combine into a single thickness without depth.

Fire: flames in the middle of the night. A small flame at first licks the log, attacking it from underneath, searching for its weakest spot, hoping for a draft to secure its hold on the wood. Burning furiously at last, it progressively absorbs the strength of the material, consuming it until little is left. Such powerful fire helps keep at bay our terror of the night. The crackling sputters and fills the ears. The flames dance furiously, protecting us, bringing us warmth, making us capable of seeing our immediate surroundings. Others learn from this: the night watchmen who walk the city at night with their torches, reminding all that the power of the law never sleeps. Indeed, as Gaston Bachelard put it, "everything that casts a light sees,"[5] helping in this case the lawmen identify and control those who would otherwise take advantage of the darkness to prey on the weak or plot against the regime. In contrast, there is also the fire of Bachelard's reverie, the one that shows up after the combustion has reached its climax and the most forceful sparks have been ejected. It is a different kind of fire, more gentle, more civilized, its animus now yielding to its anima, when, instead of the raging flames, burning embers smolder quietly, enduringly, on their own.[6] This is a time for reflection, for compassion, for sharing love. To set a fire then, to watch over it, is to attend to the most basic need of life. Through it all however, eyes remain hypnotized by the endless flicker. In a fire, one watches nothing but the light.

## II

Light dominates our universe: it functions as its heartbeat, helping us count the days. Daily life responds to its rhythm. We are at home in its tempo. We respond to its changes, its moods. We adapt ourselves to a world punctuated by its presence. Throughout our entire life, we bathe in it.

From this, we would assume that of all motion picture techniques lighting would be the one audiences would be the most familiar with. Far from it. Year after year, a few films are nominated for an Academy Award in cinematography, yet most viewers would be at a loss to explain why. At best, people might reflect upon the beauty of some landscape shots or the splendid warm light that reminds them of sunset, but no more. It may be indeed that the phenomenon of light is too familiar, making it difficult to imagine its use in film as a trope. Whatever shows up on the screen is automatically rationalized as the duplication of some natural phenomenon. Even when the lighting is absolutely bizarre (e.g., the blue and pink motif in Rainer Werner Fassbinder's *Lola* [1981]), it is either justified as an effect from some unknown source beyond the limits of the frame or discounted as mere "noise," some strange filtering not really essential for the understanding of the narrative.

One does not get more enlightened when turning to the writing of the professionals in the field (books of interviews or articles about filmmaking in *American Cinematographer*). Vilmos Zsigmond, certainly one of the best and most vocal directors of photography working in Hollywood, is typically hazy when, on the same page, he explains his approach to lighting in the following way: "The first consideration in lighting a set is the nature of the story. . . . The mood of the scene within the story is equally important. . . . The light that establishes the mood of the set is the first lamp I turn on."[7] What are we to make of this, since each consideration may run counter to the other two? Which is the determining factor and why? Is the film's genre—a comedy, a gangster film—the important factor or is it at times overridden by what happens between the characters in one scene? Or should location be the dominant ingredient in establishing Zsigmond's mood? In his writing (and it is representative of most books on lighting), the mood of the locale conveniently also happens to be that of the individual scene as well as that of the film as a whole. No clue is offered to help us out of the morass when that is not the case. Of course, Zsigmond and his peers in the American Society of Cinematographers would know exactly what to do were that situation to arise, but their solution would be hatched more out of experience and intuition rather than clear-cut rules that could be rationally explained.

I do not call attention to Zsigmond's writing to single out the one aberration in an otherwise rational system. Rather it is indicative, in my view, of the vagueness that infiltrates even the best efforts by professionals to explain their work. Put even more bluntly, one could argue that the function of light in motion pictures has never been clearly articulated. Its "history" consists of no more than a bundle of recognizable styles (e.g., "expressionist" lighting which keeps popping up now and then), or a series of authorial motifs on the part of the director of photography (for instance, Zsigmond's own "diffusion" period in his 70's films from *McCabe and Mrs. Miller* [Robert Altman, 1971]and *The Long Goodbye* [Robert Altman, 1973], all the way to *Heaven's Gate* [Michael Cimino, 1980]). On a day-to-day basis, however, lights are being placed on the set here or there because this position has worked well in the past and there is neither the time nor the inclination to study the ramifications of what is being done or investigate possible alternatives. Hence, to understand film lighting, one had better go back to its sources: the Renaissance.

### III

Although a lot has been written about the introduction of monocular perspective in painting (especially its ideological impact on film), the importance of light in the construction of the Renaissance scheme has been left relatively unexamined.[8] In fact, as Oswald Spengler correctly recognized, the introduction in Western painting of light and shadow (the former's acolyte) was absolutely critical in making the visual space inviting or Faustian.[9] Let us take two opposing examples. If we look first at the *Annunciation* by Domenico Veneziano (ca. 1445)—certainly one of the classic texts of the early Renaissance movement in Italy—we can see that its visual construction very much follows the new formula for perspective discovered by Brunelleschi and propagated by Alberti: depth is rendered by retreating lines leading to a vanishing point. With Gabriel on the left and Mary on the right, diminishing tiles on the ground and receding vertical columns help lead the eyes to a garden with a bolted door in the background. Despite the new technique, however, the image fails to convince the viewer that he or she is witnessing an actual scene. Why is that?

Although the light enters from the top right (affiliating it to the natural source in the church where the painting was to be displayed), the effect is too mild and too uniform to truly convince the eyes that what we see is for real. Depth in this instance is told to the mind rather than actually experienced by the senses. The protagonists are pasted on a background instead of standing in it. As a result, the picture remains a communication by the Church rather than a personal viewing. On that level at least, the image is not radically different from the traditional style in pre-Renaissance paintings. Used alone, the adoption of the new perspective rendering kept the pictured space distant, foreign, other.

It is only when light is added alluringly to the scenery that our relation to it is changed radically. Technically, this was done by moving the light more decisively to the side and by emphasizing the effects that normally ensue from that change of position. What are the advantages over the blander approach proposed by Veneziano? For Rudolf Arnheim, side lighting, in Caravaggio's paintings for example, keeps the eyes from wandering.[10] This is true only to some extent: the strong side light used by the painter keeps a portion of the painting in darkness, thus circumscribing what there is to watch. It does not, however, fixate the eyes. In *Doubting Thomas* (ca. 1602), one of Caravaggio's most successful works, the apostles poke the side wound of the resurrected Jesus to make sure it is really him. And, indeed, we do not see beyond the little group. There are no hints to tell us where the scene is taking place. The painting therefore lacks the usual architectural clues, such as those used by Veneziano. To the contrary, everything here is dependent on the lighting to make the viewer accept the scene as a real event. Most importantly, the light source (from the rear on the left of the group) is responsible for the stupendous effects in the foreground. The placement alone makes it possible for the light to wink at the viewer, to invite him or her to come in and visit. As doubting Thomases ourselves, we too get convinced of the reality of Christ's resuscitated body by personally visiting the site. We too poke our gaze in Christ's wound and believe. More irreverently maybe, one could counter Arnheim's argument and suggest that Caravaggio's pictured space becomes the equivalent of an amusement park for the eyes. Surely it makes the eyes want to meander around, from light to darkness and back again, to frolic with the bodies as if they were but jumbles of flesh and cloth. They could also easily get lost in the texture of a someone's skin, climb along the wrinkles of a forehead, reach over the ridge of a nose, slide down the deep furrow of a cheek, spin like a carousel along the folds and pleats of the gowns and garments, ending the visit with a toboggan slide down the rest of the body. All effective lighting, but especially the Chiaroscuro technique made famous by Caravaggio, provides such a trap for the eyes. In this case depth is no longer geometric, it is made fully sensuous. Entities are no longer just recognized, they are apprehended as they appear at that moment, in that light. Directional lighting, the use of shadows, and a clear contrast between light and dark in a scene thus greatly activate the rods and cones in our visual apparatus, provoking activity and beguiling the witness. As the eyes move along the surfaces, explore the layers, brush against the display, they fornicate with the objects in the field, taking them in, essentially internalizing something which is fully external. Light in short thoroughly glamorizes perspective, ravishing the field through its uneven radiations, bewitching viewers' eyes, engaging them in a lustful embrace. As usual André Bazin was not far from the mark when he called light "the original sin of Western Civilization."[11]

IV

Caravaggio's intuitive but forceful use of light was in time systematized, modulated, and softened by academic painters and it is their teaching that cinematographers have emulated in film. To become a member of the nineteenth century elite, to produce an "official art" agreeable to the regime, Thomas Couture reminded his pupils, "you must establish what I call [a] 'dominant' for light and shade effects. . . . Having made this your dominant, you will of course make sure that all other lights are subordinate to it."[12] In these two brief sentences we find the fundamental mystification at the core of motion picture lighting: the semblance of a single light, the reality of several. Yes, when we take a look at a scene, we believe that a single light is being used because all the shadows on the set fall in the same direction. In actuality though, other, less discernible lights are employed for all sorts of reasons. To illustrate what I am talking about, let us take a look at the famous three-point lighting system which is inevitably proposed as the model to follow in all the how-to books on the subject.

The key light, the one light that is perceivable, is generally explained as the nub of the entire lighting in a given scene. The term "key" itself is quite hazy. Is this the key that unshuts a lock, an open sesame! of sorts, implying that, after it is inserted, the natural world magically will make its appearance? Is the key rather the musical tone that connects all other notes to the keynote in a unit of music, thus underscoring the cooperation between separate entities? Or is the key but a sleight of hand that deceives the eyes, a false light whose main job is to make sure that the more marginal lights remain unnoticed? As the key ends up wearing each one of these faces in time, it can also be described as a master key, a *passe partout*, a tool vague enough to fit any situation. It is an unpredictable master to say the least.

The fill light, on the other hand, could very well be written, Derrida-like, under erasure: ~~fill light~~. Although its impact is certain on the film stock (we would not be able to read parts of the actors' faces or the decor without it), tradition dictates that its presence should never be noted by the audience. The fill, for instance, should not provide a secondary shadow anywhere, not on the body of the subject nor on the space behind it. It thus remains the invisible light par excellence.

As for the backlight—that light that shines from the top of the set behind the actors, separating their heads from the background—it usually cannot be naturalized as a light originating from diegetic sources within a scene. Rather the backlight can be described as a *parergon*, a notion explained by Immanuel Kant as an addition to a work of art, something that does not quite belong to it but is there nevertheless.[13] Kant gives as examples the drapery on the "nude" torso of statues and, in architecture, the lines of columns that are added to the main building. "A parergon," Jacques Derrida adds, thus "comes against, besides, and in addition to the *ergon*, the work done, the fact, the work, but it does not fall to one side, it touches and cooperates within the operation from a certain outside. Neither simply outside nor simply inside. Like an accessory that one is obliged to welcome on the border, on board."[14] In motion pictures, unlike the fill light whose impact is pervasive but whose materiality remains unobserved, the effect of the backlight is conspicuous in the lighting scheme. Yet audiences are not supposed to make much of it, certainly not question its origin. It is there, we see the distinctive aura, yet we should discount its presence. But why is it there in the first place? For Derrida, the parergon's "transcendent exteriority comes to play, abut onto, brush against, rub, press against the limit itself and intervene in the inside only to the extent that the inside is lacking. It is lacking *in* something and it is lacking *from itself*. . . . [The core material in fact] needs the supplementary work."[15] In our case, the backlight's very presence implies that without it the lighting would somehow be incomplete, unfinished, less visible, less glamorous. It may also express the gloss of Hollywood or a requirement of the star system. Certainly its presence is paramount in the professional cinema. To sum up, although the backlight is often dismissed by the professional as a supplement not vital to the business at hand, it reveals itself under scrutiny to be essential to the work after all.

Finally, as an extra added at the last minute to the lighting scheme, there is the kicker which from time to time lights a character's fill side from the back. The kicker is often justified by the existence of other lights on the set. It is thus a recoil from the scene itself, a light that jumps at the viewers from the depth of the lighted space. It functions therefore as a baroque light, one that, Gilles Deleuze tells us, is "*pur-dedans*,"[16] a light that owes apparently nothing to external sources. In other words, its presence verifies the self-sufficiency of the lighting scheme in toto.

There we have it, a three-point lighting system which is often a foursome: a visible key often hypostatized as a natural source, an invisible fill under erasure, a backlight-parergon that no one is supposed to notice but whose job is nevertheless beneficial for the lighting scheme as a whole, and finally a kicker, an extra, that pretends that the scene is independently capable of lighting itself.

## V

In other day-to-day practices, lighting is full of paradoxes as well. Unlike the theater where audiences always remain in the same location vis-à-vis the characters, the motion picture camera keeps moving to new positions on the set. In fact the 30-degree continuity rule even mandates that camera changes be made radical enough so as not to provoke a visual discomfort for the viewers. The problem this causes for the lighting scheme, however, is acute. Let us think: when Griffith and others ruptured the integrity of the single scene by allowing for partial views at first (the close-up), radically distinct angles later on, lighting was not yet an issue. At that time, still, the light essentially came from the sky above—glass rooftops and all—providing an unified effect regardless of where the shot was taken from. It is only later, say, with *The Cheat* (Cecil B. De Mille, 1915), that Alvin Wyckoff, the first great lighting director, had to face head-on the massive problems occasioned by this expansion of film language. When light indeed is no longer falling on the set unidimensionally, lighting all in the same manner, when there is instead an uneven distribution of light throughout, with someone's key, fill, and backlight clearly differentiated, what happens to the original apportionment of light when the camera discovers a new angle on the scene? Should the lights stay exactly as they were in the master shot or should they be adjusted to reflect the change in position that has taken place? In other words, do the lights belong to the space or are they floating around the set, endlessly rearranging themselves to accommodate the new visual relation between the characters and the camera? Although totally illogical within the parameters of verisimilitude that supposedly control traditional lighting, the latter situation prevailed. It is nevertheless easy to understand why. Imagine a scene at night where the fill side of a character's face is left virtually without light. This particular choice can be accommodated by throwing some light on the background behind the dark part of the face. By turning it into a silhouette, the technique maintains the integrity of the complete head of the character ahead of the background. What happens though if the camera is required to move to the side and shoot the dark side of the actor? Well, there wouldn't be much to look at. Something clearly needs to be done: for instance, increase the amount of fill light, change slightly the key's position so as to make it reach farther in the fill area, maybe add a little kicker. What this fudging around the edges means is that, in film, light is never constant. Its nature rather is ephemeral, its character volatile. All sorts of adjustments keep breaking down the desired illusion for a stable reality. As each successive shot (close-ups, etc.) modulates the master shot's original lighting setup, transcendental aspirations for a solid world vanish under the weight of vital accommodations. Internal lighting differences thus punctuate the assembly of each scene. Fundamental contradictions infiltrate the core construction of films.

## VI

Having established the dominant scheme that regulates the apportionment of lights on the set, it is now time to pay attention to the plan's overall objective: the naturalization of light. This too follows the general advice given by the academic painter Couture to his students: "Look carefully at your model, decide what is its brightest light, and *situate the light in your drawing at the place it occupies in real life.*"[17] And, true to form, in the movies, the lights we notice seem to originate from diegetic sources: windows for daylight or moonlight, lamps of one kind or another for artificial light. Of course, there are many lighting instruments behind the scene, just off the area made visible by the camera, but, for spectators looking at the finished film, all the light seems to emanate from the "practical" sources visible in the scene. John Bailey, the director of photography, is clear about this: "The first thing I look for is a light source. . . . I have to have an imaginary source even if there's no logic to it. I have to find some place where I could imagine . . . there would be illumination."[18] This insistence is somewhat paradoxical if we remember that, prior to the push for naturalistic lighting by Nestor Almendros and others, movies were far from rigorous in their depiction of everyday light.[19] More recently too, exposure to rock videos have accustomed spectators to unmotivated lighting effects, immunizing them to some extent against the demands of realistic lighting. Taking an extreme example, what do viewers think when Peter Greenaway repeatedly fades daylight in and out during a scene in *A Zed and Two Noughts* (1985)? If they must, spectators may rationalize the unusual event as clouds passing in front of the sun. Most, I would imagine, would simply park the strange phenomenon in the mental annex reserved for all the mysteries normally generated by a text's narrative unfolding. The astonishing event is thus quickly forgotten and does not affect permanently the status of the film.

Why the obsession with naturalistic lighting then? If indeed it is not essential to the fundamental storytelling taking place in a film, what benefits are to be gained from its use? In effect, it is used as a lure. If what we see appears to be but the ordinary display of the world, no special connotations should be derived from the actual activation of light in the studio. Lighting therefore operates with the impunity of an ordinary word in language. Paul de Man explains how the operation works: "In everyday use words . . . are used as established signs to confirm that something is recognized as being the same as before."[20] In a similar manner, natural light (sunlight, moonlight, lamps, etc.) can be used or duplicated so as to hide a profound discontinuity between the characters in a story and the real world they ostensibly live in. "The natural object," de Man continues, "safe in its immediate being, seems to have no beginning and no end. Its permanence is carried by the stability of its being, whereas, a beginning implies a negation of permanence, the discontinuity of a death. . . ."[21] In de Man's own example, no one would question the reason for the being of a flower. Thus the job of the "flower" in a poem is to carry the rest of the words, to invest them as well with "the absolute identity with itself that exists in the natural object."[22] Similarly, as an index of the ordinary world, its guarantor so to speak, naturalized light in film safely hides the presence and exercise of language. It seduces us, making us believe that the characters and their actions belong to the natural order of things. The cover-up hence provides the entire narrative operation with an apparent legitimacy: the scene is for real since it takes place in the real world.

## VII

Although an ideological dividend is already realized from such an operation, other benefits can be gleaned as well. Let us explicate. Say the scene is lighted with a beautiful "sunset" that penetrates the room through Venetian blinds. Certainly, even though the effects may be more beautiful than any we may recall, the light nevertheless reminds us of similar views we have personally experienced. Thus, as Henri Alekan, the grand old man of French cinematography, puts it, such light becomes a

> mood that gives its tone to a film. It calls upon our memory to react to physical phenomena such as cold, rain, fog, sun, heat, or dryness, and come up with psychological equivalents such as annoyance, sadness, mystery, fear, anguish, comfort, joy, gaiety, etc. As these effects produce immediate impressions in viewers, the cinematographer is able to obtain psychological reactions out of mere technical means.[23]

For Alekan then, a mood originating in the external world cues viewers into a specific state of mind. To explain what is at stake here it may be useful to go back to Martin Heidegger's discussion of mood or *Stimmung*. The key to the German thinker's entire philosophy is that we are not beings functioning independently from the rest of the world. Rather, we must deal with a specific, historical world from day one. *Stimmung* as a result reflects more than the momentary internal feeling of an individual.[24] Although experienced within the body, it nevertheless springs from the outside, expressing affinity or disjunction toward some aspect or situation encountered there. Far from a *personal* sentiment, it evidences the reflex action of the body to nonsubjective, extraneous conditions. As Heidegger puts it, moods are "the sort of thing that determines being-with-one-another in advance. It seems as if, so to speak, a mood is in each case already there, like an atmosphere in which we are steeped and by which we are thoroughly determined."[25]

*Stimmung* can thus express someone's alienation when visiting, say, a solicitor's waiting room and finding oneself out of place because the people there look, speak, and behave in totally unexpected ways, a situation well described by Christine Edzard in her *Little Dorrit* (1988). Worse, as in Bergman's *The Silence*, a traveler can find herself in a country whose foreignness is impenetrable: not only is the language unintelligible but the street manners are baffling and the men are all somewhat threatening. On the contrary, in most films, there is no discontinuity between what characters are experiencing and the external *Stimmung*. Not only does naturalized light manifest the *Stimmung* of the locale, the arrangement, somewhat miraculously, also fits the tone of the scene and the concerns of the characters. An entire bundle of separate functions are thus made to coincide within a single package. As the lighting seemingly duplicates the mood of one and all, nature is made to synchronize itself with the ups and downs of mere humans. It is domesticated, made to service individuals (the diegetic characters as well as the technicians who orchestrate it all). The combination thus provides a powerful Wagnerian *Gesamtkunstwerk* effect: everything moves at once in complete synchronicity. Nature as a result manifests the same uncanny behavior as a Disney animal. By hiding the discontinuities between the personal feelings of fictional characters, the *Stimmungen* belonging to a group, a place, or a historical situation, and the real world of everyday life, film lighting invests the fiction with hallucinatory powers.

## VIII

Other filters may also be at work in film lighting. To uncover them, I would like to bring in the phenomenological questioning attempted by Edmund Husserl at the beginning of the century. In *Logical Investigations*, Husserl strove to bracket the thorny philosophical issue of the actual existence of the world beyond our sense awareness of it by focusing exclusively on the intentionality of consciousness. In his view, "there are . . . not two things present in experience, we do not experience the object and beside it the intentional experience directed upon it, there are not even two things present in the sense of a part and a whole which contains it: only one thing is present, the intentional experience, whose essential descriptive character is the intention in question."[26] Husserl's insight therefore involves the absolute intertwining of the mind's commandeering drive and the perception that is the object of its quest. We cannot just "think," we always think of someone or something in particular. The internal thrust thus attaches itself onto the object. In the philosopher's words, the intentional act will "present *just this object in just this manner.*"[27]

For Husserl, the stream of consciousness method, the phenomenological description of the object as it appears to the mind alone, made possible a true description of the world. Leaving aside Husserl's grand design, what interests me here is the idea that we cannot access the world independently from our informing consciousness, that the latter always projects some understanding over whatever one is exposed to (a reverse *Stimmung* so to speak). Nothing, in other words, remains for very long just there, outside of us, on its own. Everything is immediately reified. Now in exceptional encounters, there may be a small delay because of the novelty of a situation but, generally speaking, as the transmission arrives from the visual apparatus, the mind seizes upon a facet of the object out there and holds it for our potential use. Instantly, the clues activate a search for meaning based on what shows up in our memory bank. There are thus always markers to read, hints to decipher, plays that refer back to our own experience. Soon enough, we end up categorizing what was new or foreign just seconds before, making it possible to proceed forward assured that nothing is remiss.

Film lighting uses this drive for meaning by the mind by parceling the visual text with all sorts of cues. Like Little Red Riding Hood, the director of photography carefully lays his/her gems along the way to make sure spectators easily pick up the track. In the end, the "sunset" is not just a sunset anymore. It is fused with intentionality. Its job is to clarify the scene, pointing to what is essential in it. This is why Alekan prefers "sunlight" as a source: "Sunlight is not only unidirectional, it is also partisan in nature. It models forms and contours, *it designates the object*, it underlines, defines, sharpens, sculpts, and emphasizes what is essential in forms, putting aside what is less important. It is a light that hierarchizes and classifies: it speaks loud and clear."[28] The lighting choice thus spells out the meaning of the scene: it brings one's attention quickly to the main character, the principal action. It helps us find our way through the mass of informations present on the screen. It functions as a kind of editing: underlining the main object, erasing or softening the unnecessary details.

But what if another type of daytime lighting is used, one that Alekan is suspicious of? He writes: "To the contrary, diffuse lighting—

through the multiplicity of the rays that wrap up the object from all sides—disperses one's attention to what is around; it drowns the essential in a sea of secondary details. Light in this case, far from defining, combines, fuses, and synthesizes. Such a light is troubling for it cancels out the clarity of the object."[29] Almendros could not disagree more. For him, "very seldom do people have spotlights in their houses."[30] It is therefore in the name of realism that he subverts the old regime in his films. In earlier days, artists (Mondrian) and theorists (Eisenstein) might have connected sunlight with a masculine outlook, diffuse light with a feminine one. And Bazin could have deemed indirect light more democratic in spirit than hard light. Realism notwithstanding, Almendros no less than Alekan makes sure the image can be decoded quickly and efficiently. His indirect light still happens to call attention to the character in the middle of the room and if it does not, he will immediately provide other mechanisms that will direct the viewers' eyes toward that area: motion, color, or the graphic positioning of lines and other vectors in the shot. All in all, in perfect accord with Husserl's principle, a light cannot just be itself, it is always invested with extrinsic intentions.

Subtle or not, hierarchical or not, lighting ends up regulating our access to the field. It tells us where to look. It ameliorates daily conditions by pointing out the important players. It signifies rather than shows. To put it in Sharon A. Russell's words, "the object no longer exists as a real thing but rather as a potential image."[31] To explicate the issue, let us make use of Emmanuel Levinas's summation of Husserl's idea of intentionality: "What emerges outside the subject is made sense of, 'enlightened'—that is to say: it is made to spring back [as if it originated] from within. It is through this internal light that objects become a world . . . that the world is given and apprehended . . . that the object, while arising from without, is grasped inside within a horizon that precedes its arrival."[32] The very process of intentionality therefore "makes possible this enveloping of the external by the inward. . . ."[33] Even in plain, unadorned meetings, the other quickly becomes ensnared within a construct of which he/she knows nothing. If we agree with the argument, it becomes clear that motion picture lighting takes full advantage of the necessary working of the mind. Not only does it do this in a general sense insofar as spectators witness what appears to be a natural phenomenon, it also manipulates that process from within the very core of the scene.[34] We have already seen how strong atmospheres suggest specific moods in the minds of spectators. But lighting operates beyond this, for everything else it touches is similarly impregnated with meaning. Peter Baxter is quite right when he insists that lighting does not impose meaning from the outside; rather "it beats in the very atmosphere through which the players walk."[35] For example, by sharply isolating certain elements in a shot at the expense of others, the delineation brings the image forward as a text that is easy to read. These accommodations of course are fabricated in advance by the technicians in charge and positioned within the field. Later on they are picked up by the viewers as they scan the scene. Lighting thus subverts the individual psychic process by loading up the scene with effects whose sole function is to comment on that very same scene. In other words, a whole group of intentional notations are projected onto the elements of the scene, incorporated in them, fused to the point where it becomes impossible for spectators to separate the object from its wrapping. Husserl's understanding of intentionality projected by the subject has thus been hijacked: the sticky stuff of intentionality is now professionally manufactured by outsiders and made to adhere onto the scene. This technique underlines not only Hollywood practice but most other cinemas as well. On the plus side, to be sure, the meaning of the scene is keynoted in a world that becomes effortlessly decodable. The world appears to speak to us simply, effectively, no questions asked. Every word, every gaze, every gesture, every mood is immediately imbricated within an interpretative web within the text. Desire is satisfied and pleasure is granted.

Since a scene which appears to be drenched in natural light is now permeated with a signification external to itself, a wrench has been thrown into the perceptual process. In other words, a semiotic screen sheathes the characters, the action, and the locale. Something has been added to the scene out there—a veil, a coloring, a veneer—to enforce a specific meaning to be picked up by the spectators. Motion picture lighting thus circumvents the mechanism that infuses everyday encounters. It deprives viewers of the precious few seconds when something is perceived in its distinct otherness before intentionality seizes and reifies the scene. Using once again his favorite example, Levinas reminds us that "the nakedness of the face is not what shows itself to me when I make sense of it—a face that is now mine, that belongs to me, to my eyes, to my senses, in a light exterior to itself. Rather the face confronts me—and that is its nudity. It *is* by itself and not in relation to somebody else's mental projection."[36] Through the cinematographer then, the director manipulates what could be different and other until it resonates with nothing but the same. Even more dramatically than in the normal day-to-day encounters described by Levinas, the meeting between characters and viewers becomes "a world of the me-only, a world that erases otherness from the picture of the other, a world in which the other becomes just another self, an alter ego known congenially through a return to one's own core."[37] Instead of keeping open the space between two entities (the character and the viewer), motion picture lighting fills the gap between them, smoothes over the difference, joins them so to speak through an umbilical cord that remains for the most part unobserved and unexamined.

Because the cloaking of the world by conventional lighting tends to make use of known stylistic figures (figures that have worked their way through mass consciousness till they have become nothing more than stereotypes), the others present in the field are siphoned through a sieve that quickly reduces them to a repertory of clichés. Even when they beg, their faces never actually demand anything of viewers. Traditional lighting thus deprives us of a defining moment of existence. Because we are not exposed to something truly outside ourselves, the movie world remains unchallenging and our responsibility toward the other nil.

## IX

So far we have taken for granted that light is a natural everyday phenomenon. Interestingly, in the Bible, God created the sun and the moon only on the third day, whereas light preceded everything else on the first day. What are we to make of this gap between sources and effect? Even more paradoxically perhaps, when God, to initiate the creation, said "'Let there be light!' and there was light," even God could not be sure that anything at all had been activated: "Darkness was [still] upon the face of the deep." This of course makes sense since light itself is invisible, its rays bouncing back and making visible only what already exists and stands in their way. In film, for example, light can be "seen" filling space only after smoke, fog, talcum powder, whatever is thrown into the air so that the light rays have a chance to hit the minute particles and join with them in the production of a beam of light. That invisible first light thus functioned as a backdrop against which all other aspects of the divine creation, including the sun and the moon, would later be revealed. In my view, this original light stands very much as an analogon for Martin Heidegger's notion of *Lichtung*.

For Heidegger, the question forgotten by Western philosophy throughout its history is the question of being. Almost immediately, from

Greek time onwards, the inquiry moved from being to human beings. Heidegger's focus, to the contrary, aims at bringing back philosophical thinking to what he was certain was the proper question: what does "to be" mean? Surely beingness is not a thing or a property that anyone can produce at his or her leisure. And certainly all the things that are, not just human beings, partake in it. Yet, although all entities share in it, only humans have the potential to question its essence. Most of the time, however, the issue of beingness remains clogged in the filter of daily life. What Heidegger called "ontic" preoccupations necessarily overwhelm factical life at the expense of ontological awareness—that which is directed toward beingness. Not unlike light therefore, beingness permeates every aspect of life, yet, most of the time, we remain strangely unaware of it. Instead, we take full advantage of what the world offers us and carry on, fully absorbed in schemes of all sorts. The externality of the world vanishes. We make it into "our" world, the world we discover through our consciousness, the world that works for us, where we can make things happen. As a result, we do not really see ourselves in that other, ontological dimension, and neither do we observe others and other entities that way. Every sight, every reaction is interpreted in terms of a personal or collective narrative. In this way, we live from day-to-day without recognizing the forbidding strangeness of our situation. Yet, for Heidegger, there is barrenness underneath our chatter. There is hollowness under our glibness. There is a radical vacuity at the core of life. Levinas goes even farther. For him "the face of the *there is* is horror."[38]

In Heidegger's terms, there is a crucial difference between *Licht* (light) and *Lichtung* (an opening, a clearing in the forest). "Light can stream into the clearing, into its openness," he writes, "and let brightness play with darkness in it. But light never first creates openness."[39] *Lichtung* then is rather like the first illumination of the Bible, the invisible illumination that preceded the work of the sun, the moon, and, later on, all sorts of artificial sources. It has therefore nothing to do with the ontic sources of light duplicated by film lighting. In other words, whereas light makes possible the world of everyday life, a *Lichtung* takes place only at the moment that one becomes conscious that something is amiss. One may suddenly feel at odds with everything familiar, disconnected from family, friends, neighbors, work, etc. For most people, such a moment arises only when facing death. As one is seized by angst, the facticity of everyday life becomes clear. At once, an unbreachable gap separates that man or woman from all that is around.

In the *Lichtung,* beingness comes briefly to the surface, breaks through the skin, makes itself known to consciousness.

Let me rehearse the argument again. In everyday life, the world is made manifest, entities appear, beings disclose themselves, etc. "Beings can be as beings," Heidegger writes, "only if they stand within and stand out within what is lighted in this lighting. Only this lighting grants and guarantees to us humans a passage to those beings that we ourselves are not, and access to the being that we ourselves are."[40] Everyday light thus allows us our humanity. Yet, as Levinas is quick to point out, this light is also deceitful. Although it makes it possible for us to see things and beings in the world as "other than myself," it is nevertheless formulated "as if it came from me," thus actually denying the otherness of these others.[41] This is the light we are familiar with, a light which, even though it originates from elsewhere, circumscribes everything in the world as a spectacle for my eyes.

For Heidegger, on the contrary, in such light, "a being can be *concealed* . . . within the sphere of what is lighted."[42] For the thinker indeed, the being displayed by the light can refuse him/herself to us or can put on a façade that keeps us at bay. In other words, something shows up in the light but we should not make too much of it. "Precisely because letting be always lets beings be in a particular comportment which relates to them and thus discloses them, it conceals beings as a whole."[43] What we access at that moment is but a facet of the entity; it is a partial illumination at best, an incomplete sketch. "The lighting in which beings stand," he concludes, "is in itself at the same time concealment."[44] In other words, light hides as much as it reveals.

There is thus another movement available to lighting. This is what Heidegger refers to when he tells us that "concealment as refusal is not simply and only the limit of knowledge in any given circumstance, but the beginning of the lighting of what is lighted."[45] Expressed differently, one could say that there is the possibility of a latent image hidden within the regular image, of a *Lichtung* within the usual lighting. Again, whereas traditional lighting reveals but one surface of things, a *Lichtung* may open up the beingness of a being. Or it can indicate that a refusal or concealment is taking place. At other times, it can allude to the darkness that permeates the very fabric of light, implying that something not yet known lurks within what is plainly lighted. Whereas light brings a scene into view, *Lichtung* denies that all is there, that everything has been said. The *Lichtung* in other words maintains the essential mystery of beingness. It therefore also expresses a more fundamental stage in film lighting.

It matters little then what kind of "ontic" lights are being used. At the beginning of *I Do Not Know What It Is I Am Like* (Bill Viola, 1986), for instance, we look at buffalo roaming on a prairie. It is bright daylight. It takes only a few seconds though to realize we are not watching a typical Hollywood Western. What makes the difference in this case is that the buffalo are kept on the screen, without zoom or cutting, much longer than we are accustomed to. They are left to themselves, in the vastness of the land and the endlessness of time. One beast pushes ahead, another takes a long pee. In the distance, a storm makes itself known. An opening is thus brought to pass. Hence *Lichtung* is not dependent upon light. The scene can be brightly or darkly lighted, the source natural or artificial, the style high key or low key, the color warm or cold. In fact, no style of lighting is really adequate to the task. As the *Lichtung* cannot be observed as a light, it is encountered through the entities themselves. On the surface, the entities have not changed but they now disclose themselves otherwise than just before. Unaccountably, something comes into the open: it is not stable and it may not last for very long, yet we come face-to-face with it. A *Lichtung* therefore extends the breadth of the film image. There is a break, a gap in the flow of the film. Time is stopped. Something transcendental insinuates itself within the discourse.

To take another example, some directors have at times become fascinated by the doubling that can take place in front of the camera. One can think of such instances in the work of Theodor Dreyer, Ingmar Bergman, and Jean-Luc Godard. Because the unusual demands of these directors expose actors in ways that force them out of zones they are comfortable with, the players may abruptly experience a breakdown of sorts. Maybe they are exhausted, maybe they have reached once too often inside themselves, but something happens and all at once they seem lost. For a short moment, the actor is done for, his or her bag of tricks empty. What is left is the face of someone who has run out of options. The words, the dialogue, the expressions, the gestures, may be the same as in previous takes but now they originate within a different context. On the screen, without notice, someone appears who is neither the character nor the actor.

In rare instances, a film may probe longer and further. One such film is *The Second Circle* (Alexander Sokurov, 1990). Darkness dominates the entire film. It is as if the world were condemned to go on in the gloom of lightlessness. Not only does the action take place mostly at night, snow continually falls, further reducing visibility outdoors. Indoors, bare bulbs keep much of the rooms in total darkness. Even the grains of the film stock contribute to the overall effect by blocking our attempt to penetrate the space. More than in most films, light, camera, and sound are not enrolled to dramatize the action. Static long takes make us confront the dread experienced by the character following the death of his father in a cabin somewhere in the Russian steppe. The man's face too is unremittingly naked, keeping our identification at bay. As a result, we are literally forced back onto ourselves, onto our own pain of being.

In a *Lichtung*, the usual world breaks down, characters are no longer coopted by the demands of a driving narrative, actors briefly forget what they otherwise know so well, and a film escapes the cultural pattern that normally keeps the world a safe and familiar place. Instead, another realm of experience is exposed, one in which the naked face of the other strips the mask that usually protects us. In the *Lichtung*, the face of the deep makes itself known.

X

There are good reasons then why the language of light has remained highly unstable, why the technical explanations by the experts do not really elucidate film practice. For them, certain things are better left unsaid. To question the foundations of their life's work would be to open a can of worms. Better to go on as before. To counter the professional attitude, take a chance, *expose* yourself. Escape the safe *pose*, the deadness of a shoot when the illumination proceeds in an orderly, methodical, unimaginative fashion. Open yourself up instead to the magical vitality of light. Sense the kind of wonderment the Greeks experienced when looking at the world around them. How do you engage the process? It is night. Obscurity surrounds you. Take a lamp in your hands. Switch it on. Now slowly move the beam of luminous rays across the surrounding space. Notice how shapes and forms appear and disappear, how they reveal themselves, then change as you move the lamp around. Feel your power as you do so: the entities respond to your call, they manifest themselves. Switch off the light. Sense the loss as everything falls back into darkness, into the unknown, into nothingness once again.

When you strike a light you partake in something momentous. Remember that light is one of the four elements. Light rays consist of *air*.

They enter a lens (from its Latin root: something convex like a lentil, a pod that belongs to the *earth*). The rays go through the iris (Iris is the goddess of the rainbow which shines when *water* is present). They end up on the film, focused (in Latin: the hearth), starting a *fire* there, branding its skin. To light and shoot a film thus calls less for a filmmaker than a firemaker. To light the fire, to carry the torch: there is your challenge, your duty, your mission.

# CHAPTER SEVEN

# *The Frame*

## I

What is a camera? Are they all alike? Jean-Luc Godard does not think so, astutely pointing to the changes that are bound to take place on the set depending on whether you use one type or another.[1] Essentially, for him, there is the large professional camera, such as the one seen at the beginning of *The Bad and the Beautiful* (Vincente Minnelli, 1952): the Mitchell, the Technicolor camera, the Panaflex. These cameras dominate the set. They sit on their throne as obese monarchs, surrounded by a bevy of attendants, constantly being fed, spritzed, made plumb. Worse, they command the budget, demand the top stars, and dictate how the film will be shot. Who the director is does not matter anymore: the system is in charge. And then there is the more modest camera that Godard so wanted: the Aaton 35, more portable, more personal, a lightweight camera that can be used as a writer uses a pen.[2]

Fat or lean, each camera always exceeds your own use of it. You cannot ever own one. (Very few professionals actually do; they are too expensive). A *camera*, let us remember, is but a little dark room with a gate and a shutter: through the former you welcome some guests, through the latter you time their entrance just right. This process of inclusion and exclusion, of coordination and duration, is never final though: midway through shooting, you may reconsider your options and greet visitors you never thought of inviting in the first place. And, of course, others using

171

the same camera would have a completely different selection of guests. The camera therefore stands metaphorically for everything one can possibly shoot. It is but another word for language. Speaking like Heidegger, one could say that the camera is the little dark house of being.

II

Many people never consider the presence of the frame at all. For them, the left and the right borders are more like book ends, the bottom line is the floor and the top the ceiling. They just do not see beyond these markings. The only thing they care about is that, in the middle of the screen, there is a hole through which they have a clear view of what is important: the action that is taking place or the face of the person who is talking. The rectangular screen is therefore just a place that offers an opening onto the narrative universe, a world that makes perfect sense, where one easily understands what is going on. One can relax and enjoy the show. For such viewers then, to use Jacques Derrida's words, "there is frame, but the frame does not exist."[3]

Quite possibly we do not question the existence of strong horizontal and vertical borders around images because we are so accustomed to them. Yet, these perfectly perpendicular lines that we take for granted do not exist anywhere in nature, which is the reason why Rudolf Arnheim labels them "Cartesian coordinates."[4] For him indeed, the use of rigid lines "visibly ruptures the fraternity of all things in nature through a promotion of only a few of its aspects."[5] In other words, we isolate certain features at the expense of others. From this we should learn that these perpendiculars press upon us a very unnatural way of seeing, that the end product is a cultural display rather than an indigenous phenomenon.

What should the contours of the cadre be like? In painting and photography, the frame often supports the general outlook of the subject matter. To take Arnheim's own examples, a distant landscape calls for a dominant horizontal shape whereas waterfalls and full-size portraits generally summon a vertical shape.[6] Alas, the need to standardize the equipment has kept the motion pictures' aperture gate much less adaptable to the patterns of specific subjects. It is therefore shocking to recall the consistent failure of the industry to come up with a sensible solution to the question of a uniform frame. Early on, many formats vied for dominance. Obviously each variation provided advantages and disadvantages when compared to others. For instance, W. K. L. Dickson, Thomas Edison's point man in the invention of the Kinetograph, once experimented with the circle back in the early 1880s. This would have brought to film the *tondo* dear to many Renaissance painters, the perfect round shape that is totally self-sufficient. And, in 1930, Eisenstein submitted to the Academy a strong defense of the "dynamic square," for him the only shape capable of answering all the visual demands of a multiform cinema. It was only when horizontals met verticals on a neutral ground, he wrote, that "the struggle, the conflict of both tendencies" could be activated.[7] In Hollywood, unsurprisingly, the idea of a square image was received with little enthusiasm. It was judged to be "static, nondynamic, and inappropriate for typical motion picture dramatic content."[8] For American filmmakers indeed, content had always been synonymous with the expansive action of individual characters in space, hence their preference for the horizontal rectangle, whereas Eisenstein was more concerned with the dialectical possibilities offered by a frame that did not impose the same vector on all scenes. In this part of the film, he thought, the horizontal elements within the shot should triumph, elsewhere the vertical factors should best their opponents. Once in a while, they would clash for dominance. And, throughout, there would be relations, conflicts, and counterpoints to the rest of the formal values present in the film: light, shadows, angles, volumes, planes, sounds, etc. In the end, it was no contest: the "creeping rectangles" won out—first the moderate ones that Eisenstein already condemned in his day, later the exacerbated ones that came in with anamorphic technology and other "wide screen" formats in the fifties.[9]

What is disgraceful about the endless format wars is the fact that aesthetic considerations never prevailed over more pedestrian concerns. Dickson, for instance, worked out the first aspect ratio as a compromise between technical and financial determinants.[10] As for the Academy, in 1930, it sheepishly went back to a slightly modified version of Dickson's format after a debate full of generalizations and commonplaces. And, in the fifties, 20th Century Fox was more concerned with making a commercial splash with Cinemascope than establishing a better standard for the industry in general. The riposte of the other studios—the "wide screen" nonanamorphic system—was also standardized without a thought given to compositional requirements. Finally, no format has been able to play on television without some loss of the original picture surface. What we see there involves either a shrinking of the frame, some modification of its original borders, or a complete reframing and recutting of the film—the infamous pan-and-scan technology. Practically then, unlike painters and photographers, filmmakers have continually worked with less than secure markers.

## III

Regardless of the size and shape of the gate, do all professionals organize their images the same way? Is there a governing principle justifying what they do? What is composition really about? For Vilmos Zsigmond, clarity is the most important job of the cinematographer. "It's very important," he tells us, "where you place the main actors within the composition so that the eye will be attracted to them right away. . . . It helps sort out what things the eye wants to see and in what order it wants them."[11] For him then the first job of composition is to simplify the view, to isolate what is important in it, dramatizing it to some extent. So far so good: nobody in the American Society of Cinematographers would disagree with him. Where we get into something of a squabble is with the other motifs that also influence the composition of a shot. For Gordon Willis, for instance, there is also the impact of "symmetry, first of all. . . . After that, the rest of these elements finish it off and make it right. But the initial thrust of it is always on symmetry."[12] Conrad Hall, however, is not so sure. To him this way of thinking is old fashioned:

> I think it's valuable to learn how to compose the way Michelangelo or other great painters did. . . . They're great artists, no question about it . . . but hell, you've got to be able to do it yourself. You've got to be able to do it the way you want to and know why it is you're doing it. And at least if you don't know intellectually, you know emotionally that it's right. It feels right to you.[13]

John Bailey shares that view as well: "I think that for any given shot there are a number of elements that, at different times, may have greater or lesser value. . . . So there's really no formula for it." In his view, the important elements in composition are "color, the focal length of the lens, movement, structural balance and focus."[14] But that is not all, as Laszlo Kovacs is quick to add, for "the major criterion of a good composition is whether it supports emotionally the scene and its dramatics. . . . You don't make beautiful compositions just for the sake of making compositions."[15]

Composition therefore is not just a pictorial matter: what happens in the narrative also helps the cinematographer in deciding the exact disposition within each shot. But how do we coordinate all these objectives? Is clarity more important than structural balance? Should colors also provide symmetry? Do these considerations vary with each shot? And what do we do when they clash with one another? To top off the discussion, Billy Williams even questions whether composition can ever be learned. He says: "It's something that you're born with. . . . There are people who can never compose properly."[16] For professionals, of course, the operation is instinctive. They know it when they see it. Zsigmond, for instance, declares: "composition is in my blood. I walk into a room and I set the camera and it's there; I cannot explain why."[17]

What do we gather from this discussion? Mostly that clarity is the leading consideration of cinematographers and that the other parameters (symmetry, color, movement, etc.) most often remain subservient to the meaning of the scene as a whole. Beyond that, cinematographers fall back upon intuition to explain how the job gets done rather than point to clear cut rules. What this innate sense consists of is not certain: one suspects it could very well be no more than a largely unconscious assimilation of compositions in thousands of films the technicians have seen and admired.

IV

How do we make the composition clear? What does it mean in practice? In many films, the solution is to bring the frame around the subject. This makes sense because traditionally the center is the place of honor, it is where the eye goes first. The very action of shooting something implies that we value it on some level and therefore it stands to reason we would offer it the position in the picture against which everything else is balanced. Furthermore, as Rudolf Arnheim remarks, "a sense of permanence goes with the central position."[18] What is less important or transitory is therefore pushed back to the periphery. If we have a group of people in the frame, for instance, they are often positioned within the field according to their relative importance. This approach goes all the way back to religious paintings where the divinity necessarily occupies the visual center of the picture, surrounded first by angels and saints, then by bishops and other servants of the Church, and finally, on the outskirts or very small at the bottom, by the faithful. Similarly, in many family group pictures, the center is generally occupied by the elders, their children behind them, the in-laws farther out, and the grandchildren sitting down at the feet of the grown-ups. One way to conceptualize the power of the central position is to think of it as a strong magnet surrounded by a series of concentric circles: the farther out, the less "attached" or dependent the individuals are.

Likewise, what does it mean to have someone isolated at the margins of a frame? For Arnheim, "every component not located in the center needs a justification for that deviation from the base, i.e., there must be a clearly defined force that keeps the object away from that base."[19] Whoever stands at the margins is therefore either banished by the strong center or is creating some breathing room between that center and him/herself. If the former, it is a question of authority. If the latter, a stand is being taken, an affiliation rejected, and a challenge evoked. In both cases then, someone's position in the frame is indicative of power relations and visual dramatics are used to tell us what is going on between these people.

Any visual organization, applied continuously without variations, may, however, become tedious for the artist as well as the viewers. It makes sense therefore that, almost from the start, Renaissance artists investigated alternatives to the centrality of the most important character and the hier-archical staging favored by the painters who preceded them. In clear oppo-sition to Leonardo's conventionally staged, frontal *Last Supper* (ca.1495–98), Tintoretto radically rearranged Christ and the apostles in unconventional diagonal formations. As a result, a tiny Jesus is relocated to the furthest region of the painting. Although a Christian contemporary of the painter would have no trouble locating him in the little group because of his halo, the actual center of the painting is nevertheless no longer occu-pied by the most important personage in the narrative. The gain for Tin-toretto is that his somewhat irreverent treatment infused his paintings with a visual dynamism lacking in Leonardo's classic deployment of the apostles around a safe, stable leader. Clearly these rule-breaking views expanded our repertoire so that today it is possible to position the action in all areas of the frame without fear of losing clarity by doing so.

## V

Composition involves more than the mere disposition of people and objects within a frame. Paradoxically this became evident through the use of video assist technology. Today indeed, more often than not, directors are watching the scene on a video monitor instead of looking at it directly.[20] This behavior has irked some technical people who have been around long enough to know better. At a recent meeting of the American Society of Cinematographers at the University of Southern California, for instance, Victor Kemper voiced many complaints against the new generation of directors who, he said, had grown up sitting too close to their TV sets. These directors as a result feel equally at home sitting just inches away from their little video monitors. Because of that, Kemper added somewhat cryptically, they cannot see the composition of the pictures.[21] Members of the audience balked at this: after all, doesn't video assist make it possible for the director to verify the operator's composition? Kemper countered by suggesting that these directors were no longer looking at things "from the periphery of their eyes." He was right of course. *Compositio* does not relate exclusively to what is inside the frame, it involves primarily a relation between what is captured and the larger context which always exceeds it. This means remaining aware at all times of the entire surroundings *beyond* the camera's view of them. In contrast, today's directors are often ensconced in front of their monitors, protected left and right by large shades that keep ambient light away from their video screens. So, unlike Robert Bresson who urges himself (and others) to "find, for each shot, a new urgency over and above what I had imagined,"[22] these directors function as if nothing else could possibly be gathered from the scene once they have laid out their initial plans. In other words, they give up on possibilities yet unexpressed by the scene at its rehearsal stage. To shoot, for them, becomes merely a question of recording on film what has been planned during the rehearsal: did this show up well, was it done effectively? For Kemper, something gets lost in this approach. To counter the impact of video assist, the filmmakers should get back on track, remaining "ubiquitous in some way—one eye in the viewfinder, the other open to the outside—so as to become available to what is taking place beyond the borders of the frame."[23] Video assist directors instead, with blinders left and right, display only tunnel vision. No longer experiencing the open field of the world, they have let themselves become the first spectators of a premature presentation.

## VI

Yet another departure remains possible for our understanding of composition. Because a film is made up of shots and involves duration, composition can also entail sequential connections. This is probably what Jean-Luc

Godard had in mind when he remarked that "today one doesn't know how to frame anymore. Most films confuse framing with the window in the camera, whereas composition consists in knowing when to initiate the action and when to cut it."[24] If I understand Godard correctly, it is the "music" generated by a film that we should pay attention to: as a shot unrolls itself in time, it functions as a "note" answering another note, preparing us for the subsequent one. And it is only when all of them have been played out that one has a sense of the melody or the "composition" in the piece. Let us take a familiar example: a conversation between two people. The first character is shown in a close-up on the left side of the screen, looking right. For the time being, the frame is somewhat out of balance. But, as soon as we go to the reverse shot, bringing in the second character, placing him on the right side of the screen looking left, the balance between the two spaces is found anew. What happened in this case is that there was a delay in the realization of the composition. Hitchcock provides us with a marvelous example of this at the beginning of *Vertigo* (1958). In the scene, Scotty (James Stewart) is being urged by his old schoolmate to investigate the comings and goings of his wife. As the scene proceeds, shots succeed one another in almost a musical manner, all the while telling us a great deal about who is winning the argument. Masters versus singles, who is standing and who is sitting, the distance between the two men, even the room they are speaking from (the conference room that is adjacent to the husband's office happens to be two steps higher), every device in Hitchcock's arsenal is activated to modulate what would otherwise be dull exposition material. A cinematographer thus does not necessarily compose each shot as if it were a complete unit. Rather he or she must weigh the entire scene, understand the multiple units of power, their change or evolution *over time*, and find an overall scheme that will bring out visually the core meaning of that scene. In a word, film composition embraces relations between shots as much as conventional displays of forces within them.

## VII

So far we have looked at the frame from the point of view of the filmmakers. The audience, however, has nothing to look at but the image itself. Or is there more? To be sure the role of the cadre for the narrative imaginary created by the film has been the object of a lively debate among theorists. André Bazin, as usual, started the ball rolling when, using judicious examples from the mature work of Jean Renoir, he compared the borders of the frame to that of a hideout behind which the bustle of life never stops.[25] As for the other corner, it is certainly not lacking in supporters. One of them, Gilles Deleuze, hinted at the difference when he described the early cinema casing as one where participants enact "eternal poses" in perfectly "immobile sections."[26] For Deleuze these "sets" (his term for the ensemble formed by the camera position and the scene) are closed: nothing at all exists beyond what we see. One can thus oppose two very different notions of the frame: one expansive as it implies, metonymically, the continuation of the visible world of the characters beyond the borders of the frame, the other restraining as it limits the visual construct to the immediately given.

Bazin rightly postulated that, when the character exits the theater stage, there is no place for him or her to go. The actor may stand in the wings but the character is suspended without anything to do. In a movie, however, the character keeps on going. He or she may be out of sight but the diegetic world lives on. This, for the French critic, was an essential fact of the cinema. It is only more conveniently demonstrated for us when the staging systematically emphasizes the lateral possibilities of the frame as Renoir does in *The Rules of the Game* (1939). In one memorable shot in that film, the camera looks down a long hallway shot in depth. The guests say good night to each other, then enter their respective "rooms." Yet, as we see only the hallway, it is we and we alone who create these rooms in our head. By the same token, it is almost impossible, when we watch a film, not to expand mentally a few buildings into an entire street or a street into a city. For Bazin then, film technique consistently urges us to complete what is not yet provided by the shot. In other words, our experience of the world in daily life completes the partial views the movies give us with what should logically be there. There is smooth continuity between what is seen and what is imagined, between visual signifiers and everyday referents. In a Gestalt-like habit of good continuation, the picture on the screen underwrites the existence of what is fancied off screen. Or, put another way, in Maurice Merleau-Ponty's terms, "the invisible is the limit or degree zero of visibility, the opening of a dimension of visible."[27]

Jacques Derrida sees it differently. In *Writing and Difference*, he questions our tendency to expand what we see to what we do not see. For Bazin, the frame functions as a center not only for the elements within the shot but also for a homologous imaginary supplied by the spectator. On the other hand, Derrida tells us:

The function of this center [is] not only to orient, balance, and organize the structure . . . but above all to make sure that the organizing principle of the structure would limit what we might call the play of the structure. By orienting and organizing the coherence of the system, the center of a structure permits the play of its elements inside the total form. . . . Nevertheless, the center also closes off the play which it opens and makes possible. . . . The center is at the center of the totality, and yet, since the center does not belong to the totality (is not part of the totality), the totality has its center elsewhere. The center is [thus] not the center. . . . The concept of a centered structure is in fact the concept of a play . . . constituted on the basis of a fundamental immobility and a reassuring certitude. . . .[28]

There is thus, according to Derrida, a subterfuge at work here. To be sure, the motion picture frame makes it easy for us to spread into the world what is contained within the casing. By guaranteeing the intelligibility of what it shows us, the frame ends up dismissing the possibility of a dissonance in the rest of the totality. Hence the frame manages to keep spectators leashed to the organizing principle of the text, making sure they do not wander off on their own. It confirms that the figures we are given to see represent all possible figures elsewhere. Such use of the frame conservatively restricts not only the play of viewers but also, from the beginning, that of the filmmaker. Both, as a result, end up being framed by the system.

Amplifying Derrida's argument, one could say that *l'effet de réel*, the illusion of reality in the cinema, is connected less to the belief that what we see is real than to the certainty that the world beyond the borders of the frame is cast in the same mold. In fact this is not so. To investigate this issue, let us go back to two well-known paintings. First, Vincent Van Gogh's *Artist's Room in Arles* (1889). Because we have a good view of the bedroom, with its bed and red blanket, the window, the two chairs, the little table, etc., we may think it easy (Bazin-like) to come up the rest of the house: a living room, a kitchen, a hallway, a staircase leading to the second floor, etc. Even if we are familiar with the house in Arles, our generic projections are bound to remain quite conventional, for they would necessarily lack that which makes the bedroom so remarkable: Van Gogh's special vision, his erratic brush style, the slanted perspective, the attention given to colors, etc. Even if we strengthen our views with a software that would give them the "Van Gogh look," the result would still fall short of the goal because the painter's "distortions" were based on his experience of each site, transforming it in a unique manner. [29] In the end, we must realize that the bedroom as painted cannot be projected outward because it owes its existence to one man's mind, not to everyday reality or a systematic program. In like fashion, who or what stands next to the man and woman in Edgar Degas's *The Glass of Absinthe* (1876)? Unlike Van Gogh's bedroom, which was self-contained, the view here is "partial, fragmentary, contingent," thus begging us to complete the café setting. [30] Surely we should be able to imagine other customers, a waiter, more tables and chairs, bottles and glasses, and the patron behind the counter. As we do so though, we go to work with the good intentions of a Hollywood art director. Like him or her, we can only provide what our knowledge of contemporary paintings or photographs suggest could be there. Once again, the artist's own lively imagination would remain missing from such a scheme. Indeed, the man and the woman in the picture, that particular café, the emotion that suffuses the text, all of that originates from Degas's life experience (and perhaps the influence of other works). And if Degas himself had decided after all to add a waiter to the scenery, his choice would be unlike the one selected by the casting agency in our head. Again, what the work represents cannot be expanded to the rest of the world. It is inevitably distinct, autonomous, self-contained.

Understood this way, we realize there is really nothing beyond the borders of the frame. The whole that these images at first suggest is in fact "neither given nor giveable," Deleuze concludes. The frame inevitably falls apart at the edges where the world resumes its diversity, its formlessness, its non-filmic reality. What is outside—the world, the totality—cannot possibly be controlled. For "its nature," Deleuze says, "is to change constantly." [31] It is thus totally unpredictable. All in all, what is within the frame ends up being the center of nothing at all beyond itself. What is shown is all there is.

## VIII

In film, however, what we do not see can become problematic. Typically, the standard way of shooting makes sure that the spectator finds no gap or hole in the scenery. To have any area on the screen off limits is annoying to audiences because this makes clear to them that they do not own the place, that someone else is controlling what they see and do not see and that the exciting spectacle is nothing after all but a discourse, a human intervention, not a superior form of reality. Jean-Pierre Oudart, several years ago, reexamined the modalities involved in the classical shot structure. Somewhat awkwardly, he called the temporary missing area—the potential threat to the viewers' imaginary—the "Absent One," and the repair process adopted by the classical cinema, "suture."[32]

Oudart opens his argument with a typical situation: whenever a character addresses someone else off screen, the viewer feels uncertain. Who is there? What else is there? A certain tension is created which is generally relieved by the appearance on the screen of the reverse shot: the second character now answering the first one. In other words, when the protagonist actually shows up, he or she fills in for the "Absent One," which had lurched in for a brief moment. And so it is for the left side of the chamber if I only see the right one at first. And even the invisible fourth wall will make its appearance if for some reason the scene turns things around and we are now looking in the opposite direction.

The whole effort of the conventional cinema then is to plug the holes, to offer spectators unrestricted access to the actions of the characters. What happens though when, for some reason, a director does not play by the rules and refuses to make available some important area of the setting? This is exactly what takes place in *The Trial of Joan of Arc* (Robert Bresson, 1962).[33] During the long interrogation sequences, Joan is located on the left side of the room facing the accusing bishop and his acolytes on the right side. All are shot from the proscenium with the camera at a salient angle, sometimes looking this way, sometimes that way. So far so good. Between the two parties, however, there is a considerable middle ground that is never shown. Therefore, we do not know for sure how far apart Joan and her judges are, nor who in fact occupies the space between them. Because a significant part of the courtroom escapes our gaze, we feel something is amiss. As a result we do not experience the kind of "jubilation" (quoting Oudart) one normally expects from a film.[34] In a later work, *The Devil Probably* (1977), Bresson pushes the technique even further. In that film, it is very difficult to reconstruct mentally any of the spaces we are permitted to see. This is so because the views are circumscribed, partial to the extreme. Mostly we see legs advancing on street pavements or through rooms. And there are many shots of doors being opened and closed. It is not just that actions are not observed in their totality, the fragmentation is so thorough that the shots often seem to be juxtaposed on one another rather than bound into a whole. To use

Stephen Heath's words, "the shots succeed [one another] with no other tie than the fact of that succession."[35] Through it all, Bresson—this most precise of all directors—is careful never to show us in one shot anything more than the absolute minimum needed to advance that particular section of his narrative. Although the overall impact of such minimalist technique can be alienating at first, it is also enthralling insofar as it makes us rethink our access to the world of the characters.

The "Absent One" is also connected to the question of the invisible fourth wall. Typically, the offscreen place occupied by the camera, that privileged angle toward which the entire scene is organized, should never be felt as missing. Its absence should never become conspicuous. What happens though when the geography of the space we are given to see makes it difficult for us to account for our own position in the scene? Let us take Bresson's *Trial* once again.[36] On and off throughout the courtroom scene we are given a third view of the trial: it shows one of Joan's supporters. His position in the room is at first difficult to ascertain. We would like very much to locate him in the area in front of us, that location unrevealed to us between the protagonists (Joan on the left, the judges on the right), but we cannot do so for when the supporter looks at Joan he turns camera right and not left as we wish him to do. To put it briefly, there is only one spot in the courtroom where he can be stationed and that is where we—the camera—have been standing for most of the earlier shot/reverse shot series. Bresson, in other words, has crossed the stage line for only this series of shots. This unexpected location not only fails to relieve the tension, it aggravates it by suddenly assigning "our" place in the room to this man. So, not only is there an unrevealed area in front of us, but also our own position is given to someone else! As a result, we end up "booted out" of the room, just as happened in the famous *Las Meninas* (1656) painting by Velázquez. Some viewers, no doubt, have attributed the unwieldy move to a lack of directorial competence. For others, the technique is praised because it forces us to maintain some needed independence vis-à-vis the world of the characters.

## IX

Directors have also found it possible to articulate offscreen space through their staging. Such an example is provided by Jean Renoir's *Nana* (1926). It is Noel Burch who first brought our attention to a remarkable scene in this film.[37] During a conversation in Nana's room, her lover is seen seated next to her. In the following shot, he continues to address her even though the frame now cuts her off. Subsequently, he stands up and walks back and forth in "his" section of the room. In the next shot, when he goes back to his earlier position, we discover that Nana is no longer seated where we had left her, having moved elsewhere while we were concentrating on her lover. As Burch explains it, we are shocked when we realize that characters offscreen are not bound to remain where we left them but are free to roam on their own. This is obvious but we tend to forget it because the conventions of the dominant cinema have accustomed us to expect that nothing of significance for a scene can take place without our knowing about it. Because Renoir moves Nana around while we were looking away, we become aware in retrospect that our view of events was in fact quite restricted, that the world beyond the borders of the frame did not stand still during our absence. In a way, both Bazin's and Deleuze's theories are validated here: Nana's move  proves that the world indeed continues beyond the cadre. However, the fact we knew nothing of her change of position demonstrates our inability to posit anything beyond what we actually witness.

As for Miklós Jancsó, he uses the same effect but more dramatically. In *The Red and the White* (1967), a sergeant in the Red Army investigates an abandoned village during the Russian civil war. Friendly troops should be there but they are not. He climbs a church tower to have a better view of the situation. At the top, he looks in our direction, sees nothing of interest, then proceeds to walk away from us. Finding nothing there either, he turns toward us again. This time noticing something, he drops his weapon and raises his arms. A moment later, two officers of the White Army enter the field from behind us. The camera in this case is clearly no longer omniscient. It does not know where to look. In fact, it shields the White Army officers. As in *Nana*, off screen space is no longer reliable. All kinds of things can happen there without our having any clue about them. Again some people accustomed to being spoon-fed information may find the situation disconcerting. Others have found the new role given the camera stimulating and farsighted.

Recalling Jacques Lacan's distinction between everyday reality and the "real," Philippe Arnaud comments that, in such films, "the screen as a space does not bring in the world we know. In the same way that the 'real,' in one's life, consists of what remains unassimilated, on the screen the 'real' is what cannot be directly represented. It consists perhaps of what transpires between the things themselves."[38] Unlike many films which attempt to provide a smooth, sutured entertainment, without any gap in the representation, by bringing us the world we are familiar with, these films by Bresson, Renoir, and Jancsó keep reminding us that any filmic reality remains necessarily in default, that something—the "real"—continues to stand in reserve. Whereas in most films the frame keeps out anything that might remind the audience that what they are seeing is not necessarily in tune with the rest of the world, the frame in the films we have just described provides excerpts of a reality whose full scope and vista remain forever inaccessible.

## X

How is an image articulated? How is it constructed? To make sense of the issues, we might refer back to the formative difference in artistic rendering that is proposed by Heinrich Wölfflin in his *Principles of Art History*: the presentation of the background as a flat plane or three-dimensionally.[39] For this indeed is the active difference between traditional and typical everyday images: the presence beyond the participants, in Gothic and Romanesque paintings for instance, of a colorful, highly decorated, graphic background or one that appears to be but an ordinary view of the world.[40] Today, to select one or the other, as we shall see, has implications beyond personal choice.

Before I proceed further with this, it may be useful first to relate the visual formation of images to our everyday life experience. Even though, as human beings, we become aware of our surroundings through all of our senses (we may hear a car coming long before we see it, the wind may bring us the aroma of food from an apartment window, etc.), the gaze is the most Faustian of them all: it knows no bounds, surging forward until the very end of the horizon line.[41] Only the material world, objects, things, beings that stand in its way arrest the visual quest. This stopping is unpleasant for the eyes, as it implies that a reaction, a countermeasure is required. In a way the gaze functions as our avant-garde since we too, when we encounter several people conversing in front of a door, must come up with a decision. We can say "Pardon me!" and attempt to thread our way through them or we may acknowledge their mass and circumvent the area. This reaction is apparently universal for, as Konrad Lorenz once noticed, even the most primitive infusoria similarly find their way around obstacles after bouncing against them.[42] Our gaze therefore operates very much like we will once we actually get there. It detects obstacles and suggests solutions for us to continue our march. Going back to Gothic and Romanesque decorative backgrounds, we can now see how they too block our gaze but more thoroughly. Like big trucks which obstruct our view of the highway, these backgrounds corner the eyes, offering them no escape path within the pictorial scheme. The communication is thus limited to what is foregrounded. No meandering is permitted.

Conversely, the Renaissance picture surface offers an opening for the eyes, not only within the canvas itself, but also, so to speak, within the wall on which the work is hung. Its vanishing point invites the gaze within its fold, providing all the necessary cues one is accustomed to in real life. The image therefore seduces rather than confronts viewers. It does not block the gaze, allowing it instead to continue its forward search. Adding motion to the picture intensifies the experience. Think of the charge you are getting every time the camera surges forward at high speed. It does not matter what is moving you, whom you are with, or where you are going, the moving-through-space is what keeps you riveted to the screen. As Erwin Panofsky, the great art theoretician, suggested, linear perspective is thus "as much a consolidation and systematization of the external world, as an extension of the domain of the self."[43] For in the end the all-perceiving trick turns viewers into "desiring machines" of spectacular displays, greedy addicts who fancy themselves to be libidinally productive after all.[44] Through the operation, one's ego is thoroughly boosted. The make-believe activity is thus said to revitalize subjects and endow them with a power they simply do not have in real life. Between the images that block us and the ones that let us roam at will, our gaze, at first, will always favor the ones that provide us with endless vistas.

Directors who construe the image as an opening on the world naturally favor expansive views. John Ford is the absolute master at this. In *Drums along the Mohawk* (1940), he has Claudette Colbert saying goodbye to Henry Fonda who is joining a band of volunteers on their way to fight an Indian war. Instead of leaving Colbert on the side of the road, Ford has her retreat back toward her house. So, when she decides to walk some with the departing soldiers, she does so *at a distance:* she keeps pace in the foreground with the men marching in the background. The scene climaxes when, a little later, we see, in a deep focus shot, the column of soldiers walking toward the horizon while, closer to us, she waves at them a last time before settling down on the grassy hillside. The scene is nothing short of breathtaking.

In contrast, Jean-Luc Godard has often covered the background behind his characters with colorful advertisements, photographs, and posters. At other times he has chosen to interrupt the diegetic flow of images with large graphic displays aimed directly at the viewers. By bouncing visual or printed data back at us, he foregrounds his own films within a general social, political, and ideological context, confirming their own status as discourses to be appraised rather than slices of life happening without anyone's being responsible for their unfolding. Godard is also partial to arranging groups on a single frontal plane facing the camera rather than in depth, in Ford's manner. This flatness, this refusal of composition in depth, according to Brian Henderson, amounts to nothing less than "a demystification, an assault on the bourgeois world-view and self image."[45] Insofar as the technique denies our gaze a compensatory release for the lack of freedom we may experience in real life, it can indeed be said to form a political critique of society. While all this sounds like an invitation to dull, pedantic filmmaking, Godard's genius is such that his flat graphic images often end up being more exciting than conventional three-dimensional pictures.

## XI

Not all perspective views though should be construed as producing the same effect. Panofsky once pointed out the differences between what could be called the long view and the short view of a given subject. In Antonello da Messina's *St. Jerome* (ca. 1475), we look at a picture that represents the saint from far away, isolating him in his cabinet. The saint is clearly allowed to remain in his own world. We have a peek at it but our place is distinct from his. We may be given a view of it but we are certainly not invited to come in. Although no guide is physically present in the picture, he or she could easily be imagined just off to the side, telling us all that is important to know about the holy man. While we may look freely into the room, our gaze is probably synchronized to the guide's comments as they bring our attention to this or that detail. In that way, the guide becomes an important intermediary or mediator in our understanding of the scene. In opposition to this, in Albert Dürer's *St. Jerome* (1514), the holy man is closer to us. As Panofsky explains it, the saint's cabinet and our own space are now one: "We imagine that we ourselves have been admitted to it, because the floor [of the saint's cabinet] appears to extend under our own feet."[46] More precisely perhaps, one feels that way because we see less of the surrounding doorway and more of the room beyond it. The result is certainly striking: we are now part of the saint's world. We are there next to him. We are sharing his abode. The situation comes to a close in another portrayal of the saint by Dürer in 1521. By this time, the doorway has been forgotten entirely and we see Jerome reflecting on life in a tight medium shot. No doubt, we are now close friends, standing side by side. Through distance, the artist is thus able to position viewers as either distant observers or immediate participants within a scene.

These views of St. Jerome can serve as metaphors for three shooting approaches imbricating the storyteller, the action, and the camera. One technique highlights the "telling" of the story, another emphasizes its direct "showing," the third its "experiencing" by the audience. Let us take "showing" first (the second St. Jerome), because this is the classical formation par excellence. In this case, all attention is directed toward the characters and their activities without much indication that someone is orchestrating all of it behind the scenes. Using a novel by Guy de Maupassant as an example, Percy Lubbock describes the strategy:

> He relates his story as though he had caught it in the act and were mentioning the details as they passed. . . . Maupassant, the showman, is overlooked and forgotten as we follow the direction of his eyes. . . . The effect is that he is not there at all. Because he is doing nothing that ostensibly requires any judgment, nothing that reminds us of his presence . . . the story occupies us, the moving scene, and nothing else.[47]

In films that "show," just like the proverbial fly on the wall, we stand near the characters who appear to be on their own: we see and hear it all without their noticing us. We also seem to know whom and what to pay attention to, as well as when to come and go. Hence it is not as if life itself was suddenly cropping up on the screen.

No, in the films that "show," a story is being told but the techniques chosen are less than straightforward. Think how the casting of the principals predisposes us one way or the other toward a character. Then there is the choice of angles and what the light tells us about someone's face. How the protagonists express themselves and how the narrative is structured. And what about the pacing and the music? Most importantly though, we get access to the characters when their behavior opens our eyes to their true nature. Sure enough there is a narrator but he or she has chosen to remain discretely in the background. This said, the stealthy narrator can be in good form as is the case for Hitchcock in the beginning scene from *Vertigo*, or he/she can be failing at the task as is the case for the same director in the equivalent exposition scene of his last film *Family Plot* (1976). Instead of the virtuoso performance of the earlier film which made us forget that background information alone justified the scene, we have a plodding succession of uninteresting angles that fail to keep our interest in the situation or even the main character. Most films that use the "showing" approach stand somewhere in between these two examples, neither a masterful demonstration of grand cinema nor a sad display of barely competent filmmaking. Needless to say, "showing" goes hand in hand with coverage, and it is also the core concept expounded by David Mamet who insists that uninflected camera positions alone should be used in film.[48] In all of this, even though the camera remains subordinate to the characters, following them wherever they go, etc., each viewer tends to commandeer the views as his/hers because the puppeteer remains behind the scene.

In contrast, the film can introduce a narrator (our imaginary guide in the first *St. Jerome*). This narrator can be physically present in the film as someone overseeing the action, e.g., in *La Ronde* (Max Ophüls, 1950), or he/she can be heard on the soundtrack only, either as the voice of one of the protagonists (Walter Neff in *Double Indemnity* [Billy Wilder, 1944]) or of a commentator not immediately involved in the story (*Barry Lyndon*, Stanley Kubrick, 1975). Although the actual control exercised by such a narrator varies widely from film to film, we always end up in some way accessing the story through his/her point of view. As Lubbock puts it, here "the reader faces towards the storyteller and listens to him . . . ," it is her "telling" of it that we pay attention to.[49]

The storyteller, however, can pace our access to the story in an entirely different manner. For Gilles Deleuze, for example, "the sole cinematographic consciousness" in the film "is not us, the spectator, nor the hero; it is the camera. . . ."[50] Far from marrying the camera to the interest of the characters or placing it in an uninflected position, some directors find a distinct and independent standpoint for it. And this in turn has its rewards for we become aware of a double presentation: the tale that is taking place and, simultaneously, the positing of a "'center of consciousness' through which everything [can] be seen and felt."[51] For Jean Mitry indeed, there is no art without such a dialectic: "a poet," he writes, "can only offer his vision of the world, not the world at large. In fact, what interests me as a spectator is less what I am being shown than the way I access it."[52]

Let us take an example where the conspicuous composition enriches the narrative strategy. In *The Rope* (1949), one of Hitchcock's most inventive projects, there is a scene where the two murderers are entertaining James Stewart and a few other guests. Unbeknownst to the company, the body is lying in a chest just next to them. As the party is coming to an end, a maid is slowly cleaning up. Leaving the little group to the side of the frame, the camera resolutely focuses all its attention on the maid, who removes dishes, a candelabra, etc., from the top of the chest, carrying them all the way to the kitchen at the end of a long hallway and back again. While the conversation goes on with the speakers out of frame, we realize she is bound to open up the chest at any moment. The framing in other words emphasizes an event which is irrelevant for Stewart at this point but important dramatically because *we* know where the dead man is and we can also imagine the mental anguish the murderers are going through as the maid is circling around the chest. In this case then, the scene reaches beyond the protagonist's concern by establishing an independent point of view that benefits the suspense in the scene.

A second example can be found in *Orlando* (Sally Potter, 1993). At the beginning of the film, Orlando paces right and left in front of a large tree. Instead of showing us the scene in one static shot or accompanying his ambling with a pan or a dolly, Potter chooses a contrarian approach: she dollies in the opposite direction of Orlando's walk. He goes right, the camera moves left, and vice versa. Later on in the film, Orlando and her lover speak to each other. A traditional presentation would probably include the two in a static shot, a number of shots and reverse shots, maybe some over the shoulder angles. Potter's strategy instead is quite intricate. Let us say we are watching Orlando from a position alongside her lover. As Orlando talks, we dolly toward her until we reach a position next to her, looking at her all the way except for the end part when we pan back to her lover.[53] And this is followed by the reverse movement, dollying back toward the lover, keeping him in the shot until the end when we pan back toward her. In such circumstances, we realize we must take our cue from a storyteller who is not going to make us forget her own contribution to the piece overall.

A third example can be found in *The Long Goodbye* (Robert Altman, 1973). Philip Marlowe interrogates a woman about her husband's whereabouts. The questions keep flowing in the usual detective style: "Where were you on the night of . . . ?" The duo is framed against a window facing the ocean. It is night time and much of the beach between them is in darkness. Almost immediately, despite being thoroughly out of focus, a white speck drifting on the beach attracts our attention. As if it too were mildly interested, the camera initiates a slow zoom forward between the two people in the fore. By now we suspect the speck to be the white shirt of a man hobbling toward the ocean. Even though Marlowe continues his questioning, all our attention is on the man outside. Finally, as if awakening to its own drifting, the camera refocuses itself on the man we now recognize as her husband. This is great cinema! It is as if the storyteller/camera, bored by all the clichés of the detective genre, were daydreaming, realizing only ten seconds afterwards that, despite its somnambulistic straying, it had caught something of interest after all. Through it all, Philip Marlowe and the wife have no idea what is happening.

By selecting an independent course for the camera—framing a chest instead of the protagonists, moving the camera against the grain of the scene, initiating a zoom yet delaying its refocusing—we very much become aware of the presence of a quirky middleman, a guide we cannot avoid, a narrator we must trust to make our filmic journey a memorable one. Although we assimilate and enjoy the view, we must nevertheless acknowledge in the end that it is not ours. In the cinema that "tells" rather than "shows," the filmmaker has to make sure that the additional ingredient, the gaze of another, is worth the detour.

Finally, the visual strategy can depart from an external viewpoint (showing or telling), utilizing instead the subjective intake of a scene by a character (the third St. Jerome if you will). In the point of view (POV) shot, certainly the most commonly used of subjective markers, the camera "attaches" itself to a character's spatial position, bringing out his or her view of the scene.[54] This position is rarely significant and does not last very long. One notable exception is Robert Montgomery's Lady in the Lake (1946), which attempts to give us the protagonist's view of events from the beginning to the end of the film.[55] A second kind of involvement with the characters is less obvious but more pronounced. Recall the scene in Witness (Peter Weir, 1985) when Harrison Ford, having recovered his health among the Amish, is working on his car at night. Kelly McGillis has joined him. There is an initial long shot but, after that, we stay with tight shots of both characters. As the battery brings the radio to life and we hear "I don't know much about geography, etc.," the camera pans left as Ford moves toward her. This is followed by a tracking POV shot that duplicates his advance toward her. He moves in closer and again that is succeeded by a POV shot moving in toward her. They then dance in a series of tight medium shots, etc. I called the moving shots POV shots even though technically speaking that is not the case, for in them McGillis is looking camera left to match Ford's own gaze to the right. The camera is thus *duplicating* his move rather than impersonating it. It is moving in tandem with the character. To use Boris Uspensky's words, this kind of shooting involves a "contamination" of the author's speech by the character's speech.[56] Far from being "shown" the scene objectively, we end up sharing the characters' romantic transformation. As we look at the scene, we are invited to respond emotionally to their good fortune and partake in the dance.

For yet another level of participation, it might be useful to go back to a metaphor drawn by Walter Benjamin in his famous essay on the aura of the work of art. In it he compares the painter to a healer who cures diseases by laying hands on a patient's body and the cameraman to a surgeon who pokes inside the body itself. This being the case, he writes,

> the painter maintains in his work a natural distance from reality [whereas] the cameraman penetrates deeply into its web. There is a tremendous difference between the pictures they obtain. That of the painter is a total one, that of the cameraman consists of multiple fragments which are assembled under a new law.[57]

When the surgeon/cameraman is inside the body, he thus becomes one with the patient. They fuse into one organism that mixes views from the outside with "views" from the inside. The late twenties offered rich examples of this style of filmmaking with perhaps *Ménilmontant* (Dimitri Kirsanoff, 1928) the outstanding one. In the film, short salvos of subjective views so consistently overwhelm the views from outside that it becomes truly difficult to identify which is which. More recently a number of filmmakers, probably under the impact of rock videos and "in your face" commercials, have rediscovered this approach to filmmaking. In *Savage Nights* (Cyril Collard, 1993), the main character has known for quite some time that he has Aids. Tonight we find him alone in his bathroom. The camera is handheld throughout the scene. First it holds onto the pendants hanging from the man's necklace. Abruptly the camera rushes up to catch his face as he coughs several times, then it backs down again to the pendants that swing around his chest. It hurries a second time up to his face, then swishes right to his blurry image in the mirror. Swish back to the face and down to the hands, which open a box of sleeping pills. Cut to a wider shot that tilts to the side as the man puts some pills in his mouth. Cut to an extreme close-up of his hand on a faucet and the glass being filled with water. Quick tilt to the face: he swallows hard. We catch his face as he removes his jacket and notices new marks of the disease on his body. The camera jerks back up again in a close-up to note his reaction. His fingers in extreme close-up gently touch the blemishes on his skin. Back up again. Then down the arm. He hits the sink in a shot that is defocused. Etc., etc. This remarkable sequence makes us share his anguish, his pain, his anger. With the help of the handheld camera, the tight subjective shots, the defocused moments, the quick displacements on the body that are motivated by the character's own preoccupation rather than outside interests, we become one with the man. Like the surgeon, we are with him, inside of him. We respond to his impulses. We "experience" what he is going through. We become him.

Showing, telling, experiencing: these are the choices. To prefer one does not mean you have to exclude the others. Also do not forget that all three approaches involve manipulative strategies for, in Wayne C. Booth's words, "the author cannot choose *whether* to use rhetorical heightening. His only choice is of the kind of rhetoric he will use."[58]

## XII

If all three arrangements involve a level of storytelling and all three provide readers with instructions "about how to read the text and how to account for the selection and ordering of its components," does it really matter which one is selected?[59] Isn't it a question of what works best for this particular subject? Or even one of personal style? Most of the time it probably does not matter. Will the protagonists survive the sinking of the ship? Will the meteor hit the earth? Will the aliens be repelled once again? At times though the issue becomes critical. What are we to make of the scene when someone is butchered with a chain saw in Brian De Palma's *Scarface* (1983) or the car murder scene in Quentin Tarrantino's *Pulp Fiction* (1994)? In the first case we are left to imagine what is taking place in the adjacent room, in the second we are immediate witnesses of the "accidental" shooting with the blood spewing out all over the protagonists and the interior of the car. De Palma stages the scene because he believes it is important, narratively speaking, to convince us that nothing is going to stop his narcotic traffickers. As for Tarrantino, he is playing the scene for laughs with the absurdist reaction of his protagonists. What happens to us though in the meantime? We believe, within the context of the films, in the reality of these events. That is to say, we observe what happens as we would real events. Yet, because this is a "film," we do not rush out of the theater and call 911, rather we take in the mayhem, at best as reluctant but nevertheless passive spectators. We absorb it all with our eyes and our ears. It nestles in our head and eventually becomes a part of our subconscious. On the one hand, the usual storytelling mode (when the story seems to tell itself) puts us on the spot, on the other hand, we cannot respond to the emergency as we would in real life. In a complex way then, these scenes teach us to become less responsible citizens. Our lack of response slyly inserts itself within our personal memory. Little by little we take for granted that these events can happen any day. The scenes make us callous to lesser crises encountered in real life. They desensitize us in general.

To keep us from coming apart, something is needed. For Booth, "our feelings toward the perpetrators range from unconcerned amusement to absolute horror, from pitying forgiveness to hatred, depending not primarily upon any natural relation between the bare events and our reaction *but upon a judgment rendered by the author*."[60] In both *Scarface* and *Pulp Fiction*, and so many others, however, such judgment is nowhere to be found. In contrast, rather than going along with specific events, a concerned narrator holds his or her ground. For Jean-Marie Straub in particular, the camera "doesn't see like an eye but a gaze. Directors need to concern themselves with the moral rather than the focusing distance between the action and the camera. In German, framing translates as *Einstellung*, and *Einstellung* is also the word used to express one's ethical position."[61] In this light, it becomes very important for the camera to transcend the usual tight embrace through which it holds the characters. In short, Straub calls for the camera to assert a moral stand toward the scene.

Such moral ground can be observed best in a film like *Night and Fog* (Alain Resnais, 1955). One of the first documentary films to deal with the concentration camps, the film was able to maintain throughout a distinct voice and gaze. Whereas other projects on the same subject combined newsreel footage and a fresh narration to recreate the story of the Nazis and the Jews "the way it really was," Resnais chose to foreground contemporary views of the camps, what was left of them, barracks, walls, and fences, bringing out the distance that today separates us from the events themselves, making clear our inability to fathom the horror of it all. To emphasize the point, Resnais insisted on an aesthetic arrangement: a long tracking shot alongside the concrete holes that served as latrines, a slow tilt up the edge of a wall in a gas chamber. Admittedly, at first, one would imagine such aesthetic concerns to be out of place when faced with the gross reality of the Holocaust. After seeing Resnais' film, however, one is bound to concur with his decision. The material traces we observe are all that is left of the extermination. Terrible things were done to human beings here but we no longer have access to them. However much we want, we will never know "what it was really like," and it would be obscene to pretend otherwise. Only shameless directors have the indecency to conjure the extermination in sanctimonious tales made up of all the commonplaces presently available. We, on the other hand, with Resnais, have to deal with our inability to penetrate the reality of the camps and the guilty conscience that overtakes us as a result.

The pictures then make us confront the naked reality of the deadly apparatus without the safeguarding auspices of a familiar tale. They do not either, as is so often the case, encase the material remnants in a protective sheath that allows us to blame the past in contrast to the present. As the film itself points out toward the end, we should not imagine that these horrors belong to the Nazis alone, and that we today know better or are incapable of such atrocities. In fact, we too are quite willing to participate in the construction and operation of new death camps and holocausts of our own choosing: Cambodia, Bosnia, and Rwanda have made that clear. Only through his unusual but relentless confrontation with the traces of the past was Resnais able to make us see through the defensive façade that usually keeps our soul safe and sound, forcing us instead to realize that we have learned nothing at all from what happened. That is the power of a narrator who cares. That is the camera gaze Straub talks about: the moral stand we must continuously aim for regardless of how many times we have fallen short of it in the past.

# CHAPTER EIGHT

# *Sound*

## I

The actors have gone through the motions. The dialogue has been rehearsed many times. The director is ready. The production mixer and the boom operator are too. "Sound!" The Nagra or Dat recorder is activated. "Speed!" The microphone at the end of the boom swings in position, aimed at the actor who will speak first. "Action!" The scene now slowly unwraps: actors go here and there, do this and that, saying their lines at the appropriate moment. The sound mixer tracks their words on the recording device. "Cut!" The scene is over: it is "good for sound" too. In many films, this is as close as the director gets to the audio. In other words, at the crucial moment of the shooting process, sound is confined to recording the dialogue without distortion. No more. Whereas the rest of the script at this moment is finding its breadth, its full measure, the audio in effect is left alone. Somehow directors are not engaging that aspect of the film, leaving it for the time oddly undeveloped. But what about preproduction? Well, it is highly unlikely, Randy Thom tells us, that there was even a discussion regarding the narrative potential of the sound track.[1] And everything afterwards—the manufacturing and positioning of the audio on the multiple sound tracks—is left to specialists with little input from the director. Does this make sense? At the very least, it should be possible to turn the production mixer from a perfunctory member of the crew to a creative collaborator

197

who could bring to the audio the kind of imaginative assistance the cinematographer directs toward the image. Unfortunately, today, the job is mostly a passive one. Jean-Luc Godard was probably hitting below the belt when he declared that few production mixers "truly like their job: they don't understand what cinema sound is all about. They believe that the audio merely escorts the picture. . . . They don't even like to record mere sounds. . . . For the most part, they are bureaucrats who sit behind their little table and switch a knob up or down."[2] For all its unfairness, the image definitely rings a bell for anyone who has spent some time on a set! The idea here at the minimum is to rethink the situation, to reopen what can be heard and recorded at the time of the shoot. But more is needed. Sound designers like Walter Murch, who are often called upon to provide their magic after the fact, cannot emphasize it enough: think of sound (beyond dialogue) at the script stage.[3] Some skeptics would point out the achievements of sound in the last twenty years, its razzle-dazzle technology which is now an important selling point for the film. But is loud sound great sound?[4] Has sound really improved all that much? Is the director now thinking of sound when working on the shooting script? Has the sound mixer truly become a creative adjunct to the film process? Is sound itself finally the equal partner of the visuals?

## II

"The eye is superficial, the ear is profound and inventive."[5] This is how Robert Bresson expressed his sympathy for sound. If we hear what Bresson is telling us, we should realize that adding audio to images does not just allow for a greater manipulation of the images, fine tuning them so to speak. It also means that the world opened up by sounds can be radically different from the one our eyes have accustomed us to. What does it mean to listen to the world? For Jean-Pierre Beauviala (the designer of the Aaton cameras), our ears act somewhat independently from our eyes.[6] While we may concentrate our sight on someone in front of us, our ears may be paying attention to what is being said behind us. Second, our ears are less domesticated than our eyes. Whereas our eyes seem to function as an accessory of one's will, discovering in the world the constructs they have been trained to find there, our ears remain locked in a sort of preindustrial mode.[7] All kinds of raw sounds enter our body from all directions, finding their way to the deepest recesses of our brain. As a result, while it is relatively easy to function as an autonomous spectator of a meaningful world, the ears intake material that remains stubbornly insular within our bodies. This penetration even suggested to Maurice Merleau-Ponty that we cannot think of ourselves as discrete entities. On the contrary, we consist of a merging between the world and ourselves. Every sensory intake, he wrote, "is a coition . . . of our body with things."[8] The less tame the material, the more intercourse with the body. Moreover, because the content of what enters us changes all the time, the body-world entity which we are forms a field in a state of constant flux. A kind of free-for-all is thus constantly at play within the body.

This said, it remains that, though many different sounds manage their way into our ears, they do not end up equally displayed in our field of consciousness. First, as Christian Metz reminded us, there is a cultural aspect to what we choose to pay attention to.[9] For instance, one can distinguish between new and familiar sounds. We may decide to focus on the new ones if they intrigue us or if they carry a sense of urgency about them. As for the ones which have been assimilated before, they are responded to depending on what we already know about them and their likely sources. Second, the filtering that is taking place is also a very individual matter. Beauviala helps us understand what is going on: "What I'm saying here is that the sounds arriving in the ears are received in a global way. They are parked in the memory bank, then selected according to what our hearing disposition chooses to listen to after a brief analysis. One can thus listen to things retroactively."[10] In other words, we select specific audio bits over others after they have all arrived and nested safely in the brain. Although we might all react similarly to the sound of screeching tires on the pavement, not everyone seated at a table in a restaurant pays the same attention to the surrounding noises or listens to the exact same bits of conversation that waft in from other tables. Rick Altman is formal about this: every hearing "concretizes a particular story among the many that could be told about that event."[11] Each hearing thus also expresses an intentional disposition to engage this event rather than that one, to make specific connections between the different snippets, and to chart our reaction in response to what was taken in. This being the case, it remains that some "stories" are more interesting than others and anyone can misinterpret a turn of events.

## III

Most film sound tracks are far from innovative. The problem is that its usual ingredients are made up of idle talk, cheap theatrics, and a serenade—the kind of stuff, Martin Heidegger tells us, that "closes things off" for us, smoke screens that draw off attention from life-and-death issues.[12] Film sound for sure can be something else. It can help us question the visible, make us discover something we would have missed in the world, even suggest an extra dimension to ordinary life. The traditional dialogue, sound effects, and music tracks need not therefore be overturned; it is their makeup, their assemblage, their connection to the visuals that would benefit from serious reconsideration.

When looking at a scene, even the element most taken for granted—the fact that the lines seem to originate from the actors' mouths—is fraught with ambiguity. Why is it so important, Rudolf Arnheim remonstrates, to keep focusing on "the monotonous motions of the mouth," a decision he suggests that "yields little" in the long run?[13] In fact, as Altman appropriately reminds us, it is the loudspeaker, not the actors, that "'speaks' directly to the audience."[14] And even today its position in the theater may not match that of the speaking actor on the screen. The point then is that, through the technique of synchronization, a discourse by a screenwriter modulated by sound technicians "is recuperated to [mere story] when it is attributed to characters in a diegesis."[15] Indeed, for all practical purposes, we are not aware, when watching a film, that a written text precedes what we take to be direct speeches by the characters. The ideological benefit is double: (1) the discourse—the screenplay—parades as pure presence (Jacques Derrida could point to this as a typical operation through which, in our society, speech camouflages writing); and (2) the work involved in transforming the latter into the former is also nowhere in evidence as per the demands of bourgeois culture. Needless to say, these lines of dialogue are also purified of the hesitations, the repetitions, and all the other malapropisms that pervade regular conversations. Taking all of this into consideration, it becomes clear that the emphasis on synchronizing voice and mouth goes beyond mere technicality. To use Mary Ann Doane's summation, it "guarantees the singularity of a point of audition, thus holding at bay the potential trauma of dispersal, dismemberment, difference" for characters and audiences alike.[16] We are reassured that the speech we hear comes from the human being we see on the screen, not a from writer about whom we know nothing. One alternative to dialogue as genuine speech by the characters has been suggested by Bertolt Brecht, who advised his actors to produce the words as material to reflect upon. His counsel, however, has been largely ignored and the audio technique is almost always used to counter the threat inherent in a stumped image.

But that is only one side of the story. The use of dialogue in film can also be said to reenact the child's acceptance of the symbolic, of words as our trusted emissaries, our alter egos in the world. Rehearsing some key idea of Jacques Lacan, Claude Bailblé writes: "At the very moment the child accepts the Other as the space where he can be heard, he consents to the loss of all that which cannot be expressed that way."[17] Thereafter the child loses access to anything that cannot be related through words. Language, so to speak, becomes the only conduit through which we make ourselves manifest. In the same way, in film, the decision to use synchronized speech to enable the story to unfold can be said to erode other potential modes of communication. Indeed, once it became possible to hear people speak on the screen, dialogue monopolized our attention. We certainly remember that, in the thirties, many theorists lamented the loss of the silent medium and its ability to tell the action precisely without having recourse to words. Since then, dialogue has consistently been given preferential treatment: it is indented in the screenplay and, on the screen, it has often become the focus of the scene at the expense of everything else.

But what else is there? William James once noted that people cry not because they are sad but they are sad because they cry.[18] Likewise, words come out of one person's mouth because their roots are already moored elsewhere in their body. Yet we often ignore the latter in favor of the former. In fact, Béla Balázs says, this has been so since the arrival of the printing press. With it, he complained, "there was no longer any need for the subtler means of expression provided by the body. For this reason our bodies grew soulless and empty—what is not in use, deteriorates."[19] Unfortunately, the standardized system of production restrains screenwriters from exploring a character's other ways of being, behavior which could sometimes speak as efficiently as words ("what a character says is a writer's business, how she looks and behaves that's a director's job"). To reverse the trend, let us pay attention once again in our writing to the way body language speaks louder than words, through a gaze, a stand, or a walk. Beyond that, as Balázs reminds us, facial expressions and gestures can also relay "inner experiences," "non-rational emotions," which "lie in the deepest levels of the soul and cannot be approached by words that are mere reflections of concepts; just as our musical experiences cannot be expressed in rationalized concepts."[20] To shift from words to the body in order to express meaning is therefore not unlike changing from one instrument to another: you vary the players, you orchestrate the piano score.

Within the synchronized dialogue itself, it is generally the words themselves that are preeminent, not what Pascal Bonitzer called the "body" of the voice. "To meet the 'body' of the voice (its 'grain,' according to Barthes) is to encounter a disunion. On the one side, there is what it says, its content, all alone, naked, neutered . . . on the other, there is its waste, the 'grain' of that voice, its noise, its dissonance."[21] It makes sense then to explore, beyond the communication, the tone of the voice, its pitch, its timbre. Did it really matter what Bogart actually said? The voices we use in a film can be gentle or sepulchral. They can snap or hiss. They can be shrill or melodious. Unfortunately, actors are often cast based on their looks alone, and little attention is given to unique drawls, accents, innate rhythmic patterns. Acting schools probably have also contributed to the disappearance of what they often consider to be negative to a career: "unpleasant" voices, regional accents, or those manners of speech that convey class distinctions.

There is also the question of whose voices we hear in a film. In many films the only ones we hear belong to the actors as they address one another. More than anyone else, Godard has found additional roles for voices. In his films, people read to one another, they quote from books, they translate for each other if they happen to speak different languages. Verbal snippets from radio or television programs are overheard. And the director himself does not hesitate to barge in and make comments. These additional voices therefore can intrude, disrupt, even dispute what the characters are saying. This is where I think the production track would benefit most from a revision of the mixer's role. Why should the recording involve only the sanctioned dialogue? The cameraman is often busy shooting cutaways that may or may not find their place in the final picture. Similarly, the production mixer could open aural "windows" that would create worlds parallel to that of the filmed action. To use critical terms, the production track could emphasize a paradigmatic approach instead of remaining subservient to a linear or syntagmatic model.[22] For instance, the script could include diary readings or streams of consciousness originating from the protagonists. More adventurously, there could be interviews with the actors, observations by extras or passersby. An external narrator could make comments. The director could keep an audio journal. Snippets of conversations picked up on location could be recorded, unusual noises documented. And, more generally, anything uncommon happening during or around the shoot could be taken advantage of instead of being erased from the production track.

A last issue, spelled out by Altman, entails the troubling question of the point of audition.[23] This topic was highly debated in the early thirties when the common practice of sound was initially worked out. Indeed, at the time, two strategies battled it out. The choice was between a recording that duplicated the camera position, so that the volume given the dialogue would change as the picture cut, say, from a close-up to a full shot, and one that would insist on the independence of the audio from the pictures, keeping the microphone close to the mouths of the characters even when they were seen from far away. Should the sound therefore be faithful to the changing visual space or should it always stick to the characters like a second skin? The former technique offered the advantage of more overall realism, the latter smooth intelligibility. The industry eventually decided that the dialogue needed to be heard clearly regardless of what the camera did. As one of the participants in the debate said at the time, this meant that, in practice, sound recording was trying to duplicate "a man with five or six long ears, said ears extending in various directions."[24]

Just the same, to hear things differently from the way we see them introduces a disturbance within the system that is not contained by mere synchronization between speech and mouth. As the technique implies a discontinuity between the point of *view* (say a long shot) and the point of *audition* (where the closeness of the microphone suggests a close-up instead), spectators could experience, going back to Doane's argument, a "dispersal" in the construction of meaning between two distinct narrators, one in charge of the pictures, the other taking care of the dialogue. In fact, Altman astutely observes, "the referent of Hollywood sound is not the pro-filmic scene at all, but a narrative constructed as it were 'behind' that scene, a narrative that authorizes and engenders the scene, and of which the scene itself is only one more signifier."[25] In other words, dialogue recording is faithful to the story construed as existing independently from its actualization during the shooting of the film. Through the years, it has taken incredible sensitivity, experience, and technical expertise on the part of re-recording mixers to keep this fundamental discontinuity within the system from becoming obvious and confusing audiences.

## IV

To look at a film with dialogue, but without sound effects (as one does when building up a rough cut), forces us to question the *soundness* of the project. Without sound effects, the characters on the screen are not quite real: it is as if their soul had left them. As for the world they move in, it does not appear solid. It feels undeveloped, inadequate; it is found wanting. This lack of presence in fact replicates what we experience when we become aware of the emptiness of everyday life activities (the endless repetitions we go through, the waste of time on trivial issues, the time spent eating, washing, sleeping, going to work) or when we focus on what should matter most: the nothingness that awaits us in the end. When we become aware, Heidegger tells us, we are overwhelmed by angst. Hence angst emerges when the mental outlook which shapes our familiar world suddenly breaks down, often under the weight of a personal emergency of some sort. At that moment, everything one takes for granted—family, friends, lovers, work—becomes frightfully inadequate. However, the shift of perspective does not make us aware of another layer of reality hidden under the surface of things; rather, the familiar world, the "real" world, our world, is discovered to be a fiction with nothing else taking its place. "The threatening," Heidegger writes, "does not come from what is available or occurrent, but rather from the fact that neither of these 'says' anything any longer."[26] Although we see the usual objects around us, they fail to fulfill us as before. In film, the foremost raison d'être for the sound effect track then is to make sure the world remains as we know it, to combat the emptiness in the core of things, a view that would show up "when something [usually] available is found missing. . . ."[27]

Sounds effects are thus positioned throughout a film to "waken up the visual space."[28] How do they do so? As Michel Chion demonstrated in his analysis of Robert Bresson's *A Man Escaped* (1956), the sounds we hear infer successive circles of presence around a French Resistance fighter imprisoned in a Nazi jail. First, there are the immediate noises within the cell itself: those the man makes as he walks back and forth, sits on the mattress, writes something on the wall. Beyond the tiny cell, we hear what is happening in the rest of the block: the yelling of other prisoners, the guards coming and going, etc. Past that, there are the different sounds of the small town that surrounds the jail: children playing on a street, birds chirping, mostly the traffic. Then, at night, when everything quiets down, one is able to hear the whistling of a train at the outskirts of the city.[29] As the camera stays for the most part with the man in his cell, all these sounds imply an ever-receding landscape of human activity beyond that which is visually available. Therefore, it is not just that synchronized sounds anchor the presence of the man in his cell, it is that other sounds, from people and things we do not see, complete the picture so to speak, testifying to the presence of an entire world out there. The main difference between the sounds heard in *A Man Escaped* and those a real prisoner would hear in that situation is that, in the film, they have been carefully selected and articulated to have the maximum impact on the narrative. The distinct traffic sounds, for instance, are amplified just right and positioned where they matter most. For John Belton, such tactics are inherently deceitful insofar as they necessarily bring up "an idealized reality, a world carefully filtered to eliminate sounds that fall outside of understanding or significance."[30] 'Sound effects therefore do not simply "waken up the space." Even though they originate from a hodgepodge of background noises, the latter are regenerated into recognizable signs that have a definite function and impact inside the film discourse.

Although all films use "on screen" and immediately "off screen" sound effects basically the same way, the selection process and their characteristic degree of presence must be carefully thought out. For instance, do we hear the sound of the traffic through the window or not? And, if someone closes a window, do the noises die off or have they merely lessened? How far back should the world reach: should we hear through the wall the steps of someone walking up the stairs even though the protagonist never acknowledges them? Or how close: is it helpful or hindering to hear the sounds of the protagonist's clothes rustling? Also (still): what should happen when the camera changes angles? Should the visual change be echoed in the audio as well? For example, how different should the noise of the motor sound be when the camera shifts from an external long shot of a plane flying to the inside of the cockpit or vice versa?[31]

"The danger of present-day cinema," Walter Murch writes, "is that it can suffocate its subjects by its very ability to represent them." With a film image, everything "seems to be 'all there.'"[32] The countermeasure then is to use, beyond the expected, recognizable sound effects heard in *A Man Escaped*, sounds that take us by surprise because they do not seem to belong to what we see. Murch makes his point by bringing out the piercing metallic sound heard in *The Godfather* (Francis Ford Coppola, 1972), when Michael Corleone is going to commit his first murder.[33] Nothing surrounding the actors can possibly account for the noise. It seems at first to be internal rather than external: a mental scream, that sort of thing. Only a few seconds later is one able to identify the noise as that made by an elevated train negotiating a turn. The idea then is to stretch the time between the moment we hear the sound and that moment when we can safely assign it to something secure. During that time, the filmic space is stretched, unsettled, less predictable, more equivocal. It is up to the sound designer and the director to determine how far they can stretch things. An extreme example occurs in *Once Upon a Time in America* (Sergio Leone, 1984), when a telephone rings in the opium den, yet nobody seems to notice. With the telephone still ringing, we cut to another scene without any more luck. It is only in the scene after that that someone finally picks up the phone that had been ringing there all along. For Murch, the power of truly "off screen" sounds (those that cannot be immediately recuperated by the visuals, remaining for a time stubbornly independent of them) is that they open "a perceptual vacuum" which makes the film "more dimensional."[34] Chion summarizes what is taking place here very well when he writes that good sound involves "observing reality through a prism that splits at first the separate elements then recomposes them, all the time making sure they do not coincide absolutely."[35] In other words, the creative use of sound effects rests in keeping open a small but definite gap not only between the audio and the images but also between reality and the film.

Finally, it is clear that modern technology has radicalized the way we think of sound effects. During the stereo battle of the fifties Fox attempted to make an exact match between the visual action on the screen and the dissemination of the audio through multiple speakers behind it.[36] Surround sound later on made the matter even more complicated for it is not always clear "when the sound [should] (for dramatic reasons) focus down to a single point; when [it] should expand across the front of the screen to stereo; and when and how [it] should use the full dimensionality of the entire theatre."[37] What is involved here can be illustrated by one of Chion's example. In a French film (*Le Choix des armes*, Alain Corneau, 1981), a character stands close to a pinball machine. The sound bursting from the machine is clearly located on the left of the screen. As the man turns around, the camera takes a position behind him, now 180 degrees away from the first shot. Logically the sound of the game should also have shifted from the left of the screen to the right. The fact that it does not points to the difficulties associated with the point of audition. In other words, do we hear the world based upon the view we have of the character or according to other, mostly psychological factors associated with the audience's own position, a dilemma which makes blanket solutions difficult to apply? If it makes sense for the character to hear the sound of the game shift to his right side since *he* turned in relation to it, spectators, on the other hand, have not moved in their seats. For them, the noise would have traveled instantly from the left to the right side of the theater with the cut, possibly disorienting them, surely making them focus on the issue rather than the narrative. One alternative, of course, would be to keep the visuals always on the same side of the stage line—an unwelcome prospect to be sure. For Chion, one reason the American cinema has been so successful in its use of Dolby Stereo is that it stayed away from exact spatial localization, positioning, in addition to a relatively stable frontal dialogue track, the additional tracks in the background as a kind of "trash bin" for the audio remnants of the action in the fore.[38]

Beyond sound localization, there is the matter of the loudness of it all. Beginning with *Star Wars*, Altman writes, "the creation of two 'baby boom' channels realigned cinema sound with a new and unexpected model, the rock concert with its characteristic overamplification and earth-shaking bass."[39] Put differently, this means that Dolby Stereo, DTS digital sound, and THX have, to some extent at least, changed our very understanding of what cinema is. In traditional filmmaking the scene is attended by an attentive audience much as if it were a live theater performance. We overhear the world of the characters from our seat, nothing extra is added: it comes to us played back seemingly at a realistic level. Murch properly refers to these as "humble sounds."[40] The recent changes in technology, however, have altered this traditional presentation. Today the film can "cause spectators to vibrate—quite literally—with the entire narrative space. It is thus no longer the eyes, the ears, and the brain that alone initiate identification and maintain contact with the sonic source; instead, it is the whole body. . . ."[41] If someone lights up a cigarette, the striking match is heard throughout the theater as a jet engine on a take-off. Glass shatters and reverberates with the purity of a grand waterfall. Thunderous explosions burst on the ear as if orchestrated by Hector Berlioz. Through it all, the body is titillated by sensations never before experienced. The overall impact is so radically different that it becomes possible to suggest an overturning of mise en scène by *mise en espace*. Because the sounds have lost their immediate affiliation to people and things, they now soar in space, gushing in their independence, exalted in their magnification, rocking the audience through waves of low frequency throbs. In this kind of spectacle, the world is no longer "wakened" by the audio. Rather the point is to rattle spectators down to a "Wow!" Special effects have evolved into special affects.

Clearly today it is no longer enough to "put the door slams, the cat meow, and the traffic," in a film any more.[42] The advances in sound technology should not be ignored. Yet, when all is said and done, the Sturm und Drang possibilities of the technology in the theaters do not fit all films equally well. There is clearly an open conflict between two types of cinema, one which lets viewers scrutinize the world for clues as to its meaning and another which seeks above all to give spectators a corporal high. The question then boils down to you and the film you are making. Is it about the world? Or is it about getting the audience through a roller-coaster type of experience?

V

Music forms the third component of the sound track. Why music at all? Looking beyond the commonplace notion that it was needed originally to cover up the noise of the projector, Chion has suggested that the practice in fact took its cue from long-established predecessors: the music that accompanied opera singers, ballet dancers, circus performers, etc. In most of these situations, the musicians sit in a space of their own: the pit. And Chion has accurately described a similar output in film, as "pit music."[43] Too often though, this type of music, Hanns Eisler tells us disapprovingly, "sets the tone of the enthusiasm the picture is supposed to whip up in the audience. . . . Its action is advertising, and nothing else. It points with unswerving agreement to everything that happens on the screen."[44] This music thus functions as an ideal audience, totally immersed in the story and always ready to applaud regardless of the depicted occurrences and the actual performance of the film. We, of course, are not an ideal audience and our own reaction to the spectacle may be different. As a result, we may become aware of the music's efforts, grow suspicious of them, and declare them to be in vain. The problem with this type of music is that it has no ethical backbone to stand on. It agrees with everything that is placed on the screen. It has never seen a situation it does not like and cannot embrace. An example of this kind of melodious endorsement can be found at the end of *The Accused* (Jonathan Kaplan, 1988). The trial is over and the protagonist has won despite the odds. She thanks her attorney before going back to her everyday life. Right on cue, the music swells to the occasion somehow forgetting that the woman has gone through a vile group rape, that she was abused by the justice system, that she was deserted by her friends, etc. It is not that this composer was particularly shortsighted but rather that, for the film makers, since the villains were now going to jail, justice had been served, hence a happy ending had been reached. The audience as a result should not be reminded that the protagonist, far from being well, will probably remain traumatized for the rest of her life. To counter such melodramatic, even deceitful effects, Eisler has proposed that film music "should not over-eagerly identify itself with the event on the screen or its mood, but should be able to assert its distance from them and thus accentuate the general meaning."[45] At best, this "general meaning" could involve a moral point of view, separate from the action, commenting upon it. Eisler's own score for *Night and Fog* (Alain Resnais, 1955) is exemplary in this matter.

Even when the tone of the music is appropriate with regard to the visuals, Eisler sees problems. All of us have been moved indeed by what we take to be inspired notes of music arising alongside the images, investing them with weight and meaning, endowing them with a humanity that might otherwise not be explicit. John Berger has beautifully demonstrated the power of this kind of music to bring out unsuspected resonance from images. In his BBC series *Ways of Seeing* (1972), he shows Van Gogh's *Wheatfield with Crows* (1853–90), first by itself, then, after he mentions that this was Van Gogh's last work before he killed himself, with profoundly moving music. The demonstration never fails: when seen alone, in silence, the work is admired for its painterly qualities, but as soon as we hear the connection to the artist's death together with the swelling of the music, we cease to look at the text itself. Rather it becomes jumping off material for the release of vague emotional sentiments connected to our own experience of loss. Even the best directors at times use this technique to help transcend the barrenness of an action. Michelangelo Antonioni, for instance, did not hesitate to use Giovanni Fusco's delicate music on top of Monica Vitti's hand hesitating toward her lover's shoulder at the end of *L'Avventura* (1960).

All in all, Eisler sees film music as an attempt "to interpose a human coating between the reeled-off pictures and the spectators . . . [so as] to mask the heartlessness of late industrial society by late industrial techniques."[46] In his view, alienation is the common reality of most people's life. That view, however, remains unacceptable to the providers of entertainment who believe their job is to keep the audience from focusing on social and other shortcomings. Through such music we are told that everything is all right after all. To avoid such mendacious effects, one solution is not to use music at all. But this is the equivalent of a high wire act without a net. What in fact happens if the film dispenses with the "human coating" usually provided by the music? Bresson who said that music "isolates your film from the life of your film" was willing to try it.[47] His film, *L'Argent* (1983), has no music and it indisputably provides a different experience for the viewer. One pays much more attention to what we see on the screen, to the sounds we hear, and to the relation between the two tracks. One is also more aware of the shots, of the cuts, of the actors. In a word, one becomes extremely sensitive to the film as a film. And there is pleasure in that awareness as well. For a director though, there is no place to hide: your work is all exposed, its heart, its pulse, its general articulation. Mistakes and inadequacies, *your* mistakes and inadequacies, are there for others to judge. Bresson is therefore not surprised that bad directors use wall-to-wall music, for their immediate goal is to "[prevent] us from seeing that there is nothing in those images."[48]

While the complete absence of music suits only the most daring directors, less radical tactics can nevertheless prevent the usual pitfalls. A simple solution consists of having the music come diegetically from the images themselves. In *The Mother and the Whore* (1973), Jean Eustache has a scene in which a protagonist plays a record for a friend. The next three or so minutes are spent looking at the characters listening to the music or observing the motions of the needle dancing on the surface of the record. Such gazing is rare in film for everything else stops. No action is going on. One simply listens to the music with the protagonists. The advantage here is that there is no score operating on our subconscious nor is there any identification with someone singing on the screen. The music can even be soppy, for we are able to recognize its effects on the characters without necessarily having to share them.

Another way to keep the music from playing tricks on the audience is to use concrete music. The advantage, for Eisler, is that such music requires neither preamble nor sequitur.[49] Think of the shrill violins in *Psycho* (Alfred Hitchcock, 1960): they come in, do their work, that's it. This style may also be admirably suited for putting events into a larger perspective, even for providing a social or political commentary on top of the protagonists' own preoccupations. Indeed, Schönberg's dissonances, Eisler comments, echo "historical fear, a sense of impending doom."[50] A good example of this approach can be found in *Muriel* (Alain Resnais, 1963). There the linear narrative is often interrupted by views of Boulogne, a city rebuilt after World War II, with its mostly graceless landscapes, buildings standing next to ruins, streets empty of human life. Although the characters themselves may not see it that way, absorbed as they are with trying to remember their own past, the discordant notes played on top of these images suggest a life cut off from its roots.

Further up on the scale, one cannot fail to notice the more jolting tactics used by Jean-Luc Godard and Marguerite Duras in several of their films. In the first scene of *Weekend* (1967), for example, Godard pumps the music up and down several times even though nothing visually justifies such a move. As a result, we become very aware of its functioning as a signifier. Duras similarly does not hesitate to call upon music without having any psychological or aesthetic reasons. She explains: "In the cinema that falsifies, music accompanies the pictures, dresses them up, shows them up. . . . In [my films] it arrives authentically, like day or night."[51] If nothing else, these extreme examples point to the fact that there is plenty of room between movie Muzak and radical experiments.

One last point. I have mentioned earlier in this book that one should think of staging when writing the screenplay for a film. Similarly, Eisler suggests that music be composed during the writing of the screenplay. By that he does not mean that a composer should be writing blind, but rather that one should be thinking of the music (specific pieces, types, instruments, or uses) from the very beginning of the project instead of leaving the job to the last minute, putting it in the hands of a stranger. More than that, the entire audio, including "off screen" sounds, would benefit from being incorporated into the very thinking of a film.

## VI

Does it matter whether the dialogue is recorded at the time of the shoot or dubbed in later? Does it make a difference whether the sounds we hear are pure or ameliorated? There is no easy answer to these questions, for dubbing a film is advantageous as well as counterproductive for the independent filmmaker. Let us start with the professional way of doing things. Here, "the goal in initial recording is to record every sound at the optimal quality, no matter what it is supposed to sound like in the final film."[52] This of course means shooting in a controlled environment, e.g., a sound stage. Traditionally then, the actors' voices are carefully isolated from their natural background so as to keep them as intelligible as possible. A good production mixer could hope to get seventy percent of his/her production track into the finished film. Dubbing is used only as a last resort, when location shooting made it too difficult to maintain the expected standard.

To dub an entire film, on the other hand, means you do not stop for sound when you are shooting. An audio track is often recorded but its quality is irrelevant. Its purpose is simple: to register the small dialogue changes that take place between takes as the scene evolves. Hence, later on, when actors are asked to come back to synchronize their lines, they will know the exact words they spoke months ago in the take that was finally chosen. To say the least, there are many problems with that operation. When it is time to dub, actors are effectively out of character. The scene environment is not there to help them psychologically. And, instead of living the drama from within, the actors are now relating it, safely, after the fact, from the comfort of an armchair in a studio. The whole enterprise is done quickly. And the new recording of the dialogue sounds unrealistic because the microphone is placed just a few inches away from the actor's mouth. Some, Michael Rabiger for instance, have no problem condemning the technique all together: "It is a procedure to be avoided because newly recorded tracks invariably sound flat and dead in contrast with live location recordings."[53] Why do people work this way then if it sounds so bad? It all comes down to money. During the New Wave for instance, the French directors had no choice: their budgets were so tiny that, even if they had wanted to, they would have been unable to pay for the sound stages needed for live sound recording. Beyond this, they were also politically opposed to the professional gloss achieved by films produced in the studios. Somehow, they felt, studio shooting had made these films lose contact with reality. Actors were speaking unnaturally, acting instead of living their parts. One goal of the New Wave was thus to bring back a sense of everyday realism to the cinema. Shooting on location with actors and camera roaming freely, without worrying about recording good sound in these conditions, would do the job. That the human immediacy of the dialogue suffered during the dubbing was a small price to pay for the overall gain in visual authenticity and intensity of their productions. Cinema got going again: what else could one want?

Dubbing entails more than a technical choice, it also implies a philosophical stand. To explain what is at stake here, one needs to go back to Heidegger's seminal presentation of beingness as "being there" or *Dasein*. To be-in-the-world is to be *there*, with others, around objects, at that time, in a specific situation, in a certain light, in a concrete space. To be there is to be in context. "By its very nature," Heidegger writes, "*Dasein* brings its 'there' along with it. If it lacks its 'there' it is not factically the entity which is essentially *Dasein*."[54] In film too, "being there" implies an interwoven situation: a character relating to someone else in a definite space and time. To ask actors to enunciate lines spoken months earlier clearly ruptures the togetherness of being-in-the-world.

If dubbing decontextualizes the body during the second recording of the dialogue by grafting one time-space continuum over another, at least the same individual is asked to reanimate the earlier living experience. With digital technology, however, the atomization of the world and the human body within it can be pushed several notches further. To start with, when actors are asked to perform against a blue or green screen, even the original environment is totally devoid of a "there." Second, it is now easier than ever to amalgamate two human beings, casting one for his/her looks alone, adding a more seasoned voice to that body later on. After all, foreigners were satisfied they got the essence of John Wayne even though his voice was dubbed, say, in German or Arabic. Jean Renoir, early on, forcefully objected to this practice, saying that "if we were living in the twelfth century . . . the practitioners of dubbing would be burnt in the marketplace for heresy. Dubbing is equivalent to a belief in the duality of the soul."[55] Today the dubbing experience can even be pushed further. Because any body part can easily be recombined (visually or aurally) with others recruited elsewhere, film actors are and will continue to be scrutinized for specific "product characteristics," so as to increase the exchange value of the total human "package" being synthesized on the screen.[56] As a result, what Samuel Weber (reading Heidegger on technology) says about objects can be extended to actors as well, as they too now "lose their distinguishing traits and become stock-in-trade against which orders are placed."[57] The new working environment is thus one where every human organ can be detached, mined, and exploited apart from its living whole or context. To sum up, the practice of dubbing was premonitory in that it anticipated the rupture of the integrity of the human experience. That something profoundly important got lost in the process is not in question. Yet many filmmakers have no choice in this matter: they will stick with dubbing because otherwise they would not be able to shoot at all.

## VII

But what about sound effects in particular? Does anyone really care whether this tire screeching on the pavement was actually recorded at the time of the shoot or artificially made up later? Worse, what if, as Murch reminds us, "walking on cornstarch . . . happens to record as a better 'footstep in snow' than snow itself"?[58] There are gradations of authenticity here. As a director, you can decide to limit yourself to the sounds actually recorded behind the dialogue on the production track while you were shooting. This basically was the case in the very early sound films. As Murch puts it, in these films, the original recording on the film acetate could not be altered: "there was no possibility of fixing it later in the mix, because this *was* the mix."[59] Today, of course, with all sorts of alternatives beguiling you, most people would ridicule such a position as way too rigid if not damn foolish. You can indeed record genuine sounds at different times and place them alongside your pictures. You can pick up what you need from a library of prerecorded sound effects. You can digitally embellish or invigorate your original or preexisting sounds. Or you can ask specialists to Foley the whole film in a studio after the fact.

To stick to the first method is certainly to go against the grain of professional filmmaking. Yet some directors limit themselves to the original track recorded at the time of the production, for it emphasizes the indexical aspect of the sound, its existence as an event.[60] What is important to them is that the sound happened during the take, that it was heard and recorded. That consideration has precedence over the quality of its acoustics or its signification in the narrative. Other filmmakers place their priorities elsewhere. On the one hand, they may agree with Béla Balázs who looked at sound effects as "the speech of things . . . the intimate whisperings of nature . . . the vast conversational powers of life."[61] On the other hand, they do not necessarily believe that the voices of nature can be recorded incidentally. One must pay special attention to them. One must go out of one's way to find them. In this case then, the sounds are real, the noises concrete, the animal grunts genuine, but they are recorded at a different time, one by one, and selected for their ability to express the surrounding world in that part of the film. Jean Cayrol speaks for these filmmakers when he writes: "we recorded thousands of rain drops, to keep only two (and it may even be that nobody hears them in the theater). And we spent days in the forest to become aware of specific sounds, like those made by the bark of the trees."[62] The problem here is that most of us have lost our ability to listen to the world and it is extremely time-consuming to reeducate our ears. Surely, rather than go searching for birds, it is much easier to sit in a sound library and pick up a loop of birds singing. In such a repository indeed, the world truly stands in reserve; it is organized, catalogued, at your fingertips. You can choose the call of a single bird, of different kinds of birds, of a flocks of birds, etc. How likely is it, Chion wistfully wonders, that someone will actually identify the particular chirping and question the presence of that bird in the region seen on the screen?[63]

If attention to fact is not the deciding issue, what makes one choose one sound over another? Let us hear from a specialist in the field:

> [Average people] don't know it, but they have all kinds of little buttons that can be pressed. If you press the right button, it will make them feel a certain way. . . . So from an artistic standpoint one should try to develop a sensitivity or an instinct for it so you can say: "Okay, of all the choices, this explosion is the best one. That explosion sounds nasty and we want a nasty explosion at this point in the film. We don't want a kind explosion that sounds like it has a resolution to it. We want something nasty."[64]

In other words, this is the terrorist explosion that rocks the beginning of the film. Its sound must extol the power of the enemy, it must connote the impossible task facing the protagonist. Even though we see an explosion only, we invest it with a meaning "that exists only in our mind."[65] The sound tells us how to read it in relation to the rest of the narrative.

Even if one does not find the perfect bird or explosion for one's project, that can be arranged. Anything can be transformed and tweaked to bring out its maximum impact. With the help of a monitor, it is easy nowadays to alter the characteristics of any sound until it produces only what is demanded of it. More so, one can combine two or more sounds to provide the audio at that moment with even more vitality, more impact. Examples of this kind of manipulation are often quoted in the press, e.g., animal roars being added to the motor of a truck in *Raiders of the Lost Ark* (Steven Spielberg, 1981) to make the motor sound more powerful. Finally, one can also let the Foley people create the effects in their specialized studios. What is happening in this case is that the concept of the indexicality of sound is abandoned in favor of a new simulatory reality. In fact, a Foley performance calls into mind what Ernst Gombrich said about painting. "What a painter inquires into," he wrote, "is not the nature of the physical world but the nature of our reactions to it. He is not concerned with causes but with the mechanisms of certain effects. His is a psychological problem—that of conjuring up a convincing image despite the fact that no one individual shape [on the painting itself] corresponds to what we call 'reality.'"[66] Here the original sounds need not be recorded. Because the ears are not that finicky, other sounds can be substituted for them. To use Murch's example once again, walking on corn starch provides a far more convincing rendering of someone walking on snow than the snow itself. In other words, you Foley (or manipulate a sound) because an acoustical counterfeit is more convincing to the ears than the sound that actually originated from the real situation depicted on the screen.

In practice, filmmakers run the gamut from Jean-Marie Straub and Danièle Huillet, who record and play a single production track in their films, to Sergio Leone who dubbed and Foleyed everything in sight. For the French filmmaking partners, dubbing/Foleying is counterproductive: "It is not just that the lips we see on the screen did not speak the words we hear, but space itself becomes illusory." On the contrary, they continue, "when shooting with direct sound, you cannot falsify the space."[67] Direct sound, for them, thus implies more than the voice of the actors. It means that we truly get a sense that this being says these things at that time, in that space. We hear the surrounding space as much as the voice. It involves the recording of an integrated slice of time/space continuum. To do so requires all kinds of adjustments. For instance, as pointed out by Huillet, locations must be selected not just for their appearance but also for the future needs of the audio. The background must not just look right but also must be a good place to hear people speak. This does not mean an environment where you are able to record perfectly clean sound but a location whose aural ambiance adds to the scene. Furthermore, they tell us to pay attention not just to the part of the location that will be discovered by the camera but also to the entire surrounding area. "Off-screen space exists," Straub comments,

> it is something one discovers when shooting in sync. Those who shoot without a production track do not understand this. And they are wrong because they go against the essence of cinema. They believe that to make a film means to shoot only what is in front of the camera, but that's not it! One also shoots what is behind and what is around it.[68]

In their own practice, for instance, Straub and Huillet do not stop the camera when a character walks off screen, they keep it going until they cannot hear him or her any more. To understand a film in this fashion gives it suddenly an extra dimension. It involves becoming attuned to the world so as to include, beyond the conventions of what a scene is, sounds that belong to this particular environment even though you may not locate their source on the screen. The context of the place, the world surrounding the characters, the Other everywhere, all intrude in a thousand ways. And this indeed is what gets lost in the typical movie soundtrack, a professional re-recording mixer admits, "because we don't allow the random relationships [between sounds] to happen, it's so controlled, everything is in its place."[69] In contrast to professionals who reject incidental sounds as contaminated material, Straub and Huillet embrace them as a valuable contribution to their projects. In their view, the world enriches the discourse through its unpredictability. Although the lens may focus on a small fraction of the total space surrounding the camera, what it shows is nevertheless in the end connected to everything that is "behind and around." In other words, the shot breathes in the midst of the off-screen space, it lives in its context. Michel Chion has given us an excellent example that underlines the importance of a larger visual and aural space. When filming "a flute solo of a Bruckner symphony," he writes, "the silence of the orchestra is as important as the notes emerging from the flute. To go for a close-up of the flute is to destroy the dimension of the quiet but surrounding orchestral ensemble which precisely allows the flute its meaning and its strength."[70] For Straub and Huillet, to go for the flute alone would be "to falsify reality." For them, "the sole duty of the filmmaker is to open the ears and eyes of the spectators to what actually is there, to the real."[71] For them like for Heidegger, the fundamental human experience of reality must remain fully present, unsweetened, unblended.

Although they may not be as absolutist as Straub and Huillet in this matter, other directors share some of their spirit. Jacques Rivette and Eric Rohmer, for instance, have consistently insisted on using synchronized sound in their films despite their working with limited budgets. As for Robert Altman, in such films as *California Split* (1974), *Nashville* (1975), and *A Wedding* (1978), he pioneered the use of radio mikes carried by many actors simultaneously. This allowed him to get rid of cumbersome overhead booms, thus giving the players much more freedom of movement. The technique also made it possible to include background conversations behind the dialogue in the fore. Because each track is recorded separately it is possible to bring each of them up or down later on depending on the final needs of the scene. As for Jean-Luc Godard, he experimented with omnidirectional microphones in *Two or Three Things I Know about Her* (1966) and several other films. His goal though was more theoretical than practical. He wanted to make a point about sound, letting the audience hear what the world would really sound like without the usual manipulation provided by the technicians. For all their intrinsic interest, these experimentations do not have to be duplicated to the letter. Indeed, problems of audibility in some of these films quickly discouraged other filmmakers. The result, Godard disingenuously complains, is that professionally no one dares do things differently any more. His main point though is worth reiterating: "the average American film has excellent audio but it should not be the only film sound we are given to hear. It is only one view of sound out of a thousand. What is wrong is that the American model has forced the disappearance of these other nine hundred and ninety-nine ways of thinking about sound."[72] At the very least, rather than getting locked in a narrow aesthetic mode, filmmakers could rethink the issues surrounding sound recording and come up with their own solutions.

## VIII

The moment when the voices, sound effects, and music get together is called the mix. What exactly happens during a mixing session? Principally, in Claude Bailblé's words, the re-recording mixer

> runs a constant and homogeneous "ambiance" under the scenes, allowing the words to stand out by giving them color, echo, and contrast. He creates an aural landscape by adding carefully selected effects. Problems related to sound continuity between cuts are erased. Finally a mood is emphasized through the repetition of certain sounds or musical leitmotifs.[73]

The mix is certainly where the entire operation comes together. It is where the disparate parts are given the glue that seamlessly binds them in one body. For any filmmaker the mix is crucial, for this is also where the world the film attempted all along to create finally comes into being. In the mix then, one is able to gauge the results of the film against one's original expectations. When the session is successful—most often it is, re-recording mixers being extremely good at what they do—one experiences an intense pleasure at witnessing the long-awaited birth of the film. For the mix truly gives the film its form, its identity. It allows the film to breathe and speak, to become finally itself.

But let us look more closely. First of all, as mentioned by Bailblé, we find "ambiance" at the bottom of the entire edifice. Technically, this track is a recording of a space's aural existence. Before leaving the room, set, or studio where the film is being shot, the production sound mixer records a minute or so of that space's presence. Later on, that recording can be duplicated so as to provide the living background for the scene, however, long it runs. Played underneath the other tracks, the "ambiance" makes what exists on the screen palpable. It builds the necessary ground without which the individual sound effects would be incapable of performing their magic. Even more importantly, it corroborates, for the spectator, the original inscription of the characters' speech. I can hear that these people actually said these things *in that room, at that very moment*. It thus confirms the truth of that lived instant of time. This is then a typical case when, referring back to Derrida, "self-presence must be produced in the undivided unity of a temporal present so as to have nothing to reveal to itself by the agency of signs."[74] In a word, "ambiance" is the cement which holds the entire aural construction together.

For all its indexical reality, this ambiance is somewhat of a sham. Far from inscribing the actual moment of the characters' existence or speech, this track (if not a canned product in the first place) is actually a memento of another moment of time, much later in the day, when the technical personnel are ordered to freeze all activity. What we hear in the theater then is not a trace of the characters' actual breathing space, but that of the crew unnaturally at a standstill. The ambiance then does not underline the authenticity of the self-same but points instead to the other (the crew, the production mixer, the director of the picture) and an entire "agency of signs" (the filmmaking practice, the manipulation of sounds in recording, editing, and mixing). Because this track actually brings forth the residues of other beings behind the scene, our imaginary attribution of a time-space continuum to a character's life can be said to be shot through and through by the entire machinery of cinema.

Second, there is a "natural" hierarchy at work in the mixing studio, with dialogue having precedence over sound effects and music. "If I have a dialogue track that's 'perfect,'" explains a re-recording mixer, then I usually try to do the ambiance part of the sound effects track-along with the dialogue and balance any kind of room tone or bird or air or traffic beds against the dialogue. Then once I've got that, I can add the Foley, any specific sound effects, like cars or buses, and balance that against the dialogue. Everything is balanced against the dialogue . . . because that's where the information is. . . . The music is the last thing that goes in.[75]

As we see, the traditional priority in the mixing session is to make sure we hear what the actors are saying regardless of the logic of the situation. A typical example: we see a room full of people at a party but, whereas the voices from the crowd remain indistinguishable, we hear the protagonists speak in turn and distinctly. Although the rules of the game changed somewhat during the late sixties and early seventies, under the impact of the New American Cinema in general and Robert Altman in particular, today the old standards have reemerged stronger than ever. This way of thinking, continuing with Derrida's assessment, is typical of the Western philosophical credo insofar as it rates directly attributable speech higher than anything else. Written text, for instance, is suspect because it is asked to function apart from its author. On the contrary, the presence of the human being "in front" of the text guarantees the reliability of what we hear. For re-recording mixers as well, each speech must be securely located within this human being, not anyone else. The worse thing for the traditional cinema would be to have, say, two men conversing in a situation in which the camera angle makes it difficult to determine who said what to whom. Speech, in other words, should not "separate itself from itself, from its own self-presence," it should not "risk death in the body of the signifier that is given over to the world and the visibility of space."[76] Words should not float in space, be recognized as independent signifiers, stay disconnected from anyone. Clearly, in this view, it matters less *what* people say than the fact that *someone* said it.

   To mix is thus not without danger. Unless the director is quite cognizant of what is going on, his/her film will be brought to life in a standardized manner. Let us put it this way: the mixing studio, the technicians working there, and their habitual procedures, all precede the arrival of any one project. Before anything else, the mix is an institutional operation. There, things are done in a certain way. It is exactly because of this that we can talk of the influence of people like Gordon Sawyer in the Goldwyn Studios. Every mix under his regime had his imprimatur. It would have been inconceivable to challenge Sawyer's conception of good sound. Although mixing is not as systematic nowadays, there remains the fact that the technicians who work there never leave their den. They tend to be a conservative bunch, suspicious of foreign films and different aesthetic approaches. Naturally, they bring to work the only standards and conventions they are familiar with.

To sum up, it is at the mix that the world of film is usually made whole through the presence of the ambiance track under the sound effects. It is at the mix that the danger inherent in a separate point of audition for the dialogue is alleviated, that music is superimposed over the most troublesome remaining passages, that all the traces of inscriptions and manipulations by the different technicians are erased. It is here that picture/sound discrepancies are smoothed over. Photographs of the mixing apparatus in sound magazines, showing a smoothly shaped, polished long bench with hundreds of identical switches, marvelously express the rational imperative of the entire project. As for the well-groomed, well-behaved re-recording mixers, they are usually shown sitting diligently next to their desks. Out of sight though, hidden underneath the elegant, glossy console, is a jungle of wires, actual chaos, complete anarchy—Babel! What all of this points to is that mixing is an ideological operation as well as a technical one. This is where a decent film can lose its freshness, its distinctness. This is where the discordant notes struck by a director can be recuperated by the industry. In the professional mix indeed, the idea is to equalize the gaps and variances that would make films more unique.

## IX

While it is true that the audio track was originally added to the pictures as a kind of supplement on the margins of the film, it cannot be regarded any more as a mere accessory to film, something not vital to it. Very much in line with Derrida's argument in *Of Grammatology*, sound has shed its earlier subservience to the visuals to become their full-fledged partner.[77] Clearly, today, one must approach a film on both fronts.

To explain the difference, I would like to bring up two films where the relation between the pictures and the audio reaches far beyond the harmony one takes for granted. The first example is *Las Hurdes* (1932), the celebrated "documentary" Luis Buñuel made in Spain during the early thirties. In that film, the images portray the hard conditions of life in a remote village. Although they are more truthful than the information provided by the other tracks, they should not, however, be taken at face value. For instance, we see in a very long shot a goat fall from a mountain peak. Immediately afterwards there is a match cut to the goat falling from another angle. This, of course, suggests manipulation in the gathering of the images. At another time, strong motion picture lights make it possible for us to see a peasant family "sleep" at night in a barn, an image that reminds us of a similar scene in *Nanook of the North* (Robert Flaherty, 1922). On the whole, though, the visuals remain more believable than the other tracks. There is no doubt, for instance, that the voice-over narration parodies the institutional, all-knowing voice of God that so often tells us what to see in a film. In this case, however, the voice tells us nothing but lies. As for the music that accompanies the film, it is serious, beautiful, classical . . . and totally out of place in the rural, dilapidated setting. There is, in other words, a chasm between the three tracks, the three distinct discourses, and we are left without any stable meaning. There is simply no single source of information we can believe totally. In *Las Hurdes*, it is the entire concept of cinema as carrier of truth that is put in question.

The second example is *Muriel* (1963). This early film by Alain Resnais deals with the ravages of time on our memories of the past. A key moment of the film occurs when Bernard, a young man, relates his experiences of the Algerian war to an old man back in France. Visually we are shown what look like home movies of a soldier's life: maneuvers, artillery firing, digging trenches, and the like. Also depicted are more relaxed moments: soldiers eating, mugging for the camera, diving in a swimming pool, going on a boat with civilians, looking at a mosque. A French soldier shakes the hand of an Algerian child. Toward the end of the sequence, a door is broken by angry soldiers but it is not clear why they are doing this or what happens afterwards. The entire footage has the markings of something shot in 8mm by an amateur filmmaker: it is grainy, scratchy, saturated in color, handheld, and uncut. We find out only afterwards that the film we are watching is in fact projected on a wall by Bernard and shown to the old man, a friend of his.

Throughout the piece we hear Bernard's voice on top of the images. His monologue, however, has nothing to do with what the pictures show us. He talks instead about leaving his barracks one night and walking through a warehouse full of munitions. In the dark he bumps against a woman who at first looks like she is sleeping on the floor. On closer examination, he realizes she is frightened, shaking all over. Fellow soldiers are there too. They tell Bernard they are interrogating the woman, Muriel, and that it is essential she talks before daybreak. One soldier seems to hurt her. She screams. Her hair becomes wet with perspiration. Another soldier lights up a cigarette and gets closer to her. She screams again. By chance her gaze falls on Bernard while she screams. Later she throws up. Much later that night Bernard returns to the warehouse. Her dead body looks like a sack of potatoes left submerged too long in water. There is blood all over and burns cover her body. Bernard eventually goes to sleep. He sleeps well. The next day, by the time he wakes up, Muriel's body has disappeared.

The power of the sequence arises from the dissonance between the two tracks. One cannot say that the pictures are not truthful. Certainly they illustrate the routine of an average soldier. No images, however, are available to evidence what must have been the most important moment of Bernard's life, when he could have influenced what happened and did not. Sure enough, the affair took place in the middle of the night, making it impossible to shoot with amateur film stock. But even if it had been technically possible, no one would have thought of shooting this particular event. That is not what an amateur camera is supposed to record. Most directors, however, would have no qualms about marrying the two tracks, introducing, for instance, Muriel's torture in a flashback. As spectators, we would not be spared any detail of the scene: the cigarette burning the flesh, Muriel's intense scream, etc. The realism of the scene would be appropriately unbearable. The guilt would be laid heavily on the soldiers, cast as the typical "bad guys" or Neo-Nazis. Most filmmakers would even go farther—the soldiers physically restraining our protagonist, keeping him from intervening. Resnais's structure on the other hand emphasizes the impossibility of reshaping the past so as to make it serve our present interest. For the character, it is too late. He finally has to confront the fact that, although he did not join his fellows, he did nothing to stop the torture. He was even able to sleep well immediately afterwards. Today, at last, he is haunted by that night's memory and his failure to measure up to what happened.

The situation thus recalls the opening of Albert Camus's *The Fall*, where the protagonist, hearing the scream of someone who might be drowning in the Seine, convinces himself there is nothing to it. He too, at first, goes back to his everyday life. Only later, does he understand that "that cry which had sounded over the Seine behind me years before had never ceased, carried by the river to the waters of the Channel, to travel throughout the world, across the limitless expanse of the ocean, and that it had waited for me there until the day I had encountered it."[78] In *Muriel*, every time Bernard watches his 8mm film with nothing but insignificant or pleasant pictures in it, he is forced to confront his own failing to do something about the Algerian woman's torture. In this case, the camera's neglect to record images matches his own failure to speak up. The absence of images reflects his own silence. His inaction is forever encrusted in the trivial home movies. As a result, *Muriel* provides us with a most welcome lesson: we learn that films cannot tell us all there is to know about life, that what is most important may often remain undocumented. Godard once remarked that in many films the visuals and the sounds effectively "mask" each other, cancel each other out.[79] In opposite fashion, by playing the audio against the visuals, Buñuel and Resnais make clear that truth cannot be served on a plate ready for our consumption. Rather it must be sought, discussed, and revised, over and over again.

# CHAPTER NINE

# *Editing*

## I

Everyone knows that cutting involves the substitution of one image by another. But what happens at the exact moment this replacement takes effect? With motion pictures, the changeover is so fast indeed that it is almost impossible to arrest the transition and reflect on what is going on. One way to access the event, though, is to imagine a presentation much in favor in art history classes. First you project a slide of a painting and discuss it, then, using a second projector, you show just next to it a second painting. It really matters little whether we have two works by the same artist, two different painters, even two different schools or art periods, the introduction of a new image next to the old one transforms one's experience of the situation and alters the discussion that follows. Let us explain: a single image grabs the attention. Even if the aesthetic forms within it point outward, they do not go very far for there is no welcoming committee out there on the wall. However much they may attempt to escape the confines of the frame, the image remains solidly where it is and it is thus toward it, in the end, that our comments are directed. Regardless of what it represents, the picture puts forth a single world. But as soon as you project another image, the situation changes radically. Not only has a second world opened itself for our perusal, the first one ceases to be what it once was. Let us emphasize the point: even though what we have on the wall are two monads, two self-contained, apparently

windowless worlds, their co-presence on the wall connects them immediately in our mind, hooking them so to speak one onto the other, as a
dialogue of sorts is imagined between them. The dual presentation in
fact makes it as impossible to analyze the second painting by itself as to
ignore its impact on the original one. In other words, unless we switch
off one of the projectors, the relations between the two images will draw
all our attention. The eyes go back and forth, establishing rapports, ver-
ifying differences, assessing this detail in one, examining the technique
in the other. If one were to verify the exact pattern followed by our eyes
during that time, the graph would show but a series of saccadic horizontal motions, back and forth between the two sites. Another way to get at
this phenomenon is to think out the differences between Cinerama and
Abel Gance's Polyvision project. In the first apparatus, all efforts were
made to minimize the lines between the three images projected on the
screen so that the action could flow seamlessly within it. In Polyvision,
on the contrary, the three images were often different from one another
while still participating in the same narrative. For instance, there could
be a close-up of Napoleon in the center frame whereas the two adjacent
frames would show his army marching. In summation, as soon as we
abandon the single image presentation (however constructed), we stop
concentrating on what is contained within it and focus instead on the
relations between the images in question. It matters little for my argument whether this reaction is learned or not: this is what we do when a
second image intrudes into the field, altering by its very existence the
lone discourse of the first.

II

When an image succeeds another instead of lying alongside it, the
exchange just described is much less perceptible because of the instanta-
neity of the transition. We looked at something and now another image
has taken its place on the screen. Instead of an exciting juxtaposition, we
witness at once the ruthless elimination of one picture (to use Eisenstein's
language) and, in the next instant, we are forced to respond to the basic,
immediate needs of a new one: to identify people, their surroundings, the
situation, etc. Yet, despite the swiftness of the exchange, some mental
traces from the previous set of informations will remain, coloring what we
see next. And, vice versa, the new image in time may come to modulate

our memory of the earlier one. Once again then, the rapports between the two images are what become significant.

The main point is one of importance: should the grafting emphasize or camouflage the fact that we are dealing with separate entities? More precisely still, assuming one attempts to tell a continuous story, how much of a connection does one need between shots? In fact that is exactly the problem American filmmakers, in the early days, had to work through. To explicate the issue, it may be useful to bring in Noel Burch's suggestion that shots relate to one another in only three basic ways.[1] In the first technique, overlap, part of the previous space remains visible in the second shot, making it easier for the spectator to infer a continuity of action between the two scenes. The magnified insert of an object, the closer shot of a protagonist, and a view of the scene from a different axis are all examples of this basic possibility. The difficulty here, Burch tells us, lies in "integrating these close-ups and medium close-ups into the film . . . [in] achieving analytically the linearisation of the primitive tableau into a successions of pictures that would cut it up and organize it, making it *legible*."[2] This of course could not be done all at once. Indeed the sudden spotlight on the face of the protagonist (at least when encircled by an iris) could suggest to the spectator the momentary abandonment of the flowing continuity, a stopping of the action, the bringing of a monad into full view. It makes sense then that this novel enlargement was carefully introduced, at first merely duplicating what had already been witnessed in the longer shot.[3]

With proximity, the second technique, the closeness of the second space to the first must be deduced by the spectator. Often, however, the viewer is helped by the staging, as when a woman who exits a room through a door in one shot is seen immediately afterwards entering another room through a similar door. Here it is the action itself, its logic, often the direction of the motion, that conveys the link between the images. The third and most radical sequence between shots is based on alterity, when one cuts between geographically distinct locations. This is where the danger of losing the spectator is greatest for, in Walter Murch's words, "at the instant of the cut there is a total and instantaneous discontinuity in the field of vision."[4] By the same token, this is also where editing can shine.

In all three situations, Griffith was able to minimize the threat of difference by recuperating the new shots under the umbrella of a single storyline. What was temporarily lost in immediate continuity was more than compensated for by gains elsewhere. Gilles Deleuze, for instance, has suggested that the close-up "produces a miniaturization of the set," endowing "the objective set with a subjectivity which equals or even surpasses it."[5] In other words, at the very time that the close-up threatened to disrupt the continuity of an event, it helped the involvement of the viewer by bringing the impact of the story nearer and nearer to the individual protagonist. The impact of the previously seen action—its existence really—could now be verified on the faces of those who made it happen or were reacting to it. Likewise, the forceful continuity of the story line could master the otherness of any new spatial situation by emphasizing immediate connections to the earlier scene: we recognize someone, we know that a character was supposed to go to a certain place and this set looks just like such a destination, etc. The staging could thus be arranged to help viewers focus on the single component in the shot that could be tied to what was already known or had been witnessed earlier. A typical gimmick, for instance, consisted in "alternatively switching the spectator to either end of a telephone wire."[6] In such a case, all attention was focused on the "talking" on the phone rather than the unknown location. In *The Lonely Villa* (1909), that exact phone situation was followed by another one of Griffith's trademarks: the cutting back and forth between the family besieged by burglars and the father racing to their rescue. In this type of parallel cutting, the repetition of the visual motifs as well as their increasingly accelerating rhythmic pattern, also helped unify the scenes for the audience. All in all, using Tom Gunning's words, it is Griffith's ability to convey "continuity and simultaneity within a variety of spatial relations," that turned out to be his most valuable achievement.[7]

There are thus two movements at work in such an editing style. Thomas Elsaesser summarized them when he wrote that "Griffith's narratives are always based on an act of splitting the narrative core or cell, and obtaining several narrative threads which could then be woven together again."[8] The initial impulse of the narrative and the editing, which is to explode the field, is thus a mere ploy, the entire point of the crosscutting being always, at the end of the rhythmic crescendo, to merge once again the dislocated elements. So, even though such cutting appears at first to scatter the separate elements of the main action further and further afield, thus retarding their reintegration, the organic unity of the whole eventually triumphs over all disparities encountered on the way, turning them into dependent constituents after all. The entire operation therefore recalls the Freudian "fort/da" game where the little boy succeeds in controlling the pain prompted by his mother's absence by throwing away a wooden reel (saying in German "*fort*" or "gone") then retrieving it using the string attached to it (now stating "*da*" or "here"). Through the game then, the boy was able to symbolically bring back his mother and thus alleviate his fears.[9] All in all, it is possible to say that with Griffith and the American cinema in general, the job of editing became one of "collecting" (to use Deleuze's word) the miscellaneous threads originally dispersed by the narrative, gathering them progressively around a core element.[10] There is therefore a centripetal impulse at work in this kind of editing, one that is essentially in tune with the Western notion of individualism.

### III

This way of relating shots is not, however, the only way to think about the relations between two images. The Russians in the twenties based their films on an altogether different model indeed. In their way of thinking, partly based on the Constructivist program, which emphasized demystifying the technical craftsmanship of the work of art (e.g., easel painting) for the benefit of a proletarian audience, it became ideologically important to bring attention to the connection between the shots as opposed to simply glossing over their treatment as was done in the American continuity editing system. All the great Russian director-theorists shared this basic understanding. What kept them apart though, as well as endlessly bickering with one another, was the size of the gap between the two shots.

To initiate the debate let us recall the Kuleshov effect. Named after the director-theorist-teacher Lev Kuleshov, this editing demonstration has doubtlessly become, as Dana Polan puts it, "the film theorist's equivalent of a palimpsest, an ink-blot test out of which one can read almost any aesthetic position."[11] True enough, but that is precisely its strength insofar as the visual assembly opens up, not a single operation, but a whole range of reflections about editing. It can thus be appreciated as the founding metaphor not only for American editing but also for all the variations of Soviet montage that would emerge in the twenties. It is also not important in our present context to ascertain whether Kuleshov executed the experiment alone or with the help of Pudovkin.[12] Likewise we need not worry about the exact visual contents in the piece for they no longer exist and each historian recalls the tale somewhat differently.

Let us summarize the experiment: using bits of film scenes from different films, Kuleshov organized them in a simple series. Several identical shots of a famous actor (Mosjukin) in a relatively inexpressive moment were intercut with different views, e.g., some food on a plate, a dead body, a woman lying on a couch. As a result of their being assembled together, audiences were said to have linked the two separate sets (the actor and the other scenes), possibly projecting their own reactions toward the food, the woman, and the dead body onto the actor's face. Since, as already mentioned, nothing remains of the original experiment, some French professors recently attempted to verify its claims by duplicating it, first in a manner as close to the original as could be managed, then in a more modern approach. The different concoctions were then presented to students to see if their reactions matched the original findings. It became obvious, however, that dealing with such an audience, one bred on films, distorted the experimentation. Indeed everyone in the audience immediately recognized the Kuleshov effect for what it was. The students thus qualified their reactions by acknowledging that they knew what reactions the operation was supposed to originate in them in the first place.[13] This said, it made no difference whether the piece was assembled from old black and white footage picked up here and there or color footage shot especially for the occasion, "as soon as two shots are juxtaposed one next to the other, there is an irresistible urge to interpret and narrativize the connection."[14]

This impulse, Norman N. Holland reminds us, probably comes out of the very habit of watching movies.[15] Yet it is not clear whether the outcome is taught to the viewers Pavlovian style, actively created by them, or a combination of the two. For David Bordwell, who uses cognitive psychology to support his argument, "just as we project motion on to a succession of frames, so we form hypotheses, make inferences, erect expectations, and draw conclusions about the film's characters and actions."[16] We thus always draw on many clusters of data or schemata, gathered from different sources, to make sense of what we see.[17] Let us remember: the side-by-side juxtaposition of images prompted a hunt for comparisons, even a search for differences between the monads. In succession, however, one automatically assumes links of some sort between the images, some immediate connections, a direct filiation. Because the second image is presumed to be relevant to the first on some level, the viewer can be counted on to bring up some interplay between them. The key point here is that it is not necessary, for the phenomenon to take place, that kindred elements be involved. The effect works even if the two views are not connected in any way. In the French experiment, for example, whenever the physical space of the two pictures was deemed too different to be assigned to a single continuity, the viewers accounted for the discrepancy by turning whatever was in the second set of images into the dream, memory, or fantasy of the person observed in the first. The demonstration thus made clear that the same physical world does not have to be present underneath the cut for a visual narrative to take hold. On the contrary, a cut could stand up, be noticed, become the nodal point between radically distinct monads, yet bridge them in some fashion. It is this understanding that was explored to the fullest by the Russian filmmakers.

## IV

To illustrate the point, we can look at the different editing approaches Soviet directors experimented with. In *Film Technique*, Vsevolod Pudovkin recalled an incident when he observed a man cutting grass with a scythe after the rain. As a Soviet filmmaker, Pudovkin was upset by the fact that movies generally did such a poor job of depicting working people and their labor. Hence, he imagined the following sequence:

1. A man stands bare to the waist. In his hands is a scythe. Pause. He swings the scythe (in regular motion).

2. The sweep of the scythe continues. The man's back and shoulders. Slowly the muscles play and grow tense (in slow motion).

3. The blade of the scythe slowly turning at the culmination of its sweep. A gleam of the sun flares up and dies out (in slow motion).

4. The blade flies downward (regular speed).

5. The whole figure of the man brings back the scythe over the grass at normal speed. A sweep-back. A sweep-back. A sweep. . . . And at the moment when the blade of the scythe touches the grass

6. Slowly the cut grass sways, topples, bending and scattering glittering drops.

7. Slowly the muscles of the back relax and the shoulders withdraw.

8. Again the grass slowly topples, lies flat.

9. The scythe-blade swiftly lifting from the earth.

10. Similarly swift, the man sweeping with the scythe. He mows, he sweeps.

11. At normal speed, a number of men mowing, sweeping their scythes in unison.

12. Slowly raising his scythe a man moves off through the dusk.[18]

What is Pudovkin doing here? Most obviously, he is breaking down a single action into a number of views, making us pay attention to specific details within the scene. That in itself is not very different from the American style. Griffith and others did this as well. But whereas they would use the new views to single out the main characters or point out particulars important for the story, Pudovkin (in this example at least) uses a paradigmatic bundling of shots to make us confront the labor process involving the man. His insistence alone forces us to stay with the man and focus on the physical aspect of his work. "When we wish to apprehend anything," Pudovkin sums up his thinking, "we always begin with the general outlines, and then, by intensifying our examination to the highest degree, enrich the apprehension by an ever-increasing number of details."[19] And this indeed is what he does at first. Observe, for instance, how he fragments the scene from the full figure to the motion of the muscles all the way down to the scythe and the grass. But then, in a reverse movement, he moves back out again to others around the man who are working as he does. Whereas Griffith's tendency is to use close-ups to emotionalize the scene and cutting to contract the entire action back to its figural core or meaningful individual, Pudovkin uses close shots and editing to make us take note of the hard labor involved, stretching it through the entire body of the worker, finally expanding it to other workers and even the world.

This tendency to reach beyond one person's story is of course symptomatic of the entire Soviet cinema. Another example can be found at the end of *Mother* (1926), Pudovkin's first great film. Pavel, the young revolutionary, is planning a prison escape with the rest of his comrades. As the jailbreak takes place, Pudovkin keeps cutting to running water, first a trickle that runs alongside the sympathizing workers as they approach the prison to protest the imprisonment of their fellow revolutionaries, then to the formidable river that crosses the city. It so happens that it is spring time and the river is in the process of breaking its ice cap. Not only does the determination of the workers find a parallel in the gushing water, the escape as well is mirrored in the breaking up of the ice cap. And when Pavel jumps from floe to floe to escape his pursuers and secure his freedom, it is as if the joy of his freedom and the strength of his revolutionary fervor have found a sympathetic echo among the forces of the universe. For Pudovkin then, the goal of the camera is to "penetrate as deeply as possible, to the mid-point of every image. The camera, as it were, forces itself, ever striving, into the profoundest deeps of life. . . ."[20] Accordingly the liberation of a Communist sympathizer reaches all the way to the whole wide world and is enlightened by it.

## V

Sometimes, in the Odessa steps sequence of *The Battleship Potemkin* (1925) for instance, Sergei Eisenstein uses editing in a way that is not that different from Pudovkin's. As the Cossacks shoot at the assembled populace and the crowd scatters in every direction, the single event bursts into a multitude of concurrent mini-events, including the famous sequence where the baby carriage escapes from the hands of the infant's mother and ends up bouncing down the steps unattended. So, in the same way that Pudovkin used cutting to dissect something happening into multiple elements—nurturing our understanding of what is going on with shots of body parts, adjacent objects, or pictures of a nature that shows itself in harmony with the main subject—Eisenstein takes full advantage of the fusillade's impact to atomize the scene into scores of distinct incidents. With both directors then, even though the cutting opens up the action to far more scrutiny than would normally be the case with American editing (where continuity remains the paramount issue), the "bursts" at this point remain physically contiguous to the original action. The difference between the two directors so far is more a question of tactics than anything else. For Pudovkin, there is an easy glide, a natural slippage from one element of the scene to another. For Eisenstein, the cutting executes little jumps to something or someone not far away from the original action. With both directors, however, the cut takes the story away from any possible involvement with a single individual and his or her predicament. For Eisenstein indeed, it is imperative for the new Soviet art to show individuals only insofar as they appear through the grid of the collective mass.[21] Even though such cutting opens up the field, taking all in, it remains nonetheless in the same geographical region as before. The centrifugal effect accomplished thus far still maintains a metonymical relationship to the central event.

Other kinds of leaps, however, were also explored by Eisenstein. In *Battleship Potemkin*, he uses many cuts to describe a sailor washing some dishes. The man examines the ornate inscription on a dish. It reads: "Give us our daily bread." As this scene directly follows the serving of spoiled meat to the crew, the frustrated sailor vents his rage by throwing the dish to the floor. What makes the scene so remarkable is that the jump cuts used to access the action illuminate a change within the protagonist, moving the issue beyond the personal anger of an individual against his superiors. Through the breaking of the plate, the man has ceased to function as a yeoman, he has become a revolutionary. The cutting in other words makes clear a radical shift in the sailor's consciousness—a transformation that could not be photographed directly. Somehow the Bolshevik revolt comes to light through the leap created by the jump cuts. In this fashion, Eisenstein discovers the true potential of montage. Let us be precise: at this point the shots do not merely add up, they build on each other cubically so to speak, pushing the whole to a new dimension, a move that must be done to reach what is demanded of them. For Deleuze, "there is not simply an organic link between two instants, but a pathetic jump, in which the second instant gains a new power, since the first has passed into it. From sadness to anger, from doubt to certainty, from resignation to revolt. . . ."[22] Pathos, for Eisenstein indeed, allows for the transition of one state onto another. With the cut, we have literally changed dimensions, we have gone from the seen to the hidden, from merely physical action to intellectual resolution, from one man to a revolutionary cause.

Still, visually, the scene remained geographically bound to the kitchen area of the battleship. It is thus only when Eisenstein expounded on the notion of the montage cell that he moved into a totally new direction. Referring back to hieroglyphs, haikus, and other types of ideograms, Eisenstein theorized that a picture cell did not have to participate in the surrounding dominant action in order to communicate with it or add significance to it. Functioning as an independent unit, structurally and dynamically, a picture cell was essentially capable of influencing a cluster of shots with a force of its own. In this way, the full potential at stake in the Kuleshov experiment was finally activated. The cell, unlike the ordinary continuity shot, does not have to be physically connected to the action at hand or inspired by the continuing story of the characters. The link could be external, brought out by the director to produce immediate associations between the separate elements. By so doing, Eisenstein decisively pushed film assembly away from an action dominated by the participants to one that could be constructed semiotically, akin to a language. In this way he surpassed Griffith's timid venture in this area when, in *Intolerance* (1916), a number of stories were crosscut under the general banner of human prejudice. With Eisenstein, the joints would become ever more audacious in nature. In *Strike* (1924), for instance, the Soviet director cuts back and forth between workers attacked by charging Cossacks and animals being butchered in a slaughterhouse. The cuts are between different picture cells, not between adjacent events or locales. Distinct monads are grafted onto the massacre precisely to bypass the limited scope of any historical incident, heightening instead its intellectual and emotional signification. Eisenstein thus stitches a linguistic comparison onto the episode: workers are being slaughtered *as* cattle. This kind of cutting is of course radically different from more typical editing associations because it does not concern itself with the whereabouts of what is presented. The deictic considerations surrounding the contrasting event—where the slaughterhouse is, who the butcher is, when the killing of the animal is taking place—shrink back before the notion of "butchering." The here and now gives way to a linguistic leap. The notion of the cell, in other words, opens up cutting to any "conflict of two pieces in opposition to each other."[23]

But Eisenstein went further still. In a celebrated montage sequence in *October* (1927), he attempts to dereify the notion of God by bringing in quick succession "images [that] increasingly disagree with our concept of God."[24] By showing the less familiar gods of different cultures and the forbidding ones from past civilizations, Eisenstein hoped to demonstrate to his audience that the Czarist power could not claim some privileged association with the deity. Here the affiliated elements do not belong to a single place (e.g., the slaughterhouse) but to multiple sources and geographical areas. Furthermore, it does not even matter whether the statues of the gods were filmed in the field somewhere, even in a museum, or were themselves reproduced from photographs in a book. We see images that signify "divinity" rather than statues standing in some actual place in the world. Very much like a larva mutating into a butterfly, any object could therefore be liberated from its original earthly context and made to fly as an independent sign. So, whereas Griffith relied on the continuity of the diegetic narrative to help audiences make sense of an action taking place in distinct locations, Eisenstein counted on the mind's activity to figure out the meaning of independent cells stuck next to each other. "While the conventional film," the Russian director wrote, "directs the emotions . . . [this kind of editing] direct[s] the whole thought process, as well."[25] Pushing beyond Griffith, Eisenstein had in fact discovered that it was not necessary to ground the pro-filmic material in any physical space at all. The picture of something could be used to connote meaning rather than denote a fact. He could send out signifying bubbles or balloons, knowing that the audience would jump at the occasion to exercise their minds.[26] Intellectual montage had at the long last liberated editing from its pedestrian earmarks. If it could ask the question: "What is a God?," there was no limit to one's excursions into the world and pronouncements about it. No wonder that at the time, Eisenstein imagined himself capable of bringing Marx's *Capital* to the screen, speaking through images as if they were but words on a page.

## VI

Dziga Vertov's theoretical and filmic work is notoriously complex. Most problematically, his films have been pigeonholed within the general category of documentary or (the kiss of death) experimental filmmaking. True enough, he uses a lot of newsreel-type footage in his films and, in his writing, he often talks about the importance of showing life as it is and of reaching indisputable truths through the use of the camera. At the same time, many of his techniques also remind us of the avant-garde. One would be mistaken though to leave it at that for we would miss out what makes his work truly exceptional. To start with, Vertov is not interested in the regular kind of story films. These, in his eyes, sink the cinema to the level of the old Bolshoi theater—an institution he loathed. There, he writes, you find but a "scabby adjacent surrogate" for life, "an idiotic conglomerate from balletic contortions, musical squeaks, clever lighting effects" and the like.[27] Quite logically, he rejected the work of his colleagues, Kuleshov, Pudovkin, and even Eisenstein, for all of them had remained stuck in the old way of doing things. For Vertov instead, a revolutionary cinema must "tunnel under literature" and "unserfage the camera" from the limited capabilities of the human eye.[28] The problem with the human eye, he goes on to say, is that it only sees what is immediately there whereas the Kino-eye—his name for his own type of cinema—is able to find its way "into the chaos of visual phenomena filling the universe," just the right tool for revolutionary times which similarly require a radical rethinking of one's comprehension of society as a whole.[29]

The first job of the Kino-eye is to seize snatches of reality. But that is followed by editing which, far from tying up loose ends, consists in analyzing the evidence gathered, frame by frame or in slow motion perhaps, dissecting it until it reveals its innate meaning, made clear in view of other bits snared elsewhere. Deleuze writes:

> Whether there were machines, landscapes, buildings or men was of little consequence: each—even the most charming peasant woman or the most touching child—was presented as a material system in perpetual interaction. They were catalysts, converters, transformers, which received and re-emitted movements, whose speed, direction, order, they changed. . . ."[30]

In Vertov's work then, the gap opened by the cut in Kuleshov's experiment has finally reached gigantic proportions.

Let us take *The Man with a Movie Camera* (1929), a film so difficult that even Eisenstein pretended at one time to see nothing in it but "formalist jackstraws and unmotivated camera mischief."[31] Typically the film is assembled from the kind of footage one would find in newsreels. Some of it was shot for the film by Mikhail Kaufman, the director's brother, some of it even shows Kaufman getting these shots, and finally some footage was probably picked up elsewhere. Through it all, Vertov is not interested in documenting any actual event or showing something for itself. Vertov is after the big picture. He tracks the connections between things, how one event relates, responds, or completes another. Shots of individual human beings or things are valuable only insofar as they contribute to our understanding of how each part fits within the whole. Where do they place themselves? How do they function within the system? Vertov searches for the social process, the greater reality, the economic or ideological ties that connect everyone and everything. For him it is inconsequential that a room is assembled out of "twelve walls, photographed by me in various parts of the world."[32] If he connects these walls in the editing it is because he has seen in their juxtaposition something unavailable in the single walls in each location. The manipulation thus escapes the reproduction of a dumb reality. On the contrary, he hopes his editing will end up revealing the workings behind the creation of that dumb reality.

But let us take some specific examples from the *The Man with a Movie Camera*. At first viewing, we become sensitive to a kind of cutting favored by many editors and directors during the silent period: a woman splashes her face with water, the street is being washed as well, a couple divorces, tramways are seen moving in opposite directions. But that is quickly followed by another, more pronounced kind of juxtaposition: some women are having their hair done while others are at work. Hair is washed, but so is dirty laundry. Fingers are manicured here, other fingers sew sheets there. And then another element is added: in one scene, as a man is being shaved and a razor is sharpened by the barber, the blade of an ax, edged in a different space, is added to the series.[33] In all these examples then, snippets of reality are played in relation to bits gathered elsewhere with increasingly significant implications. Oppositions can be graphic, conceptual, or political in nature. The people involved in these scenes do not have to know about their participation in the grand scheme of things now under investigation. The man sharpening the ax need not be aware that his tool is now threatening to cut the neck of a bourgeois relaxing in a barber's chair, but the Kino-eye (that is to say, Vertov) does and it shows to us what could—and will—happen when the new bourgeois class, the entrepreneurs presently encouraged by Lenin to revive the economy under the auspices of the New Economic Policy, finally fall from power.

If we now look at an entire sequence, we see still other tactics at work. At some moment in the film, at a train station, several women with their baggage board an old-fashioned carriage. During the ride, one of the women protects herself from the sun with a white umbrella. Kaufman's camera car is seen following the horse-driven vehicle until it arrives at its destination where a servant picks up the suitcase of the travelers, carrying it on her shoulder. We find in this sequence much of what typifies Vertov's technique in general. The horse-cart goes from point A to point B but the voyage itself is without interest for the Russian director. In a breathtaking series of cuts, he scrutinizes the scene, making it speak beyond the simplicity of the event itself. First, he abruptly crosscuts from the women in their carriage to other carts with different passengers in them. As a result, we are no longer looking at an incidental choice of transportation by the women but discover that it is the carriage of choice of the burgeoning bourgeois class. There are also cuts to the wheels of a locomotive that slowly gain power and speed. Maybe they belong to the train that brought the women to the station in the first place. But the steel wheels can also be contrasted to the cart's wooden wheels. Here are two worlds that are opposed. Even though the bourgeois group Vertov detests may momentarily have the upper hand as they ride all by themselves in their fancy nineteenth-century carriage, they are nonetheless on the wrong side of history as the powerful, modern machine of steel—a communal mode of transportation that perfectly fits the Soviet society—will eventually wipe them from the face of the earth. Standing in the car, Kaufman catches it all, cranking his camera round and round and this too can be seen as participating in the motion of the other shots, for the mechanism inside the little box (the back and forth motion of the pulldown claw) advances the film very much like the axles of the locomotive pull the train forward. The camera and the locomotive thus share the same modern technology, they belong together, they represent the new progressive world.

But that is not all, for the Kino-eye apparatus gets the edge on the train by freeing itself from time and space, arresting its own motion, and analyzing what in fact is going on.[34] To prove it, Vertov stops the film, freezing several frames of the galloping horse, the women with the white sun umbrella, and people in another cart. Then, without warning, other shots join in: the wrinkled face of an older working woman, the smiling faces of children. These faces in fact can be seen in other sections of the film, they belong in other continuities elsewhere. What are they doing here? The woman is still working despite her advanced age. She is a member of the proletariat; her face can thus be used to express reproof and anger at the bourgeois in the carriage. The children, on the other hand, belong to a sequence seen later in the film, where they are being entertained by the tricks of a magician. Hence they are taken in by a mystification. In the new context too, they cannot see beyond the good times one must have riding in a cart. All at once, the old woman and the children no longer appear full screen, as themselves, but as images captured on a film surface edited by Yelizaveta Svilova, Vertov's wife. She is shown selecting clips of film and assembling them. The whole process of montage presently at work in the film is thus being demonstrated visually for the audience. All in all, the editing of this sequence can be seen as characteristic of the editing which drives the entire project.

Vertov is not shooting a documentary because he is not in the least interested in letting his subjects or the events speak for themselves. On the contrary, the job of the filmmaker for him is to gather visual evidence in the field, then to bring it back to a central office (the cutting room) where it can be analyzed, dissected, and its true function in the social and political world determined and demonstrated. Nothing is sacred in this kind of editing free-for-all. Every captured bit functions not only within one specific ensemble, it can also be made to serve differently in other centers of activity. With Noel Burch then, "one may safely say that there is not a single shot in this entire film whose place in the editing scheme is not overdetermined by a whole set of intertwined chains of signification. . . ."[35] In other words, the parts cannot really be understood at the time of their viewing. We need to see the entire film before being able to think back and reorganize in our mind what we saw. As with Eisenstein, the film is thus not just the sum of its parts. Instead of merely sending us new bits to be made sense of once and for all, the editing forces the viewer to continually revisit the same parts, each time armed with a different set of insights. Action and reaction do not have to be immediately contiguous any more, instead they can be inferred at any time and from any distance. Straightforward causality, as a result, does not have to be established by a witnessing camera. Rather, following Deleuze, "any point whatsoever in space itself perceives all the points on which it acts, or which act on it, however, far these actions and reactions extend."[36] Never again did the cut open such a gap in film continuity, never again were the pieces that were juxtaposed one after the other so radically held together for scrutiny. To this day, *The Man with a Movie Camera* remains the most ambitious piece of filmmaking ever assembled. It keeps on speaking, and speaking, and speaking.

VII

Montage was not revisited until after World War II when André Bazin questioned the ethics involved in the cutting operation. In "The Evolution of the Language of Cinema" and other articles, he attacked all types of editing but especially the Soviet kind insofar as, in their films, "the meaning is not within the image itself, it is in the shadow of the image projected by montage onto the field of consciousness of the spectator."[37] Let us illustrate what Bazin finds objectionable. Throughout *October*, the Mensheviks or Social Democrats are not unlike the hard-liners in general appearance. What informs us about their political philosophy is that their speeches are followed by shots of hands playing on harps or balalaikas so as to bring out their mellifluent opportunism.[38] We do not get the information by witnessing the Mensheviks at work or by reading their speeches, we figure out their wickedness through the import of an image whose circumstances are unconnected to the individuals in question. The picture of the harps, in other words, is hijacked from its own environment and tacked onto the Mensheviks, defining them once and for all in our mind. For Pascal Bonitzer, what incenses Bazin in all of this "is the contraction of the open signifying field by an image, a savage operation undertaken to satisfy extrinsic interests. . . ."[39] What is after all but political mockery by a Bolshevik director is presented as fact to the unsuspecting spectator.[40] In other words, the goal of Soviet montage is to tell us about something through extraneous ingredients rather than by letting the material speak for itself. In this way, what is there in the first place is doctored until it expresses nothing but the Party view or, at the very least, the intentions of the ventriloquist-director. For Bazin, this sleight-of-hand is dangerous because it turns the viewer into a mere receptacle, a passive attendant of the text. Indeed the vulnerable spectator might take the hocus pocus for the real thing, the insinuations for hard facts. In this kind of cinema, Bazin surmised, one is led by the nose, for what is actually there is erased under the pressure of a managerial discourse.

Through montage then, the director is pulling the strings, handling the spectators' very thought process, taking away their ability to think for themselves, to verify independently the merits of each presentation. Eisenstein, in one of his numerous articles on the subject, had indeed elaborated on what he understood to be a main constituent of composition in the work of art. "The art of plastic composition," he wrote, "consists in leading the spectator's attention through the exact path and with the exact sequence prescribed by the author of the composition. This applies to the eye's movement over the surface of a canvas if the composition is expressed in painting or over the surface of the screen if we are dealing with a film frame."[41] This idea in turn could be expanded from the single image to montage whose virtue "consists in integrating the spectator's emotional and intellectual response within the very process of creation. One forces the viewer to follow the same road worked out by the director when he conceived the film."[42] Of course, Eisenstein thought it tonic and vivifying for a spectator to be able to follow the selfsame path originated by the director because he or she is "taken in a creative ride during which, far from being enslaved to the author's personality, the viewer is enriched by becoming one with the author."[43] What Eisenstein, however, described as ecstasy sounded downright fishy to Bazin. Surely it was not incidental that montage originated in the Soviet Union insofar as it was a totalitarian way of doing things.

What is it, Bazin asked, that editing was hiding? Well, it is the event in itself, for itself, and what it contained, that is, the raw reality of an actual action. For the French critic indeed, "the events are not necessarily *signs* of something, a truth of which we are to be convinced, [on the contrary] they all carry their own weight, their own complete uniqueness. . . ."[44] Russian montage was thus but a particular instance of a much larger problem: it was editing in general that needed to be challenged. As a result his attack did not spare the American system of cutting that was based upon continuity between shots. Certainly, he conceded, when "scenes were broken down just . . . to analyze an episode according to the material or dramatic logic of the scene," its meaning would not be really different from what we would get were the scene "played on a stage and seen from a seat in the orchestra."[45] If this is indeed the case, what is Bazin fretting about? Essentially there is the fact that a "continuous homogeneous reality" is no longer witnessed in a single moment of time.[46] In other words, the very force of editing promotes "the *illusion* of being at real events" rather than their genuine unfolding in time.[47] For the French critic indeed, even the more banal use of editing in a mediocre film necessarily elevates artificiality over reality, signification over witnessing. Bazin certainly acknowledges that in daily life we too focus on different aspects of what stands before us "according to what interests or attracts" us.[48] The point though is that "the event exists continuously in its entirety . . . [and] we are the ones who decide to choose this or that aspect . . . according to the bidding of our feelings or our thinking. Someone else, however, would perhaps make a different choice."[49] In contrast, in classical editing, it is the director who, autocratically, "does the selecting that we would do in real life. We unconsciously accept his choices, because they conform to the seeming laws of ocular attraction; but they deprive us of . . . the freedom, at least the potential one, to modify at each instant our method of selection, of 'editing.'"[50] More stealthily even, as shots take the place of an event whose meaning has not be pre-assigned, they are simultaneously spiked with pointers, turning the whole thing into a signifier to be decoded.[51] A dramatic spectacle, artificially constructed, thus takes the place of raw reality. In Bazin's view then, actual reality, whether in a macrocosmic or microcosmic form, is the most valuable material for cinema. For the spectator, to attend to the genesis of the manifold world is more worthwhile in the long run than reading a text, however, great the latter may be.

But editing has yet other powers: because a cut literally transports us from one view to another, the actual length of each shot can become a factor in our experience of the film. Griffith certainly was the first director to notice this effect and to take full advantage of it in his last-minute rescues. And certainly, at the other end of the scale, Chantal Akerman in *Jeanne Dielman, 23 quai du Commerce, 1080 Bruxelles* (1977), was no less aware of the special needs of her film, playing it deliberately slow in this case. Editing thus hits us twice, first on the level of the connections between the shots, second through the rhythm, the beat, the pulse that organizes the delivery of the shots. Like music then, film can deliver phrasings whose chords can be felt resonating within one's body. Our rods and cones in the back of the eye are pulsating to the trace of the visuals. At that moment, the cadence of image change overwhelms any other consideration normally present during film viewing. Yet, as Jean Mitry has shown, motion pictures and musical rhythms are not totally alike because the former arises out of a connection between ever-changing visual components whereas the latter is based on formal relations between a limited number of notes.[52] Mitry demonstrated his argument by running in reverse for his students some celebrated pieces of "pure cinema" by Walter Ruttmann and Viking Eggeling. As the aberrant projection did not produce any change in the tempo of the pieces, he concluded that the rhythm of a film should not be based on an arbitrary meter but needed instead to relate to the content of the images.

Thus the necessity for an editor to become sensitive to the life of an image so as to respond intuitively to its demands. For there are no rules to recall here, each shot or continuity of shots bringing a new set of problems to the surface. Obviously, an editor must be responsive to the drama that is staged, to the words spoken, and to the mise en scène that brings it to visibility. Yet, because it is so irresistible, rhythm can also easily lure us into special arrangements, immediate, knee-jerk responses. A single example from *Breaker Morant* (Bruce Beresford, 1980) will illustrate the point. During the main trial, Morant is asked by the military judges whether he followed legal procedures before executing the captured Boer soldiers. Morant, angrily, responds: "We didn't carry military manuals around with us. We were out on the Veld, fighting the Boer the way he fought us. I'll tell you the rule we applied, Sir. We applied Rule 3–0–3. We caught them and we shot them on the Rule 3–0–3." As he does throughout the film, Beresford cuts from the trial to flash backs of the original event, in this case the shooting of the Boers. More precisely, Beresford cuts on the words themselves, on *Rule 3 0 3*, with soldiers aiming their guns, fingers pulling a trigger, etc. By doing so, the words in the court room are visually echoed by actions in the field. The cuts, one must admit, are truly compelling. It is "good editing" because the action is suddenly heightened by the sharp vivacissimo of the images. Yet, this is also a gimmick, the kind of cheap effect that generally incensed Bazin. For the sharp cutting does not add anything to our knowledge of what took place, it does not tell us anything new about the characters, it is there only because it is damn effective at getting a rise from everyone who sees it (from the editor and the director all the way to the audience). In other words, the film passage lures us not through its content but its percussive flamboyance, its external theatrics. This is but legerdemain for Bazin who warns us to make "no concession to dramatic tension" and to reject "the imperatives of the spectacular" when these are imported from outside the scene itself.[53] The intensity of a film should originate from its internal content only. Motion picture techniques are acceptable only insofar as they help "magnify the effectiveness of the elements of reality that the camera captures."[54] All in all, the French critic radicalized the notion of editing by suggesting that it be subordinated to the larger concerns of an aesthetic based on reality."[55]

## VIII

Having made clear what he rejected, Bazin needed to offer alternative ways of organizing narratives. The main one he offered turned around the possibility of deep focus, when the entire field of view is sharp, a technique that could make unnecessary the fragmentation of a scene into multiple shots. In the most famous example of the technique, in *Citizen Kane* (1941), Orson Welles initiates a shot with the little protagonist playing in the snow. He then pulls back from the window inside the cabin, preceding the three adults all the way to a second room where the papers are to be signed. As they go about the signing, we still see in the middle of the frame, through the window, the boy playing, totally unaware that his fate is being sealed at that very moment. In other words, we see all of it at once. We face it as we would confront any moment of life. It is up to us to grab this or that aspect at any time. Here nobody "choos[es] for us what we must see at the moment when it must be seen."[56] A more dramatic example of the potential of the technique can be observed in *The Best Years of Our Lives* (1946) where William Wyler stages the wedding scene in successive planes of interest. In the fore, the sailor who lost his arms in the war is using his prosthetic pincers to slip the ring on his soon-to-be wife. Just behind the couple we see Teresa Wright, the best girl, and her parents, who did their best to dissuade her from dating Dana Andrews who also happens to be in the room but much further back on the left.[57] As the priest goes about marrying the couple, our attention keeps shifting from one plane to the other and back again: from the sailor's difficulties, to Wright who, moved by the ceremony, turns her head halfway back toward Andrews who himself gazes intently at her. Our own bliss springs from this unusual encounter with several narrative magnetic poles, working simultaneously, all worth paying attention to.

A third example can be found in the work of Jean Renoir. In a laundry scene from *The Crime of Mr. Lange* (1936), the camera is outside the room, looking in through a window. Several laundresses are doing their work, talking to one another. Other women walk in and out of the room from the sides. Further out, through another window on the other side of the room, a couple is seen walking "upstairs" in a tight embrace. Even though we don't know them and they have no importance whatsoever in the story, their presence fully convinces us that the whole scene is for real. And this is so precisely because their action takes place in the background and the director is seemingly paying the couple no attention. Visually too Renoir's depth is in a class by itself. Although everything is sharp from foreground to background, the place does not bring attention to itself optically as is generally the case in *Citizen Kane*. Moreover, far from Welles's compositional control over his material, there is here a willingness to include everyone and everything, to share the space democratically as Bazin would say. The directing, in other words, gave the ensemble priority over the few protagonists around whom the narrative is normally tightly organized. This kind of open, dispersed mise en scène was found refreshing by the French critic because it was faithful to the multifarious activities of daily life.

Elsewhere, regardless of the particular technique involved (deep focus or not), Bazin felt it was important to see all the participants in a scene together in a shot at least once. In *Nanook of the North* (Robert Flaherty, 1922), for instance, it is essential that we discover the entire action of Nanook fishing out the seal from the hole in the ice in one shot. Flaherty's aesthetic instinct fortunately provided for this, making it possible for the audience to sense that this was not a regular fiction film where things could be manipulated at will, that Nanook was not a mere actor, and that the seal, far from some rubber decoy, was the real thing. To see Nanook using all his strength to pull the seal out of the water affirms the veracity of the recorded action over the skill of the motion picture technique. Bazin also mentions a British African adventure film where, after a banal crosscutting sequence during which we see alternatively a child and a lion, a view finally shows them in the same shot. Here again, Bazin contrasts the direct witnessing of an actual event with a series of signs that point to it without ever showing it. Yes, editing can make us believe that the lion is threatening the child but to see them in the same shot is to experience the situation on an altogether different level of credibility. What Bazin is telling us through these examples is that one can reach a higher level of cinematic tension by bypassing standard filmic procedures. Today, of course, the use of transparent materials (say, a glass between an actor and a snake) and digital compositing (people with computer generated dinosaurs) has undermined this part of Bazin's argument by making it much easier to integrate any visual element within a larger composition. Because we know this, we no longer respond to this kind of situation with the same enthusiasm as Bazin, for we now automatically suspect that a manipulation has taken place.

If spatial simultaneity has lost some of its shine through the years, duration has continued to work for Bazin's ideas. Still in *Nanook*, he pointed to "the actual length of the waiting period" before the seal is finally pulled out of the icy water.[58] Indeed, Flaherty is less interested here in telling us that Nanook manages to catch a seal than in making us participate in the hunt and share with Nanook the time it takes to bring the seal to the surface. This, of course, goes right smack against standard editing which retains only the important moments of an action, excising from it what is conventionally looked upon as dead time. Putting it differently, Bazin rejects both the "fort" and the "da" of editing, preferring to remain focused on what is there in the first place. Still, if the waiting is long, do we need to take in all of it? And should we pay equal attention to all events? While recognizing that not everything is "worth preserving" and that some things indeed "should be discarded," Bazin nevertheless affirms the value of duration as a valuable substitute for quick cutting shots.[59] Beyond personal preference though, is there some intrinsic value in "the simple continuing to be of a person to whom nothing in particular happens"?[60]

At the beginning of his master opus on cinema, Gilles Deleuze recalls Henri Bergson's fascination with having to wait for a lump of sugar to dissolve in a cup of hot coffee. For Bergson, to experience this duration in full was important, for it was only in such moments that one could become aware of time per se, in its developing fluctuation. In Deleuze's explanation, "each time we find ourselves confronted with a duration, or in a duration, we may conclude that there exists somewhere a whole which is changing, and which is open somewhere."[61] Duration allows us therefore to open ourselves up to an unsuspected dimension of existence which nevertheless continually eludes us. By the same token, duration also lays bare other beings around us. Instead of focusing on what normally reifies them in our eyes (their identity, their discourses, their manners, etc.), we are now able to pay close attention to their beingness. To confront others in this way is not easy, Maurice Merleau-Ponty warns us, for "there is something horrible, repulsive, and unchallengeable about [beings] which simply are, which express nothing."[62] A quick example will illustrate what he is talking about. Place a camcorder in your living room when you know someone will be spending some time there. Start the camera and forget about it. Later play back the tape without the sound on. What you will see is a body only. You won't have access to the internal life of that person or even the external clues which normally enliven our encounter with the world. In the end, it will be almost as if you were watching a rat in its cage. If you love the person, it will be quite unbearable. Yet, Merleau-Ponty adds, an encounter like this in real life is worthwhile because, at the end of the silent confrontation, something is gained, the realization that "if another person exists, if he too is a consciousness, then I [as well] must consent to be for him only a finite object, determinate, visible at a certain place in the world."[63] In other words, in the same way that this being is there as an other before me, I too must stand as an other in his or her eyes. Duration then sketches a humble but genuine encounter between two beings, making clear the absolute breach between them, yet demanding of each to be fully responsible for the other's welfare.

In film, where the gaze is pointing in one direction only, Bazin sets duration against editing where anything present dissipates itself in the jump to the other shot. We must, he says, pay attention to what is there, not just the door-knob-that-slowly-opens-the-door-onto-the-room-where-something-terrible-may-happen, but "the color of the enamel, the dirt marks at the level of the hand, the shine of the metal, the worn-away look. . . ."[64]

To confront what is present in its own life continuity, to pay attention to the being at hand, opens up a new window on reality based upon "pure action . . . sufficient to itself."[65] Since Bazin identified the potential of the "cinema of duration," many films have successfully taken advantage of this peculiar effect of the medium.[66] Of all of them, the one closest to Bazin's thinking is without doubt Chantal Akerman's *Jeanne Dielman*. There is nothing unusual, strictly speaking, about the editing of the film. What makes the whole experience of *Jeanne Dielman* so troublesome for so many viewers is therefore not some confrontational or disharmonious technique but the fact that the cutting lets each action run its autonomous course. When the protagonist takes the elevator to her apartment, we stay with her all the way. When she bathes, we are spared no detail of her toilette. When her son eats his soup, we watch him until he is finished. Akerman, in other words, makes us face the circumstances of daily life in real time, "fragments of concrete reality" that are called "image facts" by Bazin.[67] The offering may not be to everyone's taste but, for those who survive the initiation, cinema will never be the same again.

## IX

Ultimately, Bazin can be seen as arguing for a different kind of pro-filmic reality. For reality, unlike conventional narratives, does not carry identifying tags. Existence precedes essence and things happen, events take place in the real world without predetermined meanings being imposed on them. At the same time he is urging us to adopt filmmaking approaches that keep spectators, on some level at least, from claiming mastery over the rendering of the world in a film. Bonitzer gets it right when he writes that Bazin wants us (directors and viewers) to reconcile ourselves to a vision of things that acknowledges the ultimate mystery of nature and its works. Deep focus, spatial simultaneity, and duration are thus techniques that can complicate our imperious drive to know everything all at once. They also help us resist the temptation of drama for its own sake and the theatrics of editing in particular. Yet, even "image facts" need to be assembled somehow. One approach at least is suggested. Not surprisingly, knowing Bazin's respect for the Italian director, it originates in a film by Roberto Rossellini.

In *Paisà's* (1946) last segment, "a complex train of action is reduced to three or four brief fragments, in themselves already elliptical enough in comparison with the reality they are unfolding."[68] What appeals to Bazin here is that the editing does not seamlessly weave together separate views of a single action as is the case in classical cinema. Nor does it consist of extravagantly bridged images that stress the point the director wants to make as in the Soviet cinema. Instead, less than eloquent, even inconclusive moments are displayed on the screen one after the other. Along with a group of partisans, for example, we discover that some fishermen and their families have been shot. Yet we never find out how the Germans discovered that the fishermen had helped the partisans. A baby is left alive and this also is never explained. Certainly we are given enough informations to form "an intelligible succession of events, but these do not mesh like a chain with the sprockets of a wheel."[69] Bazin acknowledges that the mind of the spectator "has to leap from one event to the other," but, unlike what happens in montage, "facts are facts, our imagination makes use of them, but they do not exist inherently for this purpose."[70]

A last example: at the end of the film, the partisans have finally been caught by the Germans. After a quick interrogation, they lay on the ground while the Germans decide what to do with them. One of them remarks: "I've wet myself as a baby." Another one wonders: "My family will never know what happened to me." Immediately afterwards, it is morning and the men are lined up, their hands tied behind their back, on the side of a boat. One by one they are pushed into the Po river. A voice then tells us that "this happened in the winter of 1944. A few months later, spring came to Italy and the war was declared over." In other words, Rossellini's filmmaking, far from smoothing the links between discrete moments of action, evidences the gaps between them. For Bazin, the distinction between classical narrative and that originated by the Italian director can be summed up in the difference between bricks and rocks. With bricks, the material itself is irrelevant, it is the shape that is all-important, for it predetermines its use in building a wall. The rocks, on the other hand, which one uses to leap across a stream, owe their shape to thousands of microcosmic events of which one knows nothing. Also, they are not lined up for our sake. In the same way, whereas with classical cinema, "the meaning is established a priori," in Rossellini's film, "it is a posteriori."[71] Put succinctly, each event exists independently in its own unit of time, many facts have intervened between two scenes of which nothing is known, and the units are literally spliced rather than merged to each other. The power of such cinema originates not from what we see but from what we don't know.

Putting it differently, one could say that Bazin favored shooting over writing and editing because it was at that time that the film was most open, aesthetically and dramatically, to the indeterminacy of life. The work of these other moments of production could consist mostly in preparing the way or preserving the encounter with reality taking place during filming. Bazin's interest was also determinedly turned toward film practice, putting its energy on what could be done to reawaken the cinema to its full potential. He reminded us that it was indeed cinematic to discover people and their environment in a single shot, to pay attention to everything at length. And he warned us against too much dependence on film techniques which at times could be destructive of more profound values. One need not play by the rules, Bazin reiterated, for these were always terribly limiting. On the contrary, one should constantly refer back to the larger multifarious territory where choice is inexhaustible. In that he pointed to the single monad rather than the flow from shot to shot, Bazin differentiated himself from other theorists. Whereas the force of the American cinema was essentially centripetal in that it brought everything back to an individual core, and the thrust of Soviet montage centrifugal in its ability to link subjects independently of time and space, Bazin pointed to the here and now, to actual existence and the materiality of things. Editing was the enemy because it performed a cheap trick on the viewer, because the cut favored the flight of an idea over the thing itself. Editing made the world disappear behind the discourse. And this, in turn, not only impoverished cinema but made us poorer as well.

# X

It is time now to return to the Kuleshov experiment and rethink its coordinates. We have evaluated its potential effects with regard to editing but have not really examined its most disturbing quality. Kuleshov indeed pointed to the connections that show up when we look at discrete shots, but he left aside the question of their origin. To understand what is at stake here it may be useful to go back once more to Ferdinand de Saussure and his seminal ideas on linguistics. Saussure made clear that the rapport between the signifier (the specific group of letters or the sounds we use to describe something) and its signified (what is meant by it in our mind) was totally arbitrary. The fact that the signifier and the signified are not amalgamated implies that each set of letters acquires its meaning only insofar as it distinguishes itself from other combinations of letters. If h-o-u-s-e conjures something in our head it is only because other terms are absent: h-u-t, f-a-r-m, l-o-d-g-e, s-k-y-s-c-r-a-p-e-r, etc. From the start then, language is marked by absences rather than presence.

Acknowledging these circumstances, how do we manage to communicate at all? First of all, what you have in mind when you speak (your signified), however hard you may try, still comes out through less than specific signifiers. There is a polysemous aspect to the entire operation. As Roland Barthes put it, "everything signifies ceaselessly and several times" without ever "being delegated to a great final ensemble, to an ultimate structure."[72] Simultaneously, in reading something or listening to someone, we do not pay equal attention to every word. A strange phenomenon indeed takes place when word follows word in a sentence. Rather than give each of them its due, we respond to the overall flow instead. We may thus bypass articles, adverbs, and adjectives in a written text so as to get quickly to the next big word-concept that moves the sentence ahead or closes it. In live conversations, we may also pay attention to intonations, facial expressions, and hand gestures more than the actual speech for they help us grasp what is being said and cue us on how to respond. All in all, if each word by itself fails to link us to a precise signified, and a sentence is made sense of by floating over the text rather than detailing its exact content, to hear or read a sentence ends up more like a hallucination than the rational, scientific decoding we often imagine such an experience to be.

We may now have a better idea of the effect involved in Kuleshov's little trick. Let us take the shot of the actor Mosjukin. It is a signifier. Yet, from the very start, the face we observe on the screen is shot through with what Jacques Derrida calls *différance*. By this he means that our signifier brings out only differences between this signifier and others, a process that endlessly postpones the determination of what it actually signifies. However controlled it may be, Mosjukin's face cannot point to a specific signified. What is it indeed that we are looking at? A man? A young man? A charismatic individual? A Russian? An actor? A member of the bourgeoisie? In addition, rather than pointing to someone specific, the view becomes significant in that other views (woman-older-man-everyman-foreigner-non-actor-revolutionary) are not there. In other words, what is absent overwhelms any specificity we may find with Mosjukin himself. For Derrida, "no element [in a system] can function as a sign without referring to another element which itself is not simply present. This interweaving results in each 'element' . . . being constituted on the basis of the trace within it of the other elements of the chain or system."[73]

Beyond this, whatever meaning we may get from a single signifier is temporary for we must postpone its actualization until we know more about what is going on in the scene. This is the "latency" of the shot Balázs talks about.[74] Indeed it is only after we see the second shot, the woman lying on the couch, that we retrospectively conclude that Mosjukin sees her, maybe even desires her. Let us quote Derrida again on this. He writes: "The play of differences supposes, in effect, syntheses and referrals which forbid at any moment, or in any sense, that a simple element be present in and of itself, referring only to itself."[75] Confronted with a succession of shots, we posit a link between them the best way we can. Desire, which we now "recognize" in Mosjukin's eyes, is nevertheless not in his close-up (we could not see it at first), nor in the second shot of the woman alone. Where is it then? It must be in the cut, in the gap between the two shots. Not in the presence of something but in the absence of anything. How is it possible in these circumstances that we find some meaning, that we "understand something" after all, as Merleau-Ponty said?[76] Well, *we* do the job: *we* put that something in, *we* bridge the gap, *we* fill the space between the two monads. Indeed, as David Bordwell suggests, "the spectator comes to the film already tuned, prepared to focus energies toward story construction and to apply sets of schemata derived from context and prior experience."[77] How does it work? It works because we already know the story. We have seen other films just like this one before. We know the genre. We recognize patterns, etc. What Bergson says of rapid reading applies here as well: "our mind notes here and there a few characteristic lines and fills all the intervals with memory-images which, projected in the paper, take the place of the real printed characters and may be mistaken for them."[78] In the same way that whenever someone speaks or when we read a sentence, we skip quickly over the filler, the stuff we recognize as mere links, the material that merely elaborates what is already well known, we do not have to pay much attention to Mosjukin's face (as Bazin urges us to do) for the second shot immediately cues us about its purpose a posteriori. In agreement with Nietzsche then, the effect produces the cause, not the other way around.[79] Better still, the link is entirely fantasized out of disparate elements. That the effect is not in the juxtaposition per se was made clear by Mitry when he suggested that a child might not understand the implication of sexual desire, thus missing at least that part of the Kuleshov effect.[80] What makes the sentence or the film sequence comprehensible in the end is therefore the buzz of language or cinema: all the other texts that precede this one, yet saturate it through and through. Kuleshov's little sequence is meaningful because we have seen many other films and we bring to this text preexisting templates gathered elsewhere.

There is more still. Not only do viewers bring to the film clusters of informations accumulated through exposure to a shared culture, individuals can also activate some more personal input. Whereas the former material can be counted on (at least within a group or a generation), the latter may involve unpredictable emotional triggers. In *Five Readers Reading*, Norman N. Holland provides many examples of such activity: a rather innocuous image, for instance, may profoundly resonate within a given individual because of a particular childhood memory.[81] A reader is therefore not only a passive recipient of an author's intentions: feedback loops congregate and meet the text half way. A transaction in effect takes place with some material more than welcome, some other content guarded against. All in all, any cut depends on an incredible amount of connections that are never consciously articulated. Hovering over each cut is a dazzling array of background material (cultural or more personal in nature) not present anywhere in the film that nevertheless flashes and waves and sizzles back and forth, coalescing with the text in some unpredictable fashion.

In Derrida's words, "nothing, neither among the elements nor within the system, is anywhere ever simply present or absent. There are only, everywhere, differences and traces of traces."[82] Editing has always been seen as the art of joining together two meaningful pieces of film material, fusing their motion, positing coherence and continuity between them, etc. But maybe editing really consists of finessing the gap between the shots, holding on to what is absent in that juncture, balancing what is consummated (but never finalized) with what is still open. Sartre put his finger on it when he pointed out that a ring is what it is only because of the large hole within it.[83] The cut too then is where the w/hole is. Think of it as two threads intertwined in a spider's web. The workability of the knot depends on hundreds of similar splices all around. The entire structure breathes with the wind. The design is full of holes. Yet, at the end of the day, a fly shows up. . . .

When we cut a film, we probably think we organize the parts, shape the text, and define the meaning. More likely, we end up evoking rather than showing, suggesting more than presenting. We sketch more than we draw. We work with what is not there. We play with what is latent in an image. We activate an endless deferment of meaning. More than a demonstration, the finished film is like a melody, a chant. It makes sense while we are at it, but do we really know what led us from the first shot to the last?

# CHAPTER TEN

○

# *Envoi*

Hollywood is a dangerous place to be. Professionally, what it promises—a large canvas, the lure of great talent, absolute control of technique—cannot be matched anywhere in the world. The film will be slick and money will not be an issue. And then there is the glamour that goes with movie making. There will be meetings and lunches, press releases and interviews, limos and parties. There will be premieres, film festivals, and the Academy Awards. No wonder the package has proven irresistible. Generation after generation, filmmakers have made the journey to Los Angeles, full of ideas and projects, energy and optimism, but few have managed to achieve what they wanted. There are simply too many compromises to make and Hollywood, in the end, has gotten the better of all of them. It is thus truly foolish to believe that you alone will buck the trend and avoid the corruption that has contaminated everyone else. I cannot repeat it loudly enough: stay away from Los Angeles. Do not live here, do not study here, and do not shoot here. Woody Allen, Stanley Kubrick, Martin Scorsese, and Francis Ford Coppola have done well while managing to live and work elsewhere: learn from them.

At a recent lunch organized by the *Los Angeles Times*, five successful writers and directors compared notes.[1] The main complaint involved the packaging of movies before a script even exists. Another issue entailed the endless duplication of material in action movies: "hostages, terrorists, car chases, fist fights, a scene in a bar with strippers, and buddy cops—one black, one white."[2] Faced with multiple sequels of successful movies, the writers also grumbled about "constantly writ[ing] on carbon paper."[3] Having heard all of this, the youngest director in the group asked the others whether they ever did a film for the "wrong" reasons. They all laughed at this: "Is he asking if we've sold out?" "Are we whores?"[4] That question though has been at the core of the Hollywood syndrome from almost the beginning. Why indeed do creative people go along with a system they supposedly despise? The answer has not changed over time. First, nobody can say no to the money. The amount of it simply overwhelms any resistance. Second, people are afraid that if they reject one project they never will work again. Literally there is the fear of being left out of the game.

There is also a delusion at work in the Hollywood mystique. It even became the subject of a very funny film by Preston Sturges, *Sullivan's Travels* (1941). Its protagonist is a comedy director who wants to make a serious movie about the difficult times in America. Since he doesn't know the situation first hand, he makes himself up as a hobo and goes out to explore how poor people live. What he learns instead is that he can help people best by continuing to entertain them. "There is a lot to be said for making people laugh," he sums up. "Did you know that's all some people have?" To this day, blockbuster writers and directors justify what they are doing by pointing to six hundred spectators "cheering and laughing" while watching their films in a theater.[5] Of course, that is also what people do when attending an extravaganza staged by the World Wrestling Federation (I could point to worse examples). These people are your audience as well. Take a good look at them. Are they being helped? Can you see rather what entertainment is doing *to* them? Finally, it is just too convenient to pretend you are helping others when in fact you are mostly serving yourself.

As a young filmmaker, you need to take a serious look at all of this and evaluate what you are really after. What are your ultimate goals? To make films or to use filmmaking to secure the easy life? If the general idea, to quote Adorno, is to avoid becoming "pawns in [an] all-encompassing system," you should bring your expectations in line with your goals.[6] Jaco van Dormael, the writer/director of *Toto the Hero* (1991), for instance, makes a point of living frugally: no luxurious home on the top of a hill, no expensive car, etc. The less at stake, the freer you are. Having too many possessions has a way of making you do things just to sustain that lifestyle. Get a job that pays the bills and make movies on the cheap. Digital technology has made that possible.

Next, stay away from big budgets, stars, and professional crews. They bring in viewpoints and attitudes that are antagonistic to innovative filmmaking. Find a different group of people to work with. There are plenty of undiscovered but talented actors and technicians throughout the country. Hire people who believe in you, individuals who value the seriousness of a project more than fame or money. Keep in mind that you are not trying to emulate Hollywood films. It is okay to be less than perfect. Remember the carpet weaver who intentionally leaves a flaw in each rug for only God's work is perfect. What you lose in gloss, you will gain in honesty and authenticity.

You will also need to adjust your tactics. Be wary of the techno-aesthetic discourse you see everywhere on display. In their "Dogma 95" proclamation, Lars von Trier and Thomas Vinterberg took a stand against what they called the "cosmeticization" of today's movies, their predictability, their superficiality.[7] What can be done in response? They suggest shooting only on locations, forcing the camera to discover the action as opposed to staging the latter for the former, using diegetic lighting. Etc., etc. These rules of course are totally arbitrary. No film technique is inherently superior to any other. The reason, I think, von Trier and Vinterberg chose these particular ones is because they put you in a bind, they force you to abandon filmmaking by the numbers. If overnight the commercial cinema decided to go for long takes, fast cutting would be their response. The idea also is to reawaken audiences to the power and magic of a single film in contrast to a commodity whose coordinates are only too wellknown. When you adopt industrial norms you just fall into a trap: you end up being judged by rules not of your making. In the days of the electric guitar, it is time to go back to the accordion.

At the close of the *Los Angeles Times* lunch, a director finally said it straight out: "We are entertainers, plain and simple, and we're responsible to bring that money back, to make a profit."[8] Is this what cinema is really all about? Andrey Tarkovsky agrees that "no artist would work to fulfill his spiritual mission if he knew that no one was ever going to see his work." Tarkovsky continues, "Yet at the same time, when he is working he must put a screen between himself and other people, in order to be shielded from empty, trivial topicality. For only total honesty and sincerity, compounded by the knowledge of his own responsibility towards others, can ensure the fulfillment of an artist's creative destiny."[9] Is this really too much to ask? My generation has to take the blame for the present morass. We shamelessly put the "trivial" on a par with the work of Bergman, Tarkovsky, and Antonioni. We dwelled in the pleasures of popular culture knowing that these artists and others were diligently at work. Today, however, the old masters are dead, retired, or very close to it. Who is there to take their place? To use Tarkovsky's image, somebody's got to water the parched tree.[10] Somebody's got to step up and do the work. If *you* don't, who will?

For a long time, the song of the sirens will echo in your head. Their lure will be difficult to resist. To maintain your course, like Ulysses, you must wear wax in your ears and tie yourself to the helm. The ride may not be easy at first, but it is your boat, your life, and your dream. Eventually the sirens will tire of calling and switch to easier prey. From that point on, I promise you, it will be smooth sailing until the end.

Hollywood *delenda.*

# NOTES

## CHAPTER ONE.
## CINEMA: THE STATE OF THE ART

1. Wayne C. Booth, "The Company We Keep: Self-Making in Imaginative Art, Old and New," in *Television: The Critical View*, ed. Horace Newcomb, 4th ed. (New York: Oxford Univ. Press, 1987), p. 391 (his emphasis).

2. Perry Anderson, *Lineages of the Absolutist State* (London: New Left Books, 1974), p. 55.

3. Janet Staiger, "Mass-Produced Photoplays: Economic and Signifying Practices in the First Years of Hollywood," *Wide Angle*, vol. 4, no. 3 (1980), p. 20.

4. U.S. vs. Paramount (1948) started the ball rolling. By forcing the studios to sell their majority interests in theater ownership, the Justice Department compelled them to change their production strategies. The studios now had little interest in saturating the market with B movies for that would dilute the value of their best films.

5. See Michael Schudson, *Advertising, the Uneasy Persuasion: Its Dubious Impact on American Society* (New York: Basic Books, 1984), p. 30.

6. No less than 186 such venues have been mentioned for *The Lion King* (Roger Allers and Rob Minkoff, 1994), *The Economist*, 23 May 1998, p. 57.

7. *The Economist*, 23 May 1998, p. 57.

8. Theodor Adorno, *The Culture Industry: Selected Essays on Mass Culture*, ed. J. M. Bernstein (London: Routledge, 1991), p. 72.

9. I am indebted for my analysis to an excellent article by W. Brian Arthur, "Increasing Returns and the New World of Business," *Harvard Business Review*, vol. 74, no. 4 (July-August 1996).

10. Arthur, p. 100.

11. Robert H. Frank and Philip J. Cook, *The Winner-Take-All Society* (New York: Free Press, 1995).

12. See Amy Wallace, "How Much Bigger Can the Bang Get?' *Los Angeles Times*, Calendar Section, August 9, 1998, p. 8.

13. Steven E. de Souza, in Wallace, p. 8.

14. De Souza, in Wallace, p. 8.

15. In Patrick Goldstein, "The Force Never Left Him," *Los Angeles Times*, Magazine Section, February 2, 1997, p. 26.

16. Harold L. Vogel, *Entertainment Industry Economics*, 2nd ed. (New York: Cambridge Univ. Press, 1990), p. 92.

17. See Frank and Cook, note 11.

18. In Frank and Cook, p. 101.

19. Arthur, p. 104.

20. See Arthur, p. 104.

21. Robert Kuttner, *Everything for Sale: The Virtues and Limits of Markets* (New York: Knopf, 1997), p. 62.

22. Tom Hayden, quoted in *The Sixties: From Memory to History*, ed. David Farber (Chapel Hill: Univ. of North Carolina Press, 1994), pp. 187–88.

23. Quoted in Richard J. Barnet and John Cavanaugh, *Global Dreams: Imperial Corporations in the New World Order* (New York: Simon and Schuster, 1994), p. 38.

24. See note 4. The demand for foreign films can also be seen as a reply by exhibitors to the Hollywood production slowdown following U.S. vs. Paramount.

25. During the sixties, on the average, ten percent of all films released in the United States market were made abroad. Today less than one percent are.

26. See Daniel Bell, *The Cultural Contradictions of Capitalism* (New York: Basic Books, 1976), p. 39.

27. Quoted in *The Sixties: From Memory to History*, p. 219 (David Farber's emphasis).

28. Todd Gitlin, *The Sixties: Years of Hope, Days of Rage* (New York: Bantam, 1987), p. 202 (his emphases).

29. The triumph of youth culture with its antiestablishment and anticon-sumerism components was no obstacle for advertising agencies who used the movement's rhetoric as "a cultural machine for turning disgust with consumerism into the very fuel by which consumerism might be accelerated." In Thomas Frank, *The Conquest of Cool: Business Culture, Counterculture, and the Rise of Hip Consumerism* (Chicago: Univ. of Chicago Press, 1997), p. 119.

30. Richard Hofstadter, *Anti-Intellectualism in American Life* (New York: Alfred A. Knopf, 1963).

31. Hofstadter, p. 55.

32. See Alexis de Tocqueville, *Democracy in America*, ed. J. P. Mayer and Max Lerner, trans. George Lawrence (New York: Harper, 1988), vol. 2, pp. 525–26.

33. Hofstadter, p. 19.

34. Theodore Roszak, *The Making of a Counter Culture: Reflections on the Technocratic Society and Its Youthful Opposition* (New York: Doubleday, 1968), pp. 50–51.

35. Susan Sontag, *Against Interpretation and Other Essays* (New York: Octagon, 1986), p. 9.

36. Susan Sontag, quoted in David Steigerwald, *The Sixties and the End of Modern America* (New York: St. Martin's Press, 1995), p. 158.

37. Sontag, *Against Interpretation*, p. 7.

38. Steigerwald, p. 158.

39. Sontag, *Against Interpretation*, p. 14 and 303 (her emphases).

40. Sontag, *Against Interpretation*, p. 303.

41. Sontag, *Against Interpretation*, p. 304.

42. Steigerwald, p. 164.

43. See Barnet and Cavanaugh, p. 38.

44. See Bell, p. 70ff.

45. Bell, p. 70.

46. The diegetic world is the part of the film that is accessible to the characters: what other characters look like, the lines of dialogue addressed to them, the size and look of the room, etc. In contrast, non-diegetic information involves all the clues directed to viewers alone: the angle of the camera, the perspective of the lens, the "pit" music that accompanies the film, the rhythm of the cutting, that sort of thing.

47. Charles Darwin, quoted in *The Works of William James: The Principles of Psychology*, (Cambridge: Harvard Univ. Press, 1981), vol. 2, pp. 1,062–63.

48. James, p. 1,065 (his emphasis). I have altered his sentence to make it more understandable to today's readers.

49. James, p. 1,066 (his emphasis).

50. Slavko Vorkapich, "A Fresh Look at the Dynamics of Film-Making," *American Cinematographer*, (February 1972), p. 223.

51. S. M. Eisenstein, *Selected Works*, vol. 1, *Writings 1922–34*, ed. Richard Taylor (London: BFI Publishing, 1988), p. 3.

52. Bell, p. 118.

53. The same argument raged during the late twenties in France. René Clair, for instance, made clear the difference between the perception of objects in motion and the spectators themselves experiencing that motion. Talking about Abel Gance's film *La Roue*, he wrote: "We had already seen trains moving along tracks at a velocity heightened by the obliging movie camera, but we had not yet felt ourselves absorbed . . . by the screen as by a whirlpool. 'That is only a feeling.' You tell me. Maybe. But we had not come there [to the theater] to think. To see and feel is enough for us." Quoted in Alan Williams, *Republic of Images: A History of French Filmmaking* (Cambridge: Harvard Univ. Press, 1992), p. 89

54. For a more complete analysis of the impact of the Steadicam, see my article, "Visuality and Power: The Work of the Steadicam," *Film Quarterly*, vol. 47, no. 2 (Winter 1993–94).

55. Jean Baudrillard, *America*, trans. Chris Turner (London: Verso, 1988), p. 6.

56. James, p. 1,072.

57. A good place to start is with Madan Sarup, *An Introductory Guide to Post-Structuralism and Postmodernism* (Athens: Univ. of Georgia Press, 1989). All essential primary sources are listed and discussed there.

58. Theodor Adorno, *Aesthetic Theory*, ed. Gretel Adorno and Rolf Tiedermann, trans. C. Lenhardt (London: Routledge, 1972), p. 334.

59. Max Horkheimer and Theodor W. Adorno, *Dialectic of Enlightenment*, trans. John Cumming (New York: Continuum, 1993), p. 135. I altered "the purity of bourgeois art" to fit my own distinction between modern art and consumer culture.

60. Adorno, *Aesthetic Theory*, p. 323.

61. Adorno, *Aesthetic Theory*, p. 323.

62. Ferdinand de Saussure, *Course in General Linguistics*, trans. Wade Baskin (New York: McGraw-Hill, 1966), p. 120.

63. Roland Barthes, quoted in *Encyclopedia of Contemporary Literary Theory*, ed. Irena R. Makaryk (Toronto: Univ. of Toronto Press, 1993), p. 161.

64. See Hayden White, *Metahistory: The Historical Imagination in Nineteenth-Century Europe* (Baltimore: Johns Hopkins Univ. Press, 1973).

65. See Martin Heidegger, *On the Way to Language*, trans. Peter D. Hertz (New York: Harper, 1971).

66. Karl Mannheim, *Man and Society in an Age of Reconstruction* (New York: Harcourt, Brace and Co., 1941), p. 87.

67. Gerald Graff, *Literature against Itself: Literary Ideas in Modern Society* (Chicago: Univ. of Chicago Press, 1979), p. 119.

68. Adorno, *The Culture Industry*, p. 53.

69. Fredric Jameson, "Postmodernism and Consumer Society," in *The Anti-Aesthetic*, ed. Hal Foster (Port Townsend, Wash.: Bay Press, 1983), p. 112.

70. "So enterprising is capitalism," Harry Braverman writes, "that even where the effort is made by one or another section of the population to find a way to nature, sport, or art through personal activity and amateur or 'underground' innovation, these activities are rapidly incorporated into the market so far as possible." In *Labor and Monopoly Capital: The Degradation of Work in the Twentieth Century* (New York: Monthly Review Press, 1974), p. 279.

71. Quoted in André Bazin, *Jean Renoir*, ed. François Truffaut, trans. W. W. Halsey II and William H. Simon (New York: Simon and Schuster, 1973), p. 11.

72. Sarup, p. 150.

73. Booth, p. 399.

74. Adorno, *Aesthetic Theory*, p. 321.

75. Robert L. Heilbroner, *Business Civilization in Decline* (New York: W. W. Norton, 1976), p. 114.

## CHAPTER TWO.
## ART/ENTERTAINMENT

1. Quoted in José Antonio Maravall, *Culture of the Baroque: Analysis of a Historical Structure*, trans. Terry Cochran (Minneapolis: Univ. of Minnesota Press), p. 120.

2. Quoted in Maravall, p. 120.

3. I am basing my portrayal of the baroque era on Maravall's analysis.

4. Maravall, p. 72.

5. Maravall, p. 89.

6. On "interpellation," see the chapter on the Ideological State Apparatuses in Louis Althusser, *Lenin and Philosophy and Other Essays*, trans. Ben Brewster (New York: Monthly Review, 1971).

7. Maravall, p. 90.

8. Joyce G. Simpson, quoted in Maravall, p. 143.

9. The link to "the triumph of sports and games" in modern life was made by José Ortega y Gasset in *The Dehumanization of Art*, trans. Helene Weyl (Princeton: Princeton Univ. Press, 1968), p. 51.

10. Today's discontent "cannot be touched by providing more prosperity and jobs because these are the very things that produced this discontent in the first place." Harry Braverman, *Labor and Monopoly Capital: The Degradation of Work in the Twentieth Century* (New York: Monthly Review Press, 1974), p. 14.

11. Munsterberg, quoted in Matthew Hale Jr., *Human Science and Social Order* (Philadelphia: Temple Univ. Press, 1980), p. 159.

12. In Hale, p. 152.

13. Hale, pp. 152–53.

14. Oskar Negt and Alexander Kluge, *Public Sphere and Experience: Toward an Analysis of the Bourgeois and Proletarian Public Sphere*, trans. Peter Labanyi, Jamie Daniel, and Assenka Oksiloff (Minneapolis: Univ. of Minnesota Press, 1993), p. 33.

15. Hanns Eisler, *Composing for the Films* (New York: Oxford Univ. Press, 1947), p. 59.

16. Max Horkheimer and Theodor W. Adorno, *Dialectic of Enlightenment*, trans. John Cumming (New York: Continuum, 1993), pp. 139 and 137 (I have rearranged the order of the text to suit my own purpose).

17. Herbert Marcuse, *One-Dimensional Man: Studies in the Ideology of Advanced Industrial Society* (Boston: Beacon, 1964), p. 7.

18. Paul Willis, quoted in Graeme Turner, *British Cultural Studies: An Introduction* (Boston: Unwin Hyman, 1990), p. 1.

19. Horkheimer and Adorno, pp. 144 and 146.

20. Although Hollywood has offered films dealing with all sorts of social ills, the negative tends to originate with individuals rather than with the system. It is enough for the "good guy" to rid society of the "bad guy" for everything to be all right again. *On the Waterfront* (Elia Kazan, 1954) epitomizes that kind of work. For more on the topic, see Steven J. Ross, *Working-Class Hollywood: Silent Film and the Shaping of Class in America* (Princeton, Princeton Univ. Press, 1998).

21. Paul Tillich, *The Protestant Era*, trans. James Luther Adams (Chicago: Univ. of Chicago Press, 1948), p. 263.

22. Negt and Kluge, p. 37.

23. Negt and Kluge, p. 172.

24. I am surely exaggerating here. A long list of films could be offered proving me wrong. Most of them though would fall into the category mentioned in note 20. My concern here is with young filmmakers entering the system. For them, Hollywood is not a welcoming place: enormous pressure is applied from the start to keep them from going "too far."

25. On *Rausch* and Nietzsche's theory of art, see Friedrich Nietzsche, *The Will to Power*, trans. Walter Kaufmann and R. J. Hollingdale (New York: Vintage, 1968), bk. 3, chap. 4 , pp. 419–53.

26. Hans-Georg Gadamer, *Truth and Method*, 2nd rev. ed., trans. Joel Weinsheimer and Donald G. Marshall (New York: Continuum, 1994), p. 70.

27. Alain Finkielkraut, *The Defeat of the Mind*, trans. Judith Friedlander (New York: Columbia Univ. Press, 1995), p. 118.

28. Martin Heidegger, "The Origin of the Work of Art," in *Basic Writings*, ed. David Farrell Krell, trans. Albert Hofstadter (San Francisco: Harper, 1977), p. 149.

29. Martin Heidegger, *Nietzsche*, trans. David Farrell Krell (San Francisco: Harper, 1991), vol. 1, p. 101.

30. Nietzsche, no. 811, p. 421 and no. 818, p. 433 (I have slightly altered the translation).

31. Heidegger, "The Origin of the Work of Art," p. 184.

32. Heidegger, "The Origin of the Work of Art," p. 181 (I have altered the translation).

33. Herbert Marcuse, *Counterrevolution and Revolt* (Boston: Beacon, 1972), pp. 71–72.

34. Henri Bergson, *L'Evolution créatrice* (Paris: Félix Alcan, 1908), p. 7 (my translation).

35. For Heidegger, such "preserving" power is time-bound. When the "world" of a work of art stops speaking to new generations, it becomes museum art.

36. For an excellent discussion of the subject, see Meyer Schapiro, "The Still Life as a Personal Object—A Note on Heidegger and Van Gogh," in *The Reach of Mind: Essays in Memory of Kurt Goldstein,* ed. Marianne L. Simmel (New York: Springer, 1968); and Jacques Derrida, *The Truth in Painting,* trans. Geoff Bennington and Ian McLeod (Chicago: Univ. of Chicago Press, 1987), pp. 255–382.

37. The quote is from David Farrell Krell's essay that precedes Heidegger's "The Origin of the Work of Art," p. 145.

38. Martin Heidegger, *Being and Time,* trans. John Macquarrie and Edward Robinson (San Francisco: Harper, 1962), p. 51.

39. See *Being and Time,*pp. 51–55.

40. Heidegger, "The Origin of the Work of Art," p. 170.

41. Heidegger, "The Origin of the Work of Art," p. 163.

42. I am paraphrasing Joseph J. Kockelmans in *Heidegger on Art and Art Works* (Dordrecht: Martinus Nijhoff, 1985), p. 152.

43. Heidegger, "The Origin of the Work of Art," p. 164.

44. See Heidegger, *Being and Time,* pp. 219–24.

45. Heidegger, *Nietzsche,* vol. 1, p. 81.

46. On expressing versus instituting a world, I am following Robert Bernasconi in *Heidegger in Question: The Art of Existing* (Atlantic Heights, N. J.: Humanities Press Int., 1993), p. 113. On the birth of aesthetics, see Heidegger, *Nietzsche,* vol. 1, pp. 77–91.

47. Heidegger, *Nietzsche,* vol. 1, p. 82.

48. Heidegger, *Nietzsche,* vol. 1, p. 82.

49. Heidegger, "The Origin of the Work of Art," p. 183.

50. Heidegger, "The Origin of the Work of Art," p. 185.

51. See Czeslaw Milosz, *The Captive Mind,* trans. Jane Zielonko (New York: Vintage International, 1990).

52. Marcuse, *One-Dimensional Man*, p. 62.

53. On bad faith see Jean-Paul Sartre, *Being and Nothingness*, trans. Hazel E. Barnes (New York: Pocket Books, 1956), pt. 1, chap. 2, pp. 86–116. Also see *What Is Literature? And Other Essays*, no trans. (Cambridge: Harvard Univ. Press, 1988), p. 66.

## CHAPTER THREE.
## THE FILM SCHOOL

1. Jacques Derrida, "Où commence et comment finit un corps enseignant," in *Politiques de la philosophie*, ed. Dominique Grisoni (Paris: Grasset, 1976), p. 74 (my translation).

2. See Bill Readings, *The University in Ruins* (Cambridge: Harvard Univ. Press, 1996).

3. James Morgan Hart, in *American Higher Education: A Documentary History*, ed. Richard Hofstadter and Wilson Smith (Chicago: Univ. of Chicago Press, 1961), vol. 2, p. 577.

4. James Morgan Hart, quoted in *American Higher Education*, vol. 2, p. 572.

5. Readings, p. 67.

6. The Yale Report of 1828, quoted in *American Higher Education*, vol. 1, p. 252.

7. James Morgan Hart, quoted in *American Higher Education*, vol. 2, p. 573.

8. John Dewey, quoted in *American Higher Education*, vol. 2, p. 952.

9. Charles William Eliot, quoted in *American Higher Education*, vol. 2, p. 705.

10. Robert M. Hutchins, quoted in *American Higher Education*, vol. 2, p. 927.

11. Robert M. Hutchins, quoted in *American Higher Education*, vol. 2, p. 932.

12. Harry D. Gideonse, quoted in *American Higher Education*, vol. 2, p. 946.

13. Harry D. Gideonse, quoted in *American Higher Education*, vol. 2, p. 945.

14. The Harvard Report on General Education, 1945 quoted in *American Higher Education*, vol. 2, p. 965 (my emphasis).

15. Victor O. Freeburg had taught a photoplay course at Columbia as early as 1915.

16. William Stull, A.S.C., "The Movies Reach College," *American Cinematographer* (June 1929), p. 16.

17. Karl T. Waugh, quoted in Stull, p. 16.

18. Quoted in Stull, p. 16.

19. Stull, p. 29.

20. Milton Sills, quoted in *The Story of the Films: As Told by Leaders of the Industry to the Students of the Graduate School of Business Administration George F. Baker Foundation Harvard University*, ed. Joseph F. Kennedy (Chicago: A. W. Shaw, 1927), p. 194.

21. Stull, p. 16.

22. Stull, p. 29.

23. Stull, p. 29.

24. Stull, p. 29.

25. Peter Milne, *Motion Picture Directing: The Facts and Theories of the Newest Art* (New York: Falk, 1922), p. 5.

26. In Patrick Goldstein, "The Force Never Left Him" *Los Angeles Times*, Magazine Section, February 2, 1997, p. 26.

27. Stull, p. 29.

28. Mitchell W. Block, "The Training of Directors: From School to Screen," *Journal of the University Film Association*, vol. 32, no. 4 (Fall 1980), p. 35.

29. David Thomson, "Who Killed the Movies?," *Esquire* (December 1996), p. 59.

30. "I would just hope the instructors and the courses might be more relevant to the industry today" is a typical complaint of the new generation of students. In *Spotlight*, the UCLA School of Theater, Film and Television Alumni Association (Special Edition, Fall 1997).

31. Stull, p. 16.

32. Albert Boime, *The Academy and French Painting in the Nineteenth Century* (London: Phaidon, 1971), p. 4.

33. Their cost is low in absolute terms, not per day of instruction. A much better financial deal can be had in local community colleges offering film courses. Furthermore, creative filmmaking requires a long self-discovery process inaccessible in weekend schooling.

34. In the Hollywood Film Institute advertising brochure (Fall 1996), p. 4.

35. There are, of course, many film departments which operate within a Fine Arts umbrella. The School of the Art Institute of Chicago's brochure for instance reads: "the filmmaking department encourages students to embrace every phase of film production from conception to final print as an opportunity to challenge conventions and as an entry point for the creative process." I couldn't agree more. In practice, however, students function as independent artists. They are urged to use the medium to please themselves only. These schools do not offer a coordinated program dedicated to working out viable alternatives to the Hollywood mode of production.

36. Theodore Roszak, *The Making of a Counter Culture: Reflections on the Technocratic Society and Its Youthful Opposition* (New York: Doubleday, 1968), p. 16.

37. Richard J. Barnet and Ronald E. Muller, *Global Reach: The Power of the Multinational Corporation* (New York: Simon and Schuster, 1974), p. 117.

38. Madan Sarup, *An Introductory Guide to Post-structuralism and Postmodernism* (Athens: Univ. of Georgia Press, 1989), p. 125

39. All the quotes from Haskell Wexler can be found in *Getting Started in Film*, ed. Emily Laskin (New York: Prentice Hall, 1992), p. 97.

40. Frank Pierson, quoted in *Getting Started in Film*, p. 10.

41. In *Entertainment Today*, October 10–16, 1997, p. 8.

42. Peter Greenaway, quoted by Kristine McKenna, "Greenaway's Way," *Los Angeles Times*, Calendar section, June 1, 1997.

43. Peter Greenaway, interviewed in *Millimeter* (June 1997), p. 128.

44. John Dewey, *On Education*, ed. Reginald D. Archambault (New York: Random House, 1964), p. 133.

45. John Dewey, *Democracy and Education: An Introduction to the Philosophy of Education* (New York: Mcmillan, 1916), pp. 283–84.

46. John Dewey, *On Education*, p. 150.

47. John M. Kennedy, *A Psychology of Picture Perception* (San Francisco: Josey Bass, 1974), p. 15.

48. M. H. Pirenne, *Optics, Painting and Photography* (Cambridge: Cambridge Univ. Press, 1970), p. 183. Alternative views can be found in John P. Frisby, *Seeing: Illusion, Brain, and Mind* (Oxford: Oxford Univ. Press, 1980), and Marshall H. Segall, Donald T. Campbell, and Melville J. Herskovits, *The Influence of Culture on Visual Perception* (Indianapolis: Bobbs-Merrill, 1966).

49. See Nelson Goodman, *Languages of Art: An Approach to a Theory of Symbols* (Indianapolis: Bobbs-Merrill, 1968).

50. Norman Bryson, "The Gaze in the Expanded Field," in *Vision and Visuality*, ed. Hal Foster (Seattle: Bay Press, 1988), p. 91.

51. E. H. Gombrich, *Art and Illusion* (New York: Pantheon, 1960), p. 85.

52. Samuel Y. Edgerton, Jr,. *The Renaissance Rediscovery of Linear Perspective* (New York: Harper and Row, 1975), pp. 45–46. In my view, Edgerton's book is the best on the subject.

53. R. A. Sayce, *The Essays of Montaigne* (Evanston: Northwestern Univ. Press, 1972), p. 317.

54. On this topic, see the first two chapters of Bill Nichols, *Ideology and the Image* (Bloomington: Indiana Univ. Press, 1981).

55. While Botticelli makes eye contact with us, five hundred years into his future, Cosimo travels back fifteen hundred years. This painting thus offers an extraordinary example of time traveling.

56. See Jacques Lacan, *The Four Fundamental Concepts of Psycho-Analysis*, trans. Alan Sheridan (New York: W. W. Norton, 1981), chaps. 6 and 8.

57. Philip Rosen, in *Narrative, Apparatus, Ideology*, ed. Philip Rosen (New York: Columbia Univ. Press, 1986), p. 163.

58. A good place to start is with Jean-Louis Comolli, "Technique and Ideology: Camera, Perspective, Depth of Field," trans. Diana Matias, in *Movies and Methods II*, ed. Bill Nichols (Berkeley: Univ. of California Press, 1985).

59. John Dewey, quoted in Herbert M. Kliebard, *The Struggle for the American Curriculum 1893–1958*, 2nd ed. (New York: Routledge, 1995), p. 152.

60. John Dewey, quoted in Kliebard, p. 136.

61. John Dewey, *Democracy and Education*, p. 88.

62. John Dewey, quoted in Henry J. Perkinson, *Two Hundred Years of American Educational Thought* (Lanham, Maryland: Univ. Press of America, 1987), p. 223.

63. John Dewey, quoted in Kliebard, p. 68.

64. I am thinking here of USC. Other film schools often have a different arrangement.

65. Block, p. 35.

66. In Robert W. Welkos, "Hey, He Only Imported the Theory," *Los Angeles Times*, Calendar Section, June 30, 1996, p. 27.

67. Allan Bloom, *The Closing of the American Mind* (New York: Simon and Schuster, 1987), p. 338.

68. Gerald Graff, *Professing Literature* (Chicago: Univ. of Chicago Press, 1987), p. 252.

69. Harry D. Gideonse, quoted in *American Higher Education*, p. 945.

70. Peter Greenaway, interviewed in *Millimeter* (June 1997), p. 128.

71. Rick Schmidt, *Feature Filmmaking at Used-Car Prices* (New York: Penguin, 1988).

72. Roberto Rossellini, quoted in Eric Sherman, *Directing the Film: Film Directors on Their Art* (Boston: Little Brown and Co., 1976), pp. 304–05.

## CHAPTER FOUR.
## WRITING

1. Benjamin B. Hampton, *History of the American Film from Its Beginnings* (New York: Dover, 1970 reprint of the 1931 text), p. 30.

2. In the *New York Dramatic Mirror* (1912), quoted by Janet Staiger in "'Tame' Authors and the Corporate Laboratory: Stories, Writers, and Scenarios in Hollywood," *Quarterly Review of Film Studies*, vol. 8, no. 4 (Fall 1983).

3. Janet Staiger, "The Hollywood Mode of Production: The Construction of Divided Labor" Ph. D. dissertation: Univ. of Wisconsin-Madison, 1981), p. 154.

4. Quoted in Janet Staiger, "Blueprints for Feature Films: Hollywood's Continuity Scripts," in *The American Film Industry*, ed. Tino Balio (Madison: Univ. of Wisconsin Press, rev. ed., 1985), p. 191.

5. Ince, quoted in Edward Azlant, *The Theory, History, and Practice of Screenwriting 1897–1920* (Ann Arbor, Michigan: University Microfilms International, 1982), p. 165.

6. In the New York *Dramatic Mirror* (1913), quoted by Azlant, p. 164. For more on Ince's practice, see Azlant pp. 159–72.

7. Tom Stempel, *Framework: A History of Screenwriting in the American Film* (New York: Continuum, 1988), p. 48.

8. Staiger, *Quarterly Review of Film Studies*, p. 39.

9. Peter Milne, *Motion Picture Directing: The Facts and Theories of the Newest Art* (New York: Falk, 1922), p. 143.

10. Quoted in Azlant, p. 252.

11. Both examples are taken from a reprint of C. Gardner Sullivan's screenplay for *Selfish Yates* in Azlant's book.

12. Jean-Paul Torok, *Le Scénario: histoire, théorie, pratique* (Paris: Henri Veyrier-Artefact, 1986), p. 41ff.

13. Richard Walter, *Screenwriting: The Art, Craft and Business of Film and Television Writing* (New York: New American Library, 1988), p. 120.

14. Stempel, p. 48.

15. Although Truffaut aimed this particular critique at the French cinema of the fifties, he had no love for their equivalent in America: the big budget movies. See François Truffaut, "A Certain Tendency of the French Cinema," in *Movies and Methods*, ed. Bill Nichols (Berkeley: Univ. of California Press, 1976), pp. 224–37.

16. Both quotes are from Andrew Sarris, "Notes on the Auteur Theory in 1962," *Film Theory and Criticism: Introductory Readings*, 4th ed., ed. Gerald Mast, Marshall Cohen and Leo Braudy (New York: Oxford Univ. Press, 1992), p. 586.

17. On the entire issue of authorship as it was debated at the time, see *Cahiers du Cinéma, Vol. 2, 1960–1968: New Wave, New Cinema, Re-Evaluating Hollywood* (London: Routledge and Kegan Paul, 1986).

18. See Sarris's full discussion of the fight between directors and writers in *Film Theory and Criticism*, 2nd ed., pp. 658–59.

19. Quoted in Ted Elrick, "Fires . . . Floods . . . Riots . . . Earthquakes . . . John Carpenter! Hollywood's Prince of Darkness Destroys LA," *DGA Magazine* (July-August 1996), p. 29.

20. Quoted in Richard Corliss, *The Hollywood Screenwriters* (New York: Film Comment, 1972), pp. 247 and 249.

21. "They're writing for the money," Scott Frank confesses. Quoted in Benjamin Svetkey, "Who Killed the Hollywood Screenplay," *Entertainment Weekly*, October 4, 1996, p. 39.

22. In Azlant, p. 35.

23. Jean-Claude Carrière et Pascal Bonitzer, *Exercice du scénario* (Paris: Femis, 1990), p. 66 (my translation).

24. See Jean-Claude Carrière, "Les Aventures du sujet," *Cahiers du Cinéma*, no. 371–2 (May 1985).

25. Quoted in Christian Salé, *Les Scénaristes au travail* (Paris: Hatier, 1981) (my translation).

26. Quoted in Staiger, "Tame Authors . . . ," p. 36.

27. In *Film & Video* (June 1997), p. 54.

28. Quoted in Suso Cecchi d'Amico, "L'Ecrivain du cinéma," *CinémAction*, no. 61 (1991) *L'Enseignement du scénario*, p. 17.

29. Torok, p. 113.

30. Alexandre Astruc, "The Birth of the New Avant-garde: La Caméra-stylo," in *The New Wave*, ed. Peter Graham (New York: Doubleday, 1968), p. 17. I have altered the translation slightly.

31. Astruc, p. 20. I have altered the translation slightly.

32. Astruc, p. 22. I have altered the translation slightly.

33. The best discussion of these concepts can be found in Meir Sternberg, *Expositional Modes and Temporal Ordering in Fiction* (Baltimore: Johns Hopkins Univ. Press, 1978).

34. Another good introduction to these concepts is David Bordwell's *Narration in the Fiction Film* (Madison: Univ. of Wisconsin Press, 1985), chap. 4. The notion of "actualization" originates with Seymour Chatman *Coming to Terms: The Rhetoric of Narrative in Fiction and Film* (Ithaca: Cornell Univ. Press, 1990), pp. 125–26.

35. Bordwell, p. 50.

36. Carrière et Bonitzer, p. 12.

37. See Azlant, pp. 131 and.209.

38. Azlant, p. 134.

39. Quoted by Janet Staiger, "Tame Authors," p. 40.

40. See Syd Field, *Screenplay: The Foundations of Screenwriting* (New York: Dell, 1979).

41. In a John Truby brochure for his *Blockbuster* software.

42. In a *Dramatica* Pro-2 model advertisement.

43. Carrière, in Salé, p. 47.

44. *The Art of Criticism: Henry James on the Theory and Practice of Fiction*, ed. William Veeder and Susan M. Griffin (Chicago: Univ. of Chicago Press, 1986), p. 75.

45. Richard Walter, p. 79.

46. Percy Lubbock, *The Craft of Fiction* (New York: Charles Scribner's Sons, 1921), p. 157.

47. Richard Walter, p. 79 (his emphasis).

48. *Aristotle Horace Longinus: Classical Literary Criticism*, trans. T. S. Dorsch (Baltimore: Penguin, 1965), in *Poetics* 2 and 6, respectively, pp. 33 and 39.

49. James Hopkins, in *Philosophical Essays on Freud*, ed. Richard Wollin and James Hopkins (Cambridge: Cambridge Univ. Press, 1982), p. x.

50. For Freud, start with *The Interpretation of Dreams*, trans. James Strachey (New York: Discus, 1965). For Lacan, read *The Four Fundamental Concepts of Psycho-Analysis*, trans. Alan Sheridan (New York: W. W. Norton, 1981). Louis Althusser's main ideas are found in *Lenin and Philosophy*, trans. Ben Brewster (New York: Monthly Review, 1971).

51. Edward Edinger, quoted in Don Fredericksen, "Jung/Sign/Symbol/Film Part 1," *Quarterly Review of Film Studies*, vol. 4, no. 2 (1979), p. 181.

52. Georges Bataille, *L'Expérience intérieure*, in *Oeuvres complètes*, vol. 5 (Paris: Gallimard, 1973), p. 27 (my translation).

53. Terry Eagleton, *Literary Theory: An Introduction*, 2nd ed. (Minneapolis: Univ. of Minnesota Press, 199), p. 150.

54. Donald Davidson, "Paradoxes of Irrationality," in *Philosophical Essays on Freud*, ed. Richard Wollheim and James Hopkins, p. 300.

55. Davidson, p. 291.

56. Eagleton, p. 146.

57. In *Narrative, Apparatus, Ideology*, ed. Philip Rosen (New York: Columbia Univ. Press, 1986), p. 163.

58. Althusser, p. 139.

59. Many commentators have objected to the absolutism of the ideological machinery described by Althusser. Against his deterministic view, cultural studies critics have preferred to emphasize a struggle for hegemony and the possibility of resistance in everyday human practices and popular culture. Thomas Frank, on the other hand, has attacked the naïveté of such views and the tendency of its adherents "to overlook the trends, changes, and intricacies of corporate culture." For instance, for the longest time, advertising has preempted much social and political critique by making itself fun of society, consumerism, etc. (in Thomas Frank, *The Conquest of Cool* [Chicago: Univ. of Chicago Press, 1997], p. 18). After many years in Los Angeles, I also think that, insofar as Hollywood is concerned, to believe that the system can be challenged from within is quite foolish. Think of the ease with which African-American, Latino, and women directors have been absorbed within the dominant culture. Finally, the notion of resistance fits right in with that of the underdog, one of the most seductive tools of the commercial cinema.

60. Althusser, p. 172.

61. Samuel Weber, *Mass Mediauras: Form, Technics, Media* (Stanford: Stanford Univ. Press, 1996), p. 138.

62. See Fredric Jameson, *The Political Unconscious: Narrative as a Socially Symbolic Act* (Ithaca: Cornell Univ. Press, 1981).

63. Henri Bergson, *L'Evolution créatrice* (Paris: Felix Alcan, 1908), p. 51 (my translation).

64. Bergson, p. 56.

65. Bergson, p. 4.

66. Paul Feyerabend, *Farewell to Reason* (London: Verso, 1987), p. 139.

67. Field, p. 35.

68. In "Working Writer," a brochure for Truby's Writer Studio, Summer 1996, p. 3.

69. Raoul Ruiz, *Poetics of Cinema, Part 1: Miscellanies*, trans. Brian Holmes (Paris: Editions DisVoir, 1995) respectively, pp. 15 and 21.

70. Ruiz, p. 14.

71. Quoted in Azlant, p. 252.

72. Emile Benveniste, *Problems in General Linguistics*, trans. Mary Elizabeth Meek (Coral Gables: Univ. of Miami Press, 1971), p. 208.

73. Hayden White, *The Content of the Form: Narrative Discourse and Historical Representation* (Baltimore: Johns Hopkins Press, 1987), p. 24.

74. White, p. 6.

75. White, p. 7.

76. White, pp. 16 and 17.

77. Field, p. 56.

78. Jacques Derrida, "The Law of Genre," *Glyph*, no. 7, (1980).

79. In Todd Coleman, "The Story Structure Gurus," *The Journal of the Writers Guild of America, West* (June 1995), p. 20.

80. Jean-Luc Godard, *Introduction à une véritable histoire du cinéma* (Paris: Albatros, 1980), p. 44  (my translation).

81. Godard, *Introduction*, p. 57.

82. Olivier Assayas, "Du Scénario achevé au scénario ouvert," *Cahiers du Cinéma*, no. 371–2 (May 1985) (my translation).

83. The term "dialogic" was coined by Mikhail Bakhtin. Read his seminal essay, *The Dialogic Imagination*, trans. Caryl Emerson and Michael Holquist (Austin: Univ. of Texas Press, 1981). David Bordwell used "Galilean" to define the polyphony of multiple speakers in *Narration in the Fiction Film*.

84. Quoted in Azlant, p. 254.

85. Quoted in Azlant, p. 154.

## CHAPTER FIVE.
## STAGING

1. Ingmar Bergman, quoted in *Film Makers on Film Making: Statements on Their Art by Thirty Directors*, ed. Harry M. Geduld (Bloomington: Indiana Univ. Press, 1967), p. 184.

2. Sergei Eisenstein, *Selected Works: Writings 1922–34*, trans. Richard Taylor (London: BFI, 1988), p. 13.

3. Maurice Merleau-Ponty, *Signs*, trans. Richard C. McCleary (Evanston: Northwestern Univ. Press, 1964), p. 19.

4. Alfred Hitchcock, quoted in Eric Sherman, *Directing the Film: Film Directors on Their Art* (Boston: Little Brown and Co., 1976), p. 143.

5. The first quote is from Martin Heidegger, "The Question Concerning Technology," in *Basic Writings*, ed. David Farrell Krell (San Francisco: Harper, 1977), p. 298. The second is from Samuel Weber, *Mass Mediauras: Form, Technics. Media* (Stanford: Stanford Univ. Press, 1996), p. 72.

6. Blaise Cendrars, quoted in Siegfried Kracauer, *Theory of Film: The Redemption of Physical Reality* (New York: Oxford Univ. Press, 1965), p. 35.

7. Ermanno Olmi, quoted in Ellen Oumano, *Film Forum: Thirty Five Filmmakers Discuss Their Craft* (New York: St. Martin's Press, 1985), p. 146. I have modified the translation slightly.

8. Henry Jaglom, quoted in Oumano, p. 150.

9. Robert Aldrich, for one, claimed he shot a lot faster using two cameras simultaneously. See Sherman, p. 117.

10. Peter Milne, *Motion Picture Directing: The Facts and Theories of the Newest Art* (New York: Falk, 1922), p. 46.

11. Frances Taylor Patterson, *Scenario and Screen* (New York: Harcourt, Brace and Co., 1928), p. 93.

12. William de Mille, quoted in Patterson, pp. 91–92.

13. Nestor Almendros, quoted in Oumano, p. 87.

14. André Téchiné, quoted in Oumano, p. 108.

15. Dennis Hopper, quoted in John Andrew Gallagher, *Film Directors on Directing* (New York: Greenwood, 1989), p. 131.

16. See Friedrich Nietzsche, *On the Genealogy of Morals*, trans. Walter Kaufmann and R. S. Hollingdale (New York: Vintage, 1967), and *The Gay Science*, trans. Walter Kaufmann (New York: Random House, 1974).

17. Maurice Merleau-Ponty, *Phenomenology of Perception*, trans. Colin Smith (London: Routledge and Kegan Paul, 1962), p. 304.

18. The best discussion of this phenomenon can be found in part 1 of Christian Metz, *The Imaginary Signifier: Psychoanalysis and Film*, trans. Celia Britton, Annwyl Williams, Ben Brewster, and Alfred Guzzetti (Bloomington: Indiana Univ. Press, 1982).

19. The concept of the filmic narrator is described by Tom Gunning as including pro-filmic material (the control of everything that takes place in front of the camera), the enframed image (perspective, focus, angle, camera or lens motion), and editing. In Tom Gunning, *D. W. Griffith and the Origins of American Narrative Film: The Early Years at Biograph* (Urbana: Univ. of Illinois Press, 1994), chap. 1.

20. Charles Ford, *On Tourne lundi: Ecrire pour le cinéma* (Paris: Jean Vigneau, 1947), p. 121 (my translation).

21. Susan Sontag, *Against Interpretation and Other Essays* (New York: Octagon Books, 1986), p. 17.

22. Luis Buñuel, quoted in Dominique Villain, *L'Oeil à la caméra: le cadrage au cinéma* (Cahiers du Cinéma/Editions de l'Etoile, 1984), p. 155 (my translation)

23. Michelangelo Antonioni, quoted in Geduld, p. 206.

24. In David Mamet, *On Directing Film* (New York: Viking, 1991).

25. Maurice Merleau-Ponty, *Sense and Non-Sense*, trans. Hubert L. Dreyfus and Patricia Allen Dreyfus (Evanston: Northwestern Univ. Press, 1964), pp. 18–19 and 17.

26. For the notion of schema, see E. H. Gombrich, *Art and Illusion* (Princeton: Princeton Univ. Press, 1969), pp. 93–178.

27. Michelangelo Antonioni, quoted in Geduld, pp. 203 and 206.

28. Quoted in Colin Crisp, *The Classic French Cinema: 1930–1960* (Bloomington: Indiana Univ. Press, 1993), pp. 311–12.

29. Ermanno Olmi, quoted in Oumano, p. 96.

30. "Entretien avec Jean-Marie Straub et Danielle Huillet," *Cahiers du Cinéma*, no. 223 (August 1970), p. 48, (my translation)

31. Peter Brook, quoted in *Interviews with Film Directors*, ed. Andrew Sarris (Indianapolis: Bobbs-Merrill, 1967), p. 41.

32. François Truffaut, quoted in Jean-Claude Carrière et Pascal Bonitzer, *Exercice du scénario* (Paris: Femis, 1990), p. 101.

33. Milne, p. 75.

34. *Jean-Luc Godard par Jean-Luc Godard* (Paris: Cahiers du Cinéma/Editions de l'Etoile, 1985), p. 532.

35. Martin Scorsese, quoted in Oumano, p. 300.

36. Arthur Penn, quoted in *Projections 4: Film-Makers on Film-Making*, ed. John Boorman, Tom Luddy, David Thomson, and Walter Donohue (London: Faber, 1995), p. 134.

37. For the differences between ready-to-hand and present-at-hand, see Martin Heidegger, *Being and Time*, trans. John Macquarrie and Edward Robinson (San Francisco: HarperCollins, 1962), chap. 4.

38. Jean-Luc Godard, quoted in Oumano, p. 209 (I have modified the translation somewhat).

39. Henry Jaglom, quoted in Oumano, p. 211.

40. Cecil B. De Mille, quoted in Milne, p. 52.

41. Maurice Merleau-Ponty, *The Primacy of Perception and Other Essays on Phenomenological Psychology, the Philosophy of Art, History and Politics*, trans. William Cobb (Evanston: Northwestern Univ. Press, 1964), p. 116.

42. Merleau-Ponty, *Sense and Non-Sense*, pp. xii–xiii (his emphases).

43. Denis Diderot, *Dorval et moi, ou Entretien sur le fils naturel* in *Oeuvres complètes*, vol. III (Paris: Le Club Français du Livre, 1970), p. 141 (my translation).

44. Jean-Paul Sartre, *The Psychology of Imagination* (New York: Citadel, 1961), p. 91 (no translator named).

45. Edmund Burke, quoted in William James, *The Principles of Psychology* (Cambridge: Harvard Univ. Press, 1981), vol. 2, p. 1078.

46. Lawrence Olivier, quoted in Ronald Hayman, *Techniques of Acting* (London: Methuen, 1969), p. 31.

47. See Jerzy Grotowski, *Towards a Poor Theatre* (New York: Simon and Schuster, 1968) (no translator named).

48. Jean Renoir, quoted in Sherman, p. 89.

49. Constantin Stanislavski, quoted in Sonia Moore, *The Stanislavski System: The Professional Training of an Actor* (Harmondsworth, England: Penguin, 1976), p. 72.

50. Constantin Stanislavski, *An Actor Prepares*, trans. Elizabeth Reynolds Hapgood (New York: Theatre Arts Books, 1936), p. 188.

51. On the differences between Stanislavski and Strasberg, see Paul Gray, "From Russia to America: A Critical Chronology," in *Stanislavski and America*, ed. Erika Munk (Greenwich, Conn.: Fawcett, 1966). See also the *Tulane Drama Review* (1964) for a reconsideration of Stanislavski's system versus Strasberg's method.

52. Mark Rydell, in Gallagher, p. 217.

53. Uta Hagen, *A Challenge for the Actor* (New York: Charles Scribner's Sons, 1991), p. 134.

54. In *Acting (Re)Considered: Theories and Practices*, ed. Phillip B. Zarrilli (London: Routledge, 1995), p. 17.

55. Duane Krause, "An Epic System," in *Acting (Re)Considered: Theories and Practices*, p. 271.

56. Bertolt Brecht, quoted in John Rouse, "Brecht and the Contradictory Actor," in *Acting (Re)Considered: Theories and Practices*, p. 231.

57. *Brecht on Theatre*, ed. and trans. by John Wilett (New York: Hill and Wang, 1964), p. 196.

58. Uta Hagen, *Respect for Acting* (New York: Macmillan, 1973), p. 218.

59. Bertolt Brecht, quoted in Rouse, pp. 239–40.

60. Michelangelo Antonioni, quoted in Geduld, pp. 195–96.

61. Mamet, op. cit.

62. Robert Bresson, *Notes on Cinematography*, trans. Jonathan Griffin (New York: Urizen, 1977), p. 2.

63. Bresson, pp. 40 and 42.

64. Bresson, pp. 46 and 47.

65. Haskell Wexler, quoted in *Getting Started in Film*, ed. Emily Laskin (New York: Prentice Hall, 1992), p. 101.

66. Wagner was trying to counter the noxious influence of the industrial revolution by creating a powerful live experience capable of revitalizing his spectators.

67. Sergei Eisenstein, *Film Essays and a Lecture*, ed. Jay Leyda (New York: Praeger, 1970), p. 85.

68. Mikhail Bakhtin, *Problems of Dostoevsky's Poetics*, trans. Caryl Emerson (Minneapolis: Univ. of Minnesota Press, 1984), p. 6.

69. Katrin Cartlidge, quoted in Kenneth Turan, "The Case for Mike Leigh," *Los Angeles Times*, Magazine Section, September 22, 1996, p. 27.

70. In Turan, p. 28.

71. Mikhail Bakhtin, quoted by Katerina Clark and Michael Holquist, *Mikhail Bakhtin* (Cambridge: Harvard Univ. Press, 1984), p. 241.

72. Mikhail Bakhtin, *The Dialogic Imagination*, trans. Caryl Emerson and Michael Holquist, (Austin: Univ. of Texas Press, 1981), p. 299.

73. Colin MacCabe, "Theory and Film: Principles of Realism," in *Film Theory and Criticism*, ed. Gerald Mast, Marshall Cohen, and Leo Braudy (New York: Oxford Univ. Press, 1992), pp. 79–92.

74. Robby Müller, "I Am a Cameraman," *LA Weekly*, November 22–28, 1996, p. 29.

75. Lars von Trier, quoted in "The Director Talks," *LA Weekly*, November 22–28, 1996, p. 27.

76. Jean-Paul Torok, *Le Scénario: Histoire, théorie, pratique* (Paris: Henri Veyrier/Artefact, 1986), p. 92 (my translation).

77. Viktor Shklovski, "Art as a Technique," in *Russian Formalist Criticism: Four Essays*, trans. Lee T. Lemon and Marion J. Reis (Lincoln, Neb.: Univ. of Nebraska Press, 1965), p. 12.

78. Emmanuel Levinas, *Totality and Infinity: An Essay on Exteriority*, trans. Alphonso Lingis (Pittsburgh: Duquesne Univ. Press, 1969), p. 13.

79. *Totality and Infinity* provides a good introduction to Levinas's main themes.

80. See Béla Balász, *Theory of the Film: Character and Growth of a New Art*, trans. Edith Bone (New York: Dover, 1970), chap. 8.

81. Shklovski, p. 12 (his emphasis).

82. Emmanuel Levinas, *Existence and Existents*, trans. Alphonso Lingis (The Hague: Martinus Nijhof, 1978), p. 40.

83. Edward Edinger, quoted in Don Fredericksen "Jung/Sign/Symbol/Film," Part I, *Quarterly Review of Film Studies*, vol. 4, no. 2, 1979, p. 181.

84. Ingmar Bergman and Luis Buñuel, quoted in Fredericksen, p. 185.

85. Roland Barthes, *Camera Lucida: Reflections on Photography*, trans. Richard Howard (New York: Hill and Wang, 1981), pp. 27–28.

86. Quoted in *Documentary Explorations*, ed. G. Roy Levin (Garden City: Doubleday, 1971), pp. 53–54.

87. Max Ophüls, quoted in Villain, p. 50.

## CHAPTER SIX.
## LIGHTING

1. Emmanuel Levinas, *Existence and Existents*, trans. A. Lingis (The Hague/Boston: Martinus Nijhoff, 1978), p. 84.

2. Maurice Merleau-Ponty, *Sense and Non-Sense*, trans. Hubert L. Dreyfus and Patricia Allen Dreyfus (Evanston: Northwestern Univ. Press, 1964), pp. 48–49.

3. Tom O'Brien, quoted in A. Alvarez, *Night: Night Life, Night Language, Sleep, and Dreams* (New York: W. W. Norton, 1995), p. 3.

4. Maurice Blanchot, *Thomas the Obscure*, trans. Robert Lamberton (New York: Station Hill, 1988), p. 14.

5. Quoted in Wolfgang Schivelbusch, *Disenchanted Night: The Industrialization of Light in the Nineteenth Century*, trans. Angela Davies (Berkeley: Univ. of California Press, 1988), p. 96.

6. See Gaston Bachelard, *Fragments d'une poétique du feu* (Paris: Presses Universitaires de France, 1988).

7. Quoted in Roy Paul Madsen, *Working Cinema: Learning from the Masters* (Belmont, Calif.: Wadsworth, 1990), p. 240.

8. On painting, see Samuel Y. Edgerton Jr,. *The Renaissance Rediscovery of Linear Perspective* (New York: Harper and Row, 1975); on film, see Bill Nichols, *Ideology and the Image* (Berkeley: Univ. of California Press, 1981), chaps. 1 and 2.

9. See Oswald Spengler, *The Decline of the West: Form and Actuality*, trans. Charles Francis Atkinson (New York: Alfred A. Knopf, 1926), p. 183.

10. Rudolf Arnheim, *Art and Visual Perception* (Berkeley: Univ. of California Press, 1974), p. 314.

11. André Bazin, *What Is Cinema?* trans. Hugh Gray (Berkeley: Univ. of California Press, 1967), vol. 1, p. 12.

12. Quoted in Albert Boime, *The Academy and French Painting in the Nineteeenth Century* (London: Phaidon, 1971), p. 28.

13. Immanuel Kant, *Critique of Judgement*, trans. J. H. Bernard (New York: Hafner, 1951), pp. 61–62.

14. Jacques Derrida, *The Truth in Painting*, trans. Geoff Bennington and Ian McLeod (Chicago: Chicago Univ. Press, 1987), p. 54 (his emphasis).

15. Derrida, p. 56 (his emphases).

16. Gilles Deleuze, *Le Pli: Leibniz et le baroque* (Paris: Editions de Minuit, 1988), p. 39 (my translation).

17. In Boime, p. 28 (my emphasis).

18. Quoted in Dennis Schaefer and Larry Salvato, *Masters of Light: Conversations with Contemporary Cinematographers* (Berkeley: Univ. of California Press, 1984), p. 57.

19. See Nestor Almendros, "Photographing 'Days of Heaven,'" *American Cinematographer*, vol. 60, no. 6 (June 1979).

20. Paul de Man, *The Rhetoric of Romanticism* (New York: Columbia Univ. Press, 1984), p. 3.

21. de Man, p. 4.

22. de Man, p. 6.

23. Henri Alekan, *Des Lumières et des ombres* (Paris: Le Sycomore, 1984), p. 38 (my translation).

24. My understanding of *Stimmung* owes a lot to Michel Haar's essay, "Le Primat de la *Stimmung* sur la corporéité de *Dasein*," *Heidegger Studies*, vol. 2 (1986).

25. Quoted in Hubert L. Dreyfus, *Being-in-the-World: A Commentary on Heidegger's Being and Time, Division I* (Cambridge: MIT Press, 1991), p. 171.

26. Edmund Husserl, *Logical Investigations*, trans. J. N. Findlay (London: Routledge and Kegan Paul, 1970), vol. 2, p. 558.

27. Husserl, p. 737 (his emphasis).

28. Alekan, p. 38 (my emphasis).

29. Alekan, p. 38.

30. Quoted in Schaefer and Salvato, p. 7.

31. Sharon A. Russell, *Semiotics and Lighting* (Ann Arbor, Mich.: UMI Research Press, 1981), p. 35.

32. Quoted in Silvano Petrosino et Jacques Rolland, *La Vérité nomade: Introduction à Emmanuel Levinas* (Paris: La Découverte, 1984), p. 130 (my translation).

33. Emmanuel Levinas, *Existence and Existents*, p. 48.

34. On this subject, see Vivian Sobchack's argument in *The Address of the Eye: A Phenomenology of Film Experience* (Princeton: Princeton Univ. Press, 1992).

35. Peter Baxter, "On the History and Ideology of Film Lighting," *Screen* 16, no. 3 (Fall 1975), p. 104.

36. Emmanuel Levinas, *Totalité et infini: Essai sur l'extériorité* (La Haye: Martinus Nijhoff, 1961), p.47.

37. Quoted in Petrosino and Rolland, p. 134.

38. Quoted in Petrosino and Rolland, p. 23.

39. Martin Heidegger, "The End of Philosophy," in *Basic Writings*, ed. and trans. David Farrell Krell (New York: Harper, 1977), p. 384.

40. Martin Heidegger, "The Origin of the Work of Art," in *Basic Writings*, p. 175.

41. Emmanuel Levinas, *Time and the Other*, trans. Richard A. Cohen (Pittsburgh: Duquesne Univ. Press, 1987), p. 64.

42. Heidegger, "The Origin of the Work of Art," p. 175.

43. Heidegger, "On the Essence of Truth" in *Basic Writings*, p. 132.

44. Heidegger, "The Origin of the Work of Art," p. 175.

45. Heidegger, "The Origin of the Work of Art," p. 175.

## CHAPTER SEVEN.
## THE FRAME

1. *Jean-Luc Godard par Jean-Luc Godard* (Paris: Cahiers du Cinéma/Editions de l'Etoile, 1985), p. 532.

2. The "camera-stylo" of Alexandre Astruc has many meanings, this being one of them. See his article, "The Birth of a New Avant-Garde: La Caméra-Stylo," in *The New Wave*, ed. Peter Graham (New York: Doubleday, 1968).

3. Jacques Derrida, *The Truth in Painting*, trans. Geoff Bennington and Ian McLeod (Chicago: Univ. of Chicago Press, 1987), p. 81.

4. Rudolf Arnheim, *The Power of the Center: A Study of Composition in the Visual Arts* (Berkeley: Univ. of California Press, 1982), p. 215.

5. Lucien Sève, quoted in Jean Mitry, *Esthétique et psychologie du cinéma*, vol. 1: *Les structures* ( Paris: Editions universitaires, 1963), p. 167 (my translation).

6. Arnheim, pp. 59–60.

7. Sergei Eisenstein, *Film Essays and a Lecture*, ed. and trans. Jay Leyda (New York: Praeger, 1970), p. 52.

8. John Belton, *Widescreen Cinema* (Cambridge: Harvard Univ. Press, 1992), p. 44.

9. Eisenstein, p. 49.

10. See Belton, pp. 15–22.

11. Quoted in Dennis Schaefer and Larry Salvato, *Masters of Light: Conversations with Contemporary Cinematographers* (Berkeley: Univ. of California Press, 1984), p. 327.

12. Quoted in Schaefer and Salvato, p. 298.

13. Quoted in Schaefer and Salvato, pp.169–70.

14. Quoted in Schaefer and Salvato, pp. 49–50.

15. Quoted in Schaefer and Salvato, p. 185.

16. Quoted in Schaefer and Salvato, p. 276.

17. Quoted in Schaefer and Salvato, pp. 328–29.

18. Arnheim, p. 73.

19. Arnheim, p. 93.

20. See my own article, "Through the Looking Glasses: From the Camera Obscura to Video Assist," *Film Quarterly*, vol. 49, no. 3 (Spring 1996).

21. At the American Society of Cinematographers open meeting at the University of Southern California on February 19, 1995.

22. Robert Bresson, *Notes on Cinematography*, trans. Jonathan Griffin (New York: Urizen Books, 1977), p. 1.

23. Dominique Villain, *L'Oeil à la caméra: le cadrage au cinéma* (Paris: Cahiers du Cinéma Editions de l'Etoile, 1984), p. 16 (my translation).

24. Quoted in Villain, p. 134.

25. See André Bazin, *What Is Cinema?*, trans. Hugh Gray (Berkeley: Univ. of California Press, 1967), vol. 1, pp. 164–69.

26. Gilles Deleuze, *Cinema 1: The Movement-Image*, trans. Hugh Tomlinson and Barbara Habberjam (London: The Athlone Press, 1986), p. 7.

27. Maurice Merleau-Ponty, *Signs*, trans. Richard C. McCleary (Evanston: Northwestern Univ. Press, 1964), p. 21.

28. Jacques Derrida, *Writing and Difference*, trans. Alan Bass (Chicago: Univ. of Chicago Press, 1978), pp. 278–79.

29. Such digital software actually exists: *Painter.*

30. Meyer Schapiro, "On Some Problems in the Semiotics of Visual Art: Field and Vehicle in Image-Signs," *Semiotica*, vol. 1, no. 3, 1969, p. 227.

31. Deleuze, p. 9.

32. Jean-Pierre Oudart, "Cinema and Suture," *Screen*, vol. 18, no. 4 (Winter 1977–78). For a complete review of the issues surrounding suture from its psychoanalytical origin to objections to Oudart's views, see Stephen Heath, "Notes on Suture," *Screen* 18, no. 4 (Winter 1977–78), pp. 48–76.

33. Oudart is the one who first brought this film to the attention of critics with regard to the notion of suture. My reading of the scene though follows closely Philippe Arnaud' description in his book on *Robert Bresson* (Paris: Cahiers du Cinéma, 1986), pp. 97–105.

34. The translator in *Screen* used "vertiginous delight" instead.

35. Heath, p. 67.

36. Again I am following the clear analysis of Philippe Arnaud in *Robert Bresson.*

37. Noel Burch, *Theory of Film Practice*, trans. Helen R. Lane (Princeton: Princeton Univ. Press, 1981), chap. 2.

38. Arnaud, p. 18 (my translation).

39. I am referring here to the second formal idea in art as elaborated by Heinrich Wolfflin in *Principles of Art History*, trans. M. D. Hottinger (New York: Henry Holt and Co., 1932).

40. On this subject, see Miriam Schild Bunim, *Space in Medieval Painting and the Forerunners of Perspective* (New York: Columbia Univ. Press, 1940).

41. Read Oswald Spengler's discussion of the Faustian gaze in *The Decline of the West*, trans. Charles Francis Atkinson (New York: Alfred A. Knopf, 1926), p. 195ff.

42. In E. H. Gombrich, *The Sense of Order: A Study in the Psychology of Decorative Art* (Ithaca: Cornell Univ. Press, 1979), p. 2.

43. Erwin Panofsky, *Perspective as Symbolic Form* (New York: Zone Books, 1991), pp. 67–68.

44. See Gilles Deleuze and Felix Guattari, *Anti-Oedipus*, trans. Robert Hurley, Mark Seem, and Helen R. Lane (New York: Viking, 1977).

45. Brian Henderson, "Toward a Non-Bourgeois Camera Style," in *Film Theory and Criticism: Introductory Readings*, 2nd edition, ed. Gerald Mast and Marshall Cohen (New York: Oxford Univ. Press, 1979), p. 846.

46. Panofsky, p. 69.

47. Percy Lubbock, *The Craft of Fiction* (New York: Charles Scribner's Sons, 1921), p. 113.

48. David Mamet, *On Directing Film* (New York: Viking, 1991).

49. Lubbock, p. 111.

50. Deleuze, p. 20.

51. Wayne C. Booth explaining Henry James's technique in *The Rhetoric of Fiction* (Chicago: Univ. of Chicago Press, 1961), pp. 23–24.

52. Jean Mitry, *Esthétique et psychologie du cinéma* (Paris: Editions universitaires, 1963), vol. 1, pp. 392–93.

53. I refer to Orlando's gender as it is acknowledged by other characters in the film.

54. The notion of "attachment" can be found in Boris Uspensky, *A Poetics of Composition*, trans. Valentina Zavarin and Susan Wittig (Berkeley: Univ. of California Press, 1973), p. 58.

55. A good analysis of *Lady in the Lake* can be found in Vivian Sobchack, *The Address of the Eye: A Phenomenology of Film Experience* (Princeton, N.J.: Princeton Univ. Press, 1992), pp. 230–48.

56. See Uspensky, pp. 32–33.

57. Walter Benjamin, "The Work of Art in the Age of Mechanical Reproduction," in *Film Theory and Criticism: Introductory Readings*, 4th edition, ed. Gerald Mast, Marshall Cohen, and Leo Braudy (New York: Oxford Univ. Press, 1992), p. 675.

58. Booth, p. 116 (my emphasis).

59. Seymour Chatman, *Coming to Terms: The Rhetoric of Narrative in Fiction and Film* (Ithaca: Cornell Univ. Press, 1990), pp. 83–84.

60. Booth, p. 113 (my emphasis).

61. "Entretien avec Jean-Marie Straub et Daniele Huillet," *Cahiers du Cinéma* 223 (August 1970), p. 54.

## CHAPTER EIGHT.
## SOUND

1. In Randy Thom, "Designing a Movie for Sound," an unpublished paper to be part of his forthcoming book, *Sound Design, The Art of Using Sound in Storytelling*, p. 3.

2. Abraham Segal, "Jean-Luc Godard," *Image et Son*, no. 215 (March 1968), p. 82 (my translation). I have modified the order of the sentences.

3. Walter Murch, quoted in Vincent LoBrutto, *Sound-on-Film: Interviews with Creators of Film Sound* (Westport, Conn.: Praeger, 1994), p. 97.

4. Thom, p. 1.

5. Robert Bresson, *Notes on Cinematography*, trans. Jonathan Griffin (New York: Urizen Books, 1977), p. 39.

6. See "Aux deux bouts de la chaîne: entretien avec Jean-Pierre Beauviala," *Cahiers du Cinéma*, no. 287 (April 1978), p. 14.

7. See Philip Rosen, "Adorno and Film Music: Theoretical Notes on Composing for the Films," *Yale French Studies*, no. 60 (1980), p. 170.

8. Maurice Merleau-Ponty, *Phenomenology of Perception*, trans. Colin Smith (London: Routledge and Kegan Paul, 1962), p. 320.

9. See Christian Metz, "Aural Objects," in *Film Sound: Theory and Practice*, ed. Elisabeth Weis and John Belton (New York: Columbia Univ. Press, 1985), pp. 154–61.

10. Beauviala, p. 14.

11. Rick Altman, "The Material Heterogeneity of Recorded Sound," in *Sound Theory Sound Practice*, ed. Rick Altman (New York: Routledge, 1992), p. 23.

12. Martin Heidegger, *Being and Time*, trans. John Macquarrie and Edward Robinson (New York: Harper and Row, 1962), p. 214.

13. Rudolf Arnheim, "Theory of the Film: Sound," in *Film Sound: Theory and Practice*, p. 114.

14. Rick Altman, "Moving Lips: Cinema as Ventriloquism," *Yale French Studies*, no. 60 (1980), p. 75.

15. Altman, p. 75. I have translated Altman's French term for the sake of intelligibility.

16. Mary Ann Doane, "The Voice in the Cinema: The Articulation of Body and Space," in *Film Sound: Theory and Practice*, p. 171.

17. Claude Bailblé, "Programmation de l'écoute," *Cahiers du Cinéma* no. 292 (September 1978), p. 54 (my translation).

18. William James, *The Principles of Psychology* (Cambridge: Harvard Univ. Press, 1981), vol. 2, p. 1066.

19. Béla Balázs, *Theory of the Film: Character and Growth of a New Art*, trans. Edith Bone (New York: Dover Publications, 1970), p. 41. Chapter 5 of *Theory of the Film* contains excerpts from his 1924 opus *Der Sichtbare Mensch*.

20. Balázs, *Theory of the Film*, p. 40.

21. Pascal Bonitzer, "Les Silences de la voix," *Cahiers du Cinéma*, no. 256 (February/March 1975), p. 31 (my translation).

22. See Kaja Silverman, *The Subject of Semiotics* (New York: Oxford Univ. Press, 1983), pp. 102–09.

23. See Rick Altman, "Sound Space," in *Sound Theory Sound Practice*.

24. John L. Cass, quoted in Altman, *Sound Theory Sound Practice*, p. 49.

25. Altman, "Sound Space" p. 59.

26. Heidegger, *Being and Time*, p. 393. I have adopted the translation suggested by Hubert L. Dreyfus in his *Being-in-the-World: A Commentary on Heidegger's Being and Time, Division 1* (Cambridge: MIT Press, 1991).

27. Heidegger, *Being and Time*, p. 105 (here too I have adopted Dreyfus's translation).

28. Michel Chion, *La Toile trouée* (Paris: Cahiers du Cinéma/Editions de l'Etoile, 1988), p. 42 (my translation).

29. In Michel Chion, *Le Son au cinéma* (Paris: Cahiers du Cinéma/Editions de l'Etoile, 1985), p. 32.

30. John Belton, "Technology and Aesthetics of Film Sound," in *Film Sound: Theory and Practice*, p. 66.

31. I owe this example to Rick Altman, "Sound Space," in *Sound Theory Sound Practice*, pp. 54–59.

32. Walter Murch, "Sound Design: The Dancing Shadow," *Projections 4: Film-Makers on Film-Making*, ed. John Boorman, Tom Luddy, David Thomson, and Walter Donohue (London: Faber and Faber, 1995), p. 247.

33. Murch, "Sound Design" p. 249.

34. Murch, "Sound Design" p. 247.

35. Chion, *Le Son au cinéma*, p. 17.

36. On this topic, see John Belton, *Widescreen Cinema* (Cambridge: Harvard Univ. Press, 1992), pp. 205–10.

37. Walter Murch, "Sound Design," p. 246.

38. Chion, *Le Son au cinéma*, p. 68.

39. Robert Altman, "The Sound of Sound: A Brief History of the Repro-duction of Sound in Movie Theaters," *Cinéaste*, vol. 21, no. 1–2 (1995), p. 70.

40. Murch, "Sound Design," p. 240.

41. Altman, "The Sound of Sound," p. 70.

42. Gary Rydstrom, quoted in LoButto, p. 245.

43. Chion, *Le Son au cinéma*, pp. 100ff.

44. Hanns Eisler, *Composing for the Films* (New York: Oxford Univ. Press, 1947), p. 60. About Theodor Adorno's collaboration with Eisler's in the English version, see Philip Rosen, "Adorno and Film Music: Theoretical Notes on Com-posing for the Films," in *Yale French Studies*, no. 60, 1980.

45. Eisler, pp. 121–22.

46. Eisler, p. 59. I have switched around the two sentences.

47. Bresson, p. 41.

48. Bresson, p. 71.

49. Eisler, p. 39.

50. Eisler, p. 36.

51. Quoted in Chion, *Le Son au cinéma*, p. 130.

52. Bruce Mamer, *Film Production Technique: Creating the Accomplished Image* (Belmont: Wadsworth, 1996), p. 320.

53. Michael Rabinger, *Directing: Film Techniques and Aesthetics*, 2nd ed. (Boston: Focal Press, 1997), p. 455.

54. Heidegger, *Being and Time*, p. 171.

55. Jean Renoir, *My Life and My Films*, trans. Norman Denny (New York: Atheneum, 1974), p. 106.

56. Donald M. Lowe, *The Body in Late-Capitalist USA* (Durham: Duke Univ. Press, 1995), p. 47.

57. Samuel Weber, *Mass Mediauras: Form, Technics, Media* (Stanford: Stanford Univ. Press, 1996), p. 74 (both quotations).

58. Murch, "Sound Design," p. 247.

59. Murch, "Sound Design," p. 240 (his emphasis).

60. For indexical signs etc., read Peter Wollen, *Signs and Meanings in the Cinema* (Bloomington: Indiana Univ. Press, 1972).

61. Balázs, *Theory of the Film*, p. 197.

62. "Interview with Jean Cayrol," *Image et Son*, no. 215, March 1968 (my translation).

63. Michel Chion, *Audio-Vision: Sound on Screen*, trans. Claudia Gorbman (New York: Columbia Univ. Press, 1994), p. 109.

64. Ben Burtt, in Vincent LoBrutto, *Sound-on-Film*, p. 143.

65. Murch, "Sound Design: The Dancing Shadow," p. 248.

66. E. H. Gombrich, *Art and Illusion* (New York: Pantheon Books, 1960), p. 49.

67. "Sur le son: Entretien avec J.-M. Straub et D. Huillet," *Cahiers du Cinéma*, no. 260–61 (October/November 1975), p. 49 (my translation).

68. "Entretien avec Jean-Marie Straub et Danièle Huillet," p. 54.

69. In LoBrutto, *Sound-on-Film*, p. 241.

70. Chion, *Le Son au cinéma*, p. 191.

71. "Entretien avec Jean-Marie Straub et Danièle Huillet," *Cahiers du Cinéma*, no. 223 (August 1970), p. 53 (my translation).

72. Abraham Segal, "Jean-Luc Godard," *Image et Son*, no. 215 (March 1968), p. 82.

73. Claude Bailblé, "Programmation de l'écoute (Part 4)" *Cahiers du Cinéma*, no. 299 (April 1979), p. 27 (my translation).

74. Jacques Derrida, *Speech and Phenomena*, trans. David Allison (Evanston: Northwestern Univ. Press, 1973), p. 60.

75. In LoBrutto, p. 179.

76. Derrida, *Speech and Phenomena*, p. 77.

77. See Jacques Derrida, *Of Grammatology*, trans. Gayatri Chakravorty Spivak (Baltimore: Johns Hopkins Univ. Press, 1977).

78. Albert Camus, *The Fall*, trans. Justin O'Brien (New York: Vintage Books, 1956), p. 108. I am following closely Shoshana Felman's analysis in

Shoshana Felman and Dori Laub, *Testimony: Crises of Witnessing in Literature, Psychoanalysis, and History* (New York: Routledge, 1992).

79. Abraham Segal, "Jean-Luc Godard," p. 74.

## CHAPTER NINE.
## EDITING

1. Noel Burch, quoted by Tom Gunning, "Weaving a Narrative: Style and Economic Background in Griffith's Biograph Films," in *Early Cinema: Space Frame Narrative*, ed. Thomas Elsaesser (London: British Film Institute, 1990), p. 340.

2. Noel Burch, *Life to Those Shadows*, trans. Ben Brewster (Berkeley: Univ. of California Press, 1990), p. 155 (his emphasis).

3. See Jean Mitry, *Esthétique et psychologie du cinéma*, vol. 1, *Les structures* (Paris: Editions universitaires, 1963), p. 163.

4. Walter Murch, *In the Blink of an Eye: A Perspective on Film Editing* (Los Angeles: Silman James Press, 1995), p. 55.

5. Gilles Deleuze, *Cinema 1: The Movement-Image*, trans. Hugh Tomlinson and Barbara Habberjam (Minneapolis: Univ. of Minnesota Press, 1986), p. 30.

6. Quoted by Tom Gunning, *D. W. Griffith and the Origins of American Narrative Film: The Early Years at Biograph* (Urbana: Univ. of Illinois Press, 1991), p. 189.

7. Gunning, *D. W. Griffith*, p. 26.

8. Thomas Elsaesser, *Early Cinema: Space Frame Narrative*, p. 295.

9. A good explanation of the "fort/da" game can be found in Kaja Silverman, *The Subject of Semiotics* (New York: Oxford Univ. Press, 1983), pp. 166–78.

10. Deleuze, p.33.

11. Dana Polan, "'The Kuleshov Effect' Effect" in *Iris*, vol. 4, no. 1 (1986).

12. On the historical complexity surrounding the Kuleshov effect, see Dominique Chateau "L'Effet Koulechov et le cinéma comme art" in *Iris*, vol. 4, no. 1 (1986).

13. Similarly Kuleshov himself did not go beyond colleagues and associates, as pointed out by Norman N. Holland, in "Film Response from Eye to I: the Kuleshov Experiment," in *Classical Hollywood Narrative: The Paradigm Years*, ed. Jane Gaines (Durham: Duke Univ. Press, 1992), p. 95.

14. Martine Joly and Marc Nicolas, "Koulechov: de l'experience à l'effet" in *Iris*, vol. 4, no. 1 (1986).

15. Holland, "Film Response from Eye to I," p. 95.

16. In David Bordwell, Janet Staiger, and Kristin Thompson, *The Classical Hollywood Cinema: Film Style and Mode of Production to 1960* (New York: Columbia Univ. Press, 1985), p. 8.

17. See David Bordwell, *Narration in the Fiction Film* (Madison: Univ. of Wisconsin Press, 1985), pp. 32–33.

18. V. I. Pudovkin, *Film Technique and Film Acting*, trans. Ivor Montagu (New York: Grove Press, 1978), pp. 174–78.

19. Pudovkin, pp. 90–91.

20. Pudovkin, p. 91 (I have slightly altered the translation).

21. Serge Eisenstein, *Reflexions d'un cinéaste*, trans. Lucia Galinskaia and Jean Cathala (Moscou: Editions du Progrès, 1958), p. 58.

22. Deleuze, p. 35.

23. S. M. Eisenstein, *Film Form: Essays in Film Theory* (Cleveland: Meridian, 1963), p. 37.

24. Eisenstein, *Film Form*, p. 62.

25. Eisenstein, *Film Form*, p. 62.

26. At the time, of course, that was not the case and Eisenstein, accused of formalism, was asked to change his approach to filmmaking. Today, mass audiences experience these "signifying bubbles" on a daily basis in commercials and rock videos.

27. Dziga Vertov, "Kinoks-Revolution," in *Film Culture*, no. 25 (Summer 1962), p. 53.

28. Vertov, p. 51

29. Vertov, p. 51.

30. Deleuze, p. 39.

31. Eisenstein, *Film Form*, p. 43.

32. Vertov, p. 52.

33. Read the remarkable article by Stephen Crofts and Olivia Rose, "An Essay towards Man with a Movie Camera," in *Screen*, vol. 18, no. 1 (Spring 1977), pp. 9–58.

34. Vertov, p. 53.

35. Noel Burch, "Film's Institutional Mode of Representation and the Response," in *October*, no. 11 (Winter 1971), p. 94.

36. Deleuze, p. 81.

37. André Bazin, *What Is Cinema?*, trans. Hugh Gray (Berkeley: Univ. of California Press,1967), vol. 1, p. 25. I have slightly altered Hugh Gray's translation.

38. Sergei Eisenstein, *Film Form*, p. 245.

39. Pascal Bonitzer, *Le Regard et la voix: Essais sur le cinéma* (Paris: Union Générale d'Editions, 1976), pp. 38–39.

40. See Pascal Bonitzer's analysis of Bazin's thinking in *Le Champ aveugle: Essais sur le cinéma* (Paris: Cahiers du Cinéma/Gallimard, 1982), p. 121.

41. Eisenstein, *The Film Sense*, trans. Jay Leyda (New York: Meridian, 1963), p. 190.

42. Eisenstein, *Réflexions d'un cinéaste*, p. 84 (my translation from the French).

43. Eisenstein, *Réflexions d'un cinéaste*, p. 85 (my translation from the French).

44. André Bazin, *What Is Cinema?*, trans. Hugh Gray (Berkeley: Univ. of California Press, 1971), vol. 2, p. 52 (my emphasis).

45. Bazin, vol. 1, pp. 24 and 32.

46. Bazin, quoted by Dudley Andrew, *The Major Film Theories: An Introduction* (London: Oxford Univ. Press, 1976), p. 161.

47. Bazin, quoted by Andrew, p. 161 (my emphasis).

48. *Bazin at Work: Major Essays and Reviews from the Forties and Fifties*, ed. Bert Cardullo, trans. Alain Piette and Bert Cardullo (New York: Routledge, 1997), p. 7.

49. *Bazin at Work*, p. 8.

50. *Bazin at Work*, p. 8.

51. Bazin, *What Is Cinema?*, vol. 2, pp. 35–38.

52. See Mitry, vol. 1, pp. 329–54.

53. Bazin, *What Is Cinema?*, vol. 2, p. 59.

54. Bazin, *What Is Cinema?*, vol. 2, p. 27.

55. See, for instance, in *What is Cinema?*, "In Defense of Mixed Cinema," "Theater and Cinema," and "*Le Journal d'un curé de campagne* and the Stylistics of Robert Bresson" in vol. 1, pp. 53–143 and "An Aesthetic of Reality: Neo-realism," "Bicycle Thief," and "De Sica: Metteur en scène" in vol. 2, pp. 16–78.

56. *Bazin at Work*, p. 233.

57. See *Bazin at Work*, p. 16.

58. See Bazin, *What Is Cinema?*, vol. 1, p. 27.

59. Bazin, *What Is Cinema?*, vol. 2, p. 26.

60. Bazin, *What Is Cinema?*, vol. 2, p. 76.

61. Deleuze, p. 9.

62. Maurice Merleau-Ponty, *Sense and Non-Sense*, trans. Hubert L. Dreyfus and Patricia Allen Dreyfus (Northwestern: Northwestern Univ. Press, 1964), p. 75. I have altered "things" to a more Heideggerian "beings" to ease the reading.

63. Merleau-Ponty, *Sense and Non-Sense*, p. 29.

64. Bazin, *What Is Cinema?*, vol. 2, pp. 37–38.

65. Bazin, *What Is Cinema?*, vol. 2, p. 77.

66. See Bazin *What Is Cinema?*, vol. 2, pp. 76–77 and *Orson Welles: A Critical View*, trans. Jonathan Rosenbaum (New York: Harper and Row), p. 67ff.

67. Bazin, *What Is Cinema?*, vol. 2, p. 37.

68. Bazin, *What Is Cinema?*, vol. 2, p. 35.

69. Bazin, *What Is Cinema?*, vol. 2, p. 35.

70. Both quotes: Bazin, *What Is Cinema?*, vol. 2, p. 35.

71. Bazin, *What Is Cinema?*, vol. 2, p. 99.

72. Roland Barthes, *S/Z*, trans. Richard Miller (New York: Hill and Wang, 1974), p. 12.

73. Jacques Derrida, *Positions*, trans. Alan Bass (Chicago: Univ. of Chicago Press, 1981), p. 26.

74. Béla Balázs, *Theory of the Film: Character and Growth of a New Art*, trans. Edith Bone (New York: Dover, 1970), p. 118.

75. Derrida, *Positions*, p. 26.

76. Maurice Merleau-Ponty, *Signs*, trans. Richard McCleary (Evanston: Northwestern Univ. Press, 1964), p. 81.

77. Bordwell, *Narration in the Fiction Film*, p. 34.

78. Henri Bergson, *Matter and Meaning*, trans. Nancy Margaret Paul and W. Scott Palmer (London: George Allen and Unwin, 1919), p. 126.

79. See Friedrich Nietzsche, *The Will to Power*, trans. Walter Kaufmann and R.J. Hollingdale (London: Weidenfeld and Nicolson, 1968).

80. Mitry, vol. 1, p. 283.

81. See Norman N. Holland, *Five Readers Reading* (New Haven: Yale Univ. Press, 1975).

82. Derrida, *Positions*, p. 26.

83. See Jean-Paul Sartre, *Being and Nothingness: A Phenomenological Essay on Ontology*, trans. Hazel E. Barnes (New York: Philosophy Library, 1956), p. 485.

# CHAPTER TEN.
## ENVOI

1. Amy Wallace, "How Much Bigger Can the Bang Get?," *Los Angeles Times*, Calendar Section, August 9, 1998, p. 8.

2. Steven E. De Souza, quoted in Wallace, p. 10.

3. De Souza, quoted in Wallace, p. 10.

4. In Wallace, p. 10.

5. Michael Bay, in Wallace, p. 27.

6. Theodor W. Adorno, *Aesthetic Theory*, ed. Gretel Adorno and Rolf Tiedermann, trans. C. Lenhardt (London: Routledge, 1972), p. 344.

7. Lars von Trier's and Thomas Vinterberg's "Dogma 95" proclamation. I want to thank my student Mikhael Forsberg for making it available to me.

8. Michael Bay, in Wallace, p. 28.

9. Andrey Tarkovsky, *Sculpting in Time: Reflections on the Cinema*, trans. Kitty Hunter-Blair (Austin: Univ. of Texas Press, 1989), p. 165.

10. Tarkovsky, p. 229.

# INDEX

4410919

Made in the USA
Lexington, KY
22 January 2010